# Protect Your Life!

## A Health Handbook
### for
## Law Enforcement
## Professionals

*– 2nd Edition –*

Edited by
## Davidson C. Umeh

Foreword by
**Dr. Alberto A. Gotay**
**Commanding Officer, (Ret.)**
**Physical Education Unit, New York City Police Department**

**Looseleaf**
Law Publications, Inc.

ISBN 978-1-60885-060-0

Digital ISBN 978-1-60885-097-6


**Library of Congress Cataloging-in-Publication Data** – Pending


**Printed in the United States of America**

To the glory and honor of the
men and women in uniform
services who work relentlessly
to protect the public.

# TABLE OF CONTENTS

# ACKNOWLEDGMENTS

This anthology would not have been possible without the insight from people in the uniform services departments. I am particularly grateful to Leslie Dawkins and Edward Ngwu for sharing their experiences with me. I am greatly indebted to Dr. Albert Gotay, Thomas J. Eich and Michael Jacobson for writing the foreword and preface to this book.

I thank Elias A. Guevara, Milagros E. Duque and John Taveras for technical assistance and typing the manuscript. Finally, I thank my publisher, Mike Loughrey, and his staff for their competence in managing the project.

# FOREWORD

At this time over 65 percent of Americans are overweight and many of these are obese. Diets and the management of nutrition are apparently not being managed adequately to ensure good health. Physical activity and exercise are not reaching the levels that are needed to keep the public in good physical condition. Additionally, many are saddled with higher levels of stress for longer periods of time than that with which the body can cope with efficiently and effectively.

Law enforcement professionals, as a part of American society are plagued by the same health problems that affect the general population. Those men and women charged with protecting society have an increased problem with maintaining their health because of the very nature of the job. The responsibilities of the positions in law enforcement, the fluctuating hours, the nonavailability of nutritious food at mealtime, the stresses of the job, and dealing with difficult and changing societal conditions all combine to increase the propensity for law enforcement professionals to have their health negatively affected.

The World Health Organization (WHO) has defined health as "a state of complete physical, mental, and social well-being, not merely the absence of disease or infirmity" (World Health Organization, 2010). This broad application of health concepts has led to the coining of the term "wellness." In turn the concept of wellness has evolved into a reflection of six dimensions. They are physical health, mental/ intellectual health, emotional health, social health, environmental health, and spiritual health. The literature tells us that overall health may be increased by "the adoption of healthy lifestyle habits that will enhance well-being while decreasing the risk of diseases" (Floyd, Mimms, & Yelding, 2008, p. 12).

The six dimensions of wellness are expertly addressed by Dr. Davidson Umeh in the second edition of his book *Protect Your Life! A Health Handbook for Law Enforcement Professionals*. With specific attention to the health needs of the men and women sworn to law enforcement duties, the book is divided into nine parts. They are: 1) Cardiovascular Diseases Issues, 2) Drug and Alcohol Issues, 3) Infectious and Non-Infectious Disease Issues, 4) Stress Issues, 5) Nutrition Issues, 6) Physical Fitness Issues, 7) Suicide Issues, 8) Environmental Issues, and 9) Safety Issues. Several articles were added in Part Seven to highlight the issues of suicide in law enforcement. Additionally, a new section Part Nine was added to discuss safety issues. The articles in this second edition give law enforcement officers comprehensive background knowledge to prepare and protect their health for the difficult tasks they encounter in the line of duty.

Dr. Alberto A. Gotay
Commanding Officer (Ret.)
Physical Education Unit
New York City Police Department

# PREFACE I

There is arguably no more stressful and difficult job in the uniformed services than that of a correction officer. Greatly outnumbered by prisoners, unarmed and locked inside secure facilities with society's most violent members result in high levels of stress and fatigue. Prisoners also have very high rates of infectious diseases, such as tuberculosis, that can spread in the frequently overcrowded jails and prisons where correction officers work. Additionally, it is not unusual for officers to work two and, in emergencies, three straight eight-hour shifts. Coupled with all this is the fact that at barely a moment's notice an officer may have to respond to an inmate disturbance, escort a notorious prisoner to court or to the hospital, participate in a difficult cell extraction or, possibly, be attacked by a prisoner. Correction officers have one of the most stressful jobs in government.

Other than constant training, the most important thing correction officers can do to successfully handle the physical, emotional, and psychological stress inherent in their jobs is to stay healthy and fit. The job demands it. Cardiovascular fitness and excellent nutrition in particular are tremendously important. Immediate and emergency response, unanticipated use of force with recalcitrant prisoners and being clear-headed enough to diffuse potentially violent situations, all require a high level of fitness and alertness that cardiovascular exercise and eating well provides. Officers who are fit and who successfully manage the stress of their jobs also do not need to rely on force nearly as much as someone who is stressed out and tired. Maintaining the level of physical fitness achieved upon graduation as recruits from the Correction Training Academy is essential given the rigors of the job.

Correction officers who do not stay fit are ill prepared to handle the stress and fatigue inherent in the job. In addition, the likelihood of contracting communicable diseases increases, the chances of becoming obese are far greater (especially when officers eat the always available and usually high calorie prison food), and the risk of heart attacks and other cardiovascular diseases increases in the absence of good nutrition and fitness.

Good health is not simply an ephemeral concept that is only tangential to the nature of correction work. Correction officers' well-being and their lives depend on it. Dr. Umeh's collection of essays contributes much to our understanding of the various factors that affect the health of uniform services personnel. It is the responsibility of every uniform service personnel to use this book as a useful resource in the effort to protect his/her health.

Professor Michael Jacobson
Department of Law and Police Science
John Jay College of Criminal Justice
Former Commissioner
NYC Dept. of Corrections and Probation

# PREFACE II

Probation and Parole Officers are increasingly concerned about their safety both in the office and in the field. More than ever, community corrections agencies are asking officers to supervise serious drug offenders and abusers, mentally ill offenders, high risk violent offenders, and career criminals who reside in dangerous and hostile neighborhoods. These contacts often take place after daylight at the offender's home and workplace. In view of these concerns many agencies are allowing officers to arm themselves with personal defense sprays, such as pepper gas and firearms.

In recent times, throughout the country, we are seeing a proliferation of training in defensive tactics and street survival skills, as well as the legal issues surrounding civil liability for probation and parole personnel. Officers who are both mentally and physically prepared greatly improve their possibility of surviving a critical incident.

Davidson C. Umeh's book *Protect Your Life! A Health Handbook for Law Enforcement Professionals* reinforces the concept that each officer must accept responsibility for his/her own safety in the form of a lifelong commitment to safety. This includes staying in good physical condition, eating right, and maintaining a high level of mental awareness.

Thomas J. Eich
Supervising U.S. Probation Officer
Southern District of New York

# Introduction:
# Health and Fitness in Uniform Services:
# An Overview

Law enforcement officers encounter a more dangerous situation in the line of duty. The advancement in technology and science has equipped the new era of criminals with new modality to commit crime with more violent and deadly consequences. Terrorists can detonate bombs and nerve gases by remote control. Hence, law enforcement officers are in a more precarious position to develop knowledge to protect themselves from illness and injuries in the line of duty.

The process of industrialization and modernization have introduced many pollutants into the environment and completely changed the lifestyle of the modern person. Hence, many preventable diseases now abound in our society. Members of the uniform services personnel perform very important roles in the protection of life and property in society. It is essential to enhance the ability of members of the uniform services to take care of their health so they can effectively perform their duties in the communities. Pilant (1995) declares "the concept of wellness is certainly nothing new. Studies have shown that a healthy diet and moderate lifestyle can be tremendous contributors to long life. Unfortunately, a police officer's lifestyle is often on the other end of the wellness spectrum. Fluctuating schedules and shift work make it hard to get adequate rest, maintain a regular eating schedule or establish an exercise routine. Officers are also prone to eat too much fast food, smoke too much, drink too much and ignore the job's constant stress." The unusual expectation placed on the law enforcement officers by everyone has made them ignore their own health while they aspire to save everyone else.

Health is defined as the ability to effectively function physically, emotionally, mentally, socially, and spiritually in an environment. Physical fitness is the ability to effectively carry out the functions necessary to meet the demands of daily activities. Health and fitness are very important concepts relevant to the performance of uniform services' duties. The uniform services personnel through the requirement of duty are prone to risky situations that are susceptible to personal injury, diseases, infection from micro-organisms or poisonous gases/fumes. Fire officers respond to calls in environments where combustion of different materials creates pollutants that may be very hazardous to health. Loeb (1997) indicated that the greatest effort in fire operation is saving human lives. In this commitment sometimes, fire officers become victims themselves and suffer the same fate as those they are trying to save. Police officers respond to emergency calls in all sections of the community and may have to deal with open wounds or provide assistance to people with infectious diseases. Law enforcement officers have legitimate concerns about contracting HIV from persons they encounter on the job, because according to Thompson and Marquart (1998) police officers and correction officers on a daily basis encounter suspects, offenders, and colleagues who are HIV positive. Correction officers work with prison inmates and evidence indicates that infectious diseases are common within the prison population because of overcrowding. Champion (1998) stated that most prisoner grievances are directly or indirectly connected with overcrowding. The probation/parole officers are responsible for monitoring the movements of people released from prison. This responsibility presents the possibility of personal injury or infection in tracking the whereabouts of the released persons. Hurley (2000) stated that the number of attacks on law enforcement officers has increased dramatically. Not only are officers being attacked more frequently, the attacks are also more vicious and deadly. The necessity to perform the requirements of the job has resulted in certain health problems among uniform services personnel, such as cardiovascular diseases, poor nutrition habits, stress-related problems, poor physical fitness, substance abuse, and infectious and noninfectious diseases—HIV/AIDS, tuberculosis, and diabetes.

## Cardiovascular Health

Cardiovascular health problems have been responsible for the death or early retirement of members of the uniform services profession. Fahy et al. (2010) stated that sudden cardiac death has consistently been the number-one cause of firefighter line-of-duty death each year in the United States. Risk factors include a high-stress work environment, irregular sleeping and eating habits, poor health habits, and lack of exercise. In fact, Kales et al. (2007) identified that firefighters are 12 to 136 times more likely to die of heart disease when putting out a fire; are 3 to 14 times more likely to die of heart disease while responding to an alarm; are 2 to 10.5 times more likely to die of heart disease while returning from an alarm, and 3 to 7 times more likely to die of heart disease during physical training. These hazardous health risk factors are similarly experienced by other members of the uniform services personnel.

To combat the incidence of heart disease, adequate lifestyle changes may play a significant role in reducing cardiovascular diseases. Kales et al. (2003) indicated that improved fitness promotion, medical screening, and medical management could prevent premature death of firefighters. *Police Magazine* (March 1993) reported that officers are 25 times more likely to die on the job from heart disease than from a criminal's bullet and those that do not die young take early disability retirement due to heart disease and back problems.

There is a need to discuss specific cardiovascular diseases and risk factors related to uniform services personnel to enhance the ability of the officers to protect their health. A well-designed education program that addresses issues on nutrition, smoking and alcohol cessation, exercise, and medical screening will provide major benefit to both the officers and the department.

## Substance Abuse

Substance abuse has a very detrimental effect on health and fitness. Yet, evidence shows that it is an inherent problem among uniform services personnel. Substances usually abused include steroids, alcohol, cocaine, and marijuana. Dart III and Ferranto (1991) stated that substance abuse problems among law enforcement personnel have traditionally centered around those drugs most commonly encountered while enforcing the law—marijuana, cocaine, and methamphetamine. Officers abuse these drugs either as an escape from the stressful events inherent to the job or to enhance muscle development for body building. And according to Dart III and Ferranto (1991): "As officers become more concerned about their ability to adequately protect themselves on the job, the incidence of steroid abuse will probably increase. In their pursuit of increased fitness, some officers are innocently introduced to steroids at gymnasiums where body builders—who may also be steroid abusers—work out. Others may turn to steroids to give them the physical edge they fear they lack."

Substance abuse is responsible for different negative effects on physical, social, mental, and emotional health. Abuse of steroids and methamphetamine may result in increased blood pressure and elevated cholesterol—a condition that leads to early onset of heart disease.

## Suicide

Suicide is still a major health concern in the law enforcement professionals. Kelly and Martin (2006) stated that police officers are killing themselves at a rate much higher than they are dying in the line of duty. Miller (2006) indicated that suicide is the single most lethal factor in police work. The different expectations in the performance of law enforcement duties and other personal problems often lead to stress, depression, and other debilitating illnesses. When officers find it difficult to cope with these problems, some resort to committing suicide as a way to ease the pains they are experiencing. Ramos (2010) stated that relationship problems, coupled with alcohol abuse and the accessibility of a firearm, create a recipe for disaster among troubled officers who may view suicide as the only way out.

Suicide in the law enforcement community can be reduced through a well-designed educational program that involves the administrators, officers, and members of the officers' family.

## HIV/AIDS

HIV/AIDS is a deadly disease because at present there is no cure and no vaccine. There is a general fear about the disease due to misleading information from the different media organizations. Pilant (1995) stated that AIDS sparks the deepest fear, because there is no cure and those that develop AIDS are usually dead within a few years. The uniform services personnel come in contact with different people in the communities while on duty. Also, police officers are in unique positions to convey important health resource information to those most in need of it. Correction officers are also in the best position to provide AIDS education for prison inmates because they are in close contact in their working environment. The fire and police officers respond to emergency situations that sometimes expose them to open wounds with blood or other body fluids. The unique job requirements of uniform services personnel situates them in the best place to act as AIDS educators, but it also exposes them to possible infection by HIV. It is imperative that the more information and knowledge uniform services personnel have about HIV/AIDS, the less fearful they are about the disease and also better prepared to educate the public while protecting themselves from HIV infection.

## Tuberculosis

Tuberculosis is presently on the increase in the general population because of infection by immune deficiency viruses such as HIV. There is an increase in the number of correction officers who test positive for tuberculosis. The overcrowding in prisons and the close proximity of the correction officers to the prison inmates is responsible for TB infection. The other uniform services personnel are also susceptible to TB because they constantly respond to emergencies in different communities. Pilant (1995) stated that TB is transmitted through the air by suspects who are coughing, hacking, and wheezing in the back of patrol cars or in the jail cell. The modern strains of TB are drug resistant, and even those who test positive for it may not show symptoms. This is because TB generally affects people whose immune system is already weak, which may explain why prisons have a high rate of TB-infected inmates. Officers need proper education on TB and necessary methods of prevention so that they can protect themselves in the line of duty.

## Stress

The responsibilities of uniform services personnel are varied and complex. The complexity of their job is based on personal, departmental, and public expectations of their performance. "Exhaustion due to shift work, voluntary and mandatory overtime assignments, seemingly endless hours waiting to testify in court, physical and emotional demands of dealing with the public, and management expectations of doing more with less, combined with family responsibilities, puts the modern law enforcement professional at serious emotional and physical risk" (Lindsey, 2007). Sometimes in an effort to do the best job, one of these expectations conflicts with the other. The job sometimes requires making decisions in an emergency and mistakes may occur. These situations that are encountered on the job create stress for the officers which inevitably result in poor health. The macho image of the profession prevent officers from seeking help; rather, they may resort to alcohol or drug use. In extreme cases, officers commit suicide as a way to resolve their problems. It is essential to create awareness about the possible causes of stress for officers. Adequate background information may assist them in making the right decision for overcoming their problems.

## Nutrition

Studies indicate that uniform services personnel have very poor nutrition habits. The poor nutrition habits are blamed on the nature of the job vis-a-vis shift hours, long hours at work, and patrol duties.

Chapola (2002) stated that officers are somewhat at a disadvantage when it comes to eating right because job factors, such as overtime, shift work, and rotating schedules, usually affect dietary patterns. Because poor nutrition affects strength, endurance, and body weight, performance and health can be adversely impacted. Uniform service officers buy their food from fast-food stores and eat on the run. This habit has negative effects on the overall health of the officers. There is an increase in the level of obesity, heart diseases, and diabetes among officers as their years on the job increase. Proper nutrition knowledge and practice will help the uniform services personnel to wisely select the right foods to promote good health. Bahrke (1996) stated that police officers can make healthy choices even with their irregular schedules. Balance, moderation, and variety are important ingredients to being nutrition-wise.

**Physical Fitness**

The duties of uniform services personnel involves regular physical activities, such as lifting, carrying, pushing, dragging heavy objects, long pursuit, use of physical force, bending, and pursuit with obstacles. Adequate physical fitness is essential for one to be able to effectively perform the duties of the uniform services personnel. Hoffman (1996) stated that law enforcement work demands a high level of physical fitness to accomplish tasks that sometimes are very demanding including carrying heavy objects, running, jumping over objects, and the use of force. The basic components of physical fitness—cardiorespiratory endurance, muscular strength and endurance, flexibility, anaerobic power, and a healthy body composition—underlie the ability to perform each task. To ascertain that officers meet the minimum physical fitness requirement for the job, they are tested as a prerequisite for entry into the uniform services profession. However, soon after graduation from the academy, officers do not participate in any form of regular fitness activity to maintain their fitness and health. Collingwood (1995) stated that the problem with the testing approach is that the testing does not lead to any physical training or fitness programming. The test tends to serve only as standards for entry into a law enforcement position with nothing addressed in terms of incumbent officer standards or needs for ongoing fitness programs.

Regular participation in fitness activities is not only necessary for performance on the job, but it helps in total improvement in the officers' health. Studies show that regular involvement in fitness activities helps to improve the various components of physical fitness. Rhea (2010) stated that behavior change requires a change in one's environment, a change in one's thought patterns, and a goal to better oneself. Uniform services personnel would enhance their health with better information and knowledge on the proper methods to improve their health with physical fitness activities. Dezelan (1997) stated that because improving the health and fitness of firefighters is everybody's concern, fire service labor and management leaders met recently to begin a cooperative effort on this issue.

**Work Environment and Safety**

Uniform services personnel work under all environmental conditions. The environmental condition may be hazardous to the officer's health but his first commitment is to get the job done. Loeb (1997) stated that the number one priority for firefighters responding to a fire scene is preventing death and injury to the public. Shouldn't there also be someone to look out for firefighters? Uniform services personnel need an accurate knowledge of the possible dangers in their working environment and protective equipment and procedures to enable them to safeguard themselves from injury and infection in the line of duty. The environmental conditions of extreme cold, heat, noise, and hazardous pollutants create susceptible conditions for ill-health for the officers. The new threat of nerve gas release in the environment by terrorist or dissident groups creates a new challenge for law enforcement officers in overcoming hazardous and environmental conditions in the line of duty. Uniform officers need adequate knowledge of the environmental conditions so that they may take appropriate measures to protect their health. Levitan and Socher (1997) stated that each recognition of signs and symptoms and appropriate administration of antidote therapy and airway management will save lives, reduce injuries, and minimize adverse health effects from a nerve agent exposure.

The members of the uniform services play a significant role in the protection of the community. To effectively perform their duties, adequate effort should be made to enable them to stay healthy. This objective will best be achieved through the provision of accurate and relevant information on the development of physical fitness, causes, signs, and symptoms and methods of transmission of diseases and preventive measures to avoid infection and injury. Pilant (1995) stated that protecting the health of officers from infectious diseases does not have to be difficult or an expensive proposition. In recognition of the need to protect the health of officers, the Occupational Safety and Health Administration (OSHA) has mandated application of "universal precautions" to protect them against potentially infectious or blood-borne pathogens. OSHA's policy also requires employers to provide written education programs for their workers and a training workshop to help them learn how to protect their health in the line of duty. This text is written with the objective of providing basic and accurate information for uniform services personnel to help them maintain, protect and preserve their health, so that they can effectively and efficiently provide the best service to their communities.

## References

Bahrke, M. (April, 1996). "Eating on the run." *Muscles and Fitness*, p. 77.

Champion, D. J. (1998). *Criminal Justice in the United States*. Chicago, Nelson-Hall Inc.

Chapola, C. (Dec. 2002). "Good nutrition benefits all officers." *Law and Order*, pp. 90–94.

Collingwood, T. R. (Feb. 1995). "Physical fitness standard: Measuring job relatedness." *The Police Chief*, pp. 31–47.

Dart, R. C. III & Ferranto, D. A. (July, 1991). "Anabolic steroid abuse among law enforcement officers." *The Police Chief*, p. 18.

Department of Labor, Occupational Safety and Health Administration, Occupational Exposure to Blood borne Pathogens. 29 CFR, Part 1910.1030, Docket no. H-370 (Washington, DC: US Department of Labor, Occupational Safety and Health Administration, 1992).

Dezelan, L. A. (Feb. 1997). "Firefighter fitness is now on the front burner." *Fire Chief*, pp. 56–57.

Fahy, R. F; LeBlanc, P. R; Molis, J. L. (2010). Firefighter fatalities in the United States—2009 and US fire service fatalities in structure fires, 1077–2009. Retrieved from National Fire Protection Association Website: http://www.nfpa.org.

Hoffman, B. (April, 1996). "How today's law enforcement officers rank." *Muscles and Fitness*, pp. 76–79.

Hurley, J. (June, 2000). "Officer Survival." *Law and Order*, pp. 112–114.

Kales, S. N.; Soteriades, E. S.; Christophi, C. A. and Christiani, D. C. (2007). "Emergency duties and from heart disease among firefighters in the United States." *New England Journal of Medicine*. 356 (12): pp. 1207–1215.

Kales, S. N.; Soteriades, E. S.; Christophi, C. A. and Christiani, D. C. (2003). "Firefighters and on-duty deaths from coronary heart disease: A case control study." *Environmental Health*, Vol. 4, p. 14, Retrieved online on 11/27/12.

Kelly, P. and Martin, R. (March, 2006). "Police suicide is real." *Law and Order*, Vol. 54, pp. 93–96.

Levitin, H. W. & Socher, M. M. (Oct./Nov. 1997). "Attacking the nervous system." *Fire International*, pp. 13–14.

Lindsey, D. (Aug. 2007). "Police fatigue: An accident waiting to happen." *FBI Law Enforcement Bulletin*, pp. 1–8.

Loeb, D. L. (Nov. 1997). "Have we gone too far?" *Fire Chief*, pp. 60–65.

Miller, L. (2006). "Practical strategies for preventing officer suicide." *Law and Order*, pp. 90–93.

Pilant, L. (Nov. 1995). "Infection control." *The Police Chief*, pp.53–56.

Pilant, L. (Aug. 1995). "Physical fitness." *The Police Chief*, pp. 85–90.

Ramos, O. (May, 2010). "Police suicide: Are you at risk?" *FBI Law Enforcement Bulletin*, pp. 21–23.

Rhea, D. J. (2010). "Back to the basics: Eat right and get active." *Journal of Physical Education, Recreation and Dance*. Vol. 81. no. 3, pp. 4, 5, & 56.

Thompson, R. A. and Marquart, J. W. (1998). "Law enforcement responses to the HIV/AIDS epidemic." *Policing*, Vol. 21, Issue 4, pp. 648–665.

Violanti, J. M. (Feb. 1995). "The mystery within: Understanding police suicide." *FBI Law Enforcement Bulletin*, pp.19–23.

# PART ONE
# Cardiovascular Disease Issues

## The Cardiovascular System: An Overview
*Davidson C. Umeh*

The National Fire Protection study indicates that heart attacks have accounted for nearly half of all firefighters' deaths each year.[1] Evidence indicates that cardiovascular health problems are responsible for early retirement or disability from duty by law enforcement officers.[2] The risk factors of cardiovascular diseases relevant to uniform services personnel are lack of exercise, poor nutrition, stress, use of alcohol, drugs, and tobacco. Other risk factors are age, sex, and race. These risk factors have the ability to influence the functioning of the heart. The prevailing risk factors to uniform services personnel can be prevented through better education and a change in lifestyle.

### The Cardiovascular System

The cardiovascular system comprises the heart and the blood vessels—arteries and veins. The arteries are responsible for transporting blood containing oxygen (oxygenated blood) and the veins are responsible for carrying blood containing carbon dioxide (deoxygenated blood). The heart is a muscle and it is responsible for generating the pressure for pumping blood throughout the body. Blood travels out of the heart through the channels provided by the arteries and returns to the heart through the veins with the exception of the pulmonary artery and vein.

The heart comprises four chambers—the right and left atrium and the right and left ventricle. The heart chambers are divided into different compartments by walls but they are connected by valves. The tricuspid valve connects the right atrium to the right ventricle and the bicuspid valve connects the left atrium to the left ventricle. To generate pressure for blood circulation, the atria contracts at the same time while the ventricles also contracts simultaneously. Oxygenated blood from the lungs enters the left atrium through the pulmonary vein. During the atria contraction, the blood is forced into the left ventricle through the bicuspid valve. At the ventricular contraction, the bicuspid valve is closed to prevent a backflow of blood, hence the blood is forced into the aorta—the largest artery in the body—for transportation to the entire body. The blood branches off into smaller arteries that travel to the upper and lower part of the body. The blood loses its oxygen content in the capillaries for metabolism and collects carbon dioxide. The deoxygenated blood travels back to the heart from different veins. The veins connect to the superior and inferior venae cavae that transport the deoxygenated blood into the right atrium. During the atria contraction, the blood is forced into the right ventricle through the tricuspid valve. At the next ventricular contraction, the tricuspid valve closes and the blood flows through the pulmonary vein to the lungs where it is replenished with oxygen and the carbon dioxide is released.

In order for the heart to effectively perform its function of providing the pressure for transporting blood throughout the body, it needs its own supply of oxygen. The heart receives blood through the coronary and collateral arteries. The coronary is the large artery and the collateral is the small artery of the heart. Cardiovascular diseases are caused by the risk factors that hinder the ability of the heart and vascular system to perform their functions.

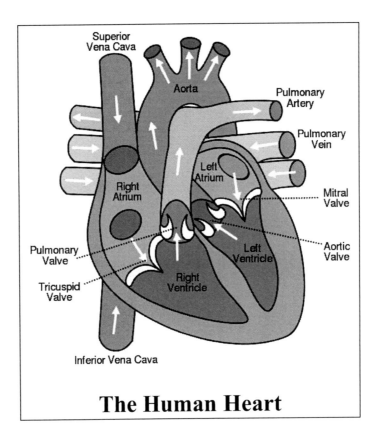

# The Human Heart

## Cardiovascular Diseases

### *Hypertension*

Hypertension is an excessive increase in the level of the blood pressure. The normal blood pressure is 120/80. Blood pressure reading is taken with a sphygmomanometer and a stethoscope. The upper reading is called the systolic pressure—when the heart muscle contracts—and the lower reading is called the diastolic pressure—when the heart muscle relaxes. Hypertension occurs when the blood pressure reading is 140/90. Increase in blood pressure occurs when the arteries are blocked by an accumulation of plaque or other substances that hinder movement of blood through the system. This situation exerts excessive demand on the heart muscle to provide the pressure needed to transport blood through the body.

### *Atherosclerosis*

This condition is the deposition of fat and other substances in the artery. Accumulation of the substances over time in the arteries will slow down the rate of blood transport through the arteries. Atherosclerosis will eventually result in hardening of the arteries—arteriosclerosis. The arteries lose their flexibility and make transportation of blood more difficult.

### *Congestive Heart Disease*

This disease occurs when the heart is unable to provide enough pressure to pump blood through the body. It is caused by a weakness in the heart muscle or dysfunction in the valves that creates a backflow of blood to the heart. The weak blood pressure may result in swelling in the lower extremities (edema) due to poor circulation of waste materials out of the system.

### Coronary Heart Disease

This disease is caused by a blockage in the coronary artery creating the inability to supply enough blood to the heart cells. This situation results in angina pectoris—pain experienced in the chest and down the left arm due to poor supply of oxygen to the heart muscle. Angina pain is the first sign of a heart attack and it is essential to consult a physician. If extended areas of the heart cells are deprived of oxygen, a heart attack or myocardial infarction occurs.

### Stroke

A stroke is caused by a lack of oxygen supply to the brain cells. The arteries may be blocked by fat deposits that create increased pressure within the system. Persistent pressure over time results in a rupture in the arterial wall that floods blood into the brain cells. The immersion of the cells in blood prevents respiration.

### Congenital Heart Disease

Congenital heart diseases are present at birth. The heart diseases are caused by malformation in the genes. It may be attributed to viral infection in vitro or abuse of drugs/alcohol by the parents. Congenital heart disease may be indicated by a hole in the heart, a block in the valve, the artery, or vein, a constriction in the flow of blood between the heart and aorta.

### Rheumatic Heart Disease

This disease is an inflammation of the heart valve caused by complication of streptococci infection. Poorly treated streptococci infection may permanently damage the heart valve. Common colds and streptococci infections should be given adequate attention.

## Endnotes

[1]  A. Miller, "A Fireman's Heart." *Public Management*, July 1987, pp. 24–26.

[2]  R. M. Arliss, "Healthy Hearts for New York City Cops." *The Police Chief*, July 1991, pp.16–22.

## Review Questions

1. Describe the structure of the heart. A diagram of the heart is essential.

2. Discuss the process of blood circulation in the heart.

# Healthy Hearts for New York City Cops
*Rebecca M. Arliss*

Coronary heart disease is the leading cause of death in the United States. It is the number one killer of men in their forties and women in their sixties. Since most officers begin their careers in their early twenties and retire by their mid-forties, this is a good time to encourage the development of health habits that will prevent heart disease, stroke and lung cancer.

Of course, the law enforcement workplace is different from other work settings. It is often difficult to schedule appointments for health services due to changes in work schedules that result from arrests, investigations, court appearances and the round-the-clock nature of the job. Yet, given the inherent stress of the job, personal health is of paramount importance. Police departments need work-site health promotion programs that are tailored to the special needs of their employees. Such programs provide educational information, structured opportunities and organizational support for health-related behavioral changes—preventive maintenance, so to speak.

Work-site health promotion programs—smoking cessation, health screening, nutrition information provide major benefits to both the police department and the individual officer. Specific examples of such programs include cardiovascular fitness programs, hypertension screening and treatment programs, health risk appraisal programs and cholesterol screening and education programs.

Changes in individual risk factors will eventually result in reduced risk of developing premature heart disease, stroke, cancers and diabetes. Specific improvements for the individual officer include enhanced self-image and self-esteem through improvements in personal appearance, weight loss through a decrease in body fat, lower blood cholesterol level. Exercise and nutrition programs also may raise the protective high-density lipoprotein (HDL) fraction of the cholesterol level and improve glucose metabolism, which may result in a delay in the development of adult-onset diabetes mellitus. Exercise may also enable the officer to cope more effectively with the stress endemic to police work.

Improvements in officers' health and appearance result in major benefits to the department. Health promotion programs produce improvements in staff morale, productivity and job satisfaction. Industry studies suggest that health promotion programs may also result in a decrease in days lost due to illness, a decline in injuries and their attendant costs and a reduction in staff turnover. In addition, improvements in personal appearance may enhance the public's response to the police officer.

## Enhancing Motivation

The primary tool for motivating New York City Police Department (NYPD) police officers to increase their personal health awareness is the measurement and interpretation of cardiovascular risk factors, a process called cardiovascular risk assessment. This is done by a team of civilian registered nurses assigned to the Health Services Division's Hypertension Screening Unit. First, the officer completes a self-administered questionnaire containing questions regarding risk factors for heart disease, including family history of premature heart disease; personal history of diabetes, stroke and heart attack; age; male gender; and cigarette smoking. Second, a registered nurse measures the officer's blood pressure and blood cholesterol level. (Cholesterol is measured using a fingertip sample of capillary blood that is analyzed in three minutes.) Finally, the nurse identifies and reviews all of the individual's risk factors for heart disease. Blood pressure and cholesterol results are explained and questions are answered. The nurse then suggests and appropriate time interval for re-measurement and provides health education materials from the American Heart Association and NYPD Hypertension Screening Unit.

At the end of the session, the nurse counsels the officer regarding the role of lifestyle factors in the prevention of heart disease, and encourages individuals with high readings to see their personal physicians for follow-up. In addition, the NYPD Hypertension Screening Unit operates a high blood pressure management clinic where individuals with elevated blood pressure readings can be re-measured, monitored and treated at six convenient work-site locations.

## National Education Programs

The NYPD Hypertension Screening Unit uses the guidelines of the National Cholesterol and High Blood Pressure Education programs, sponsored by the National Heart, Lung and Blood Institute. The National High Blood Pressure Education program began in the 1980s following conclusive research demonstrating the lifesaving benefits of lowering high blood pressure. The National Cholesterol Education program began in 1988 with a campaign to educate physicians and the public concerning the importance of lowering elevated blood cholesterol levels. A blood pressure reading greater than 140/90 or a cholesterol level greater than 200 is defined as elevated and requires re-measurement. Therefore, referral back to the usual source of medical care is an important part of the program. Diet and exercise are usually recommended by the physician as initial treatment modalities.

Continuous staff training is also essential. Hypertension Screening Unit staff regularly attend local training sessions sponsored by the New York City affiliate of the American Heart Association, as well as national training sessions sponsored by the National High Blood Pressure and Cholesterol Education programs. Health and nutrition newsletters and professional journals are also useful training tools.

## Blood Pressure and Cholesterol Screening Sites

In the NYPD, cardiovascular risk assessment is available at three locations: the Police Academy's Firearms and Tactics Section at the Outdoor Range, local precinct station houses and police headquarters. Since all officers are required to qualify with their firearms at the Outdoor Range between the months of May and December, it is an excellent place to offer voluntary blood pressure and cholesterol screening. Therefore, a team of registered nurses from the Hypertension Screening Unit is assigned to the Outdoor Range to review risk factors and provide health counseling. In 1988, 19,054 police officers qualified at the Outdoor Range and 13,714 were seen by the Hypertension Screening Unit. When the Outdoor Range closes in December, the same team of nurses provides cardiovascular risk assessments at local precinct station houses. In 1989, 3,273 police department personnel were seen at 35 precincts throughout the city. In September 1988, the NYPD Health Services Division opened a Health Education Center at police headquarters. Approximately 400 police department personnel are seen there each month by the Hypertension Screening Unit.

## The NYPD Cardiovascular Fitness Program

New York Police Department Cardiovascular Fitness Centers provide police personnel with state-of-the-art aerobic exercise equipment and instruction. Fitness centers are located at police headquarters and at precinct station houses. Department personnel, who exercise on off-duty time, must be cleared by their family physician prior to participation. The fitness centers are funded by the New York City Police Foundation.

## The NYPD Nutrition Awareness Program

The NYPD Health Services Division has also designed a nutrition awareness program for the department. The nutrition awareness program has a dual focus: the individual and the workplace. The Hypertension Screening Unit's cardiovascular risk assessment is used to enhance the individual police officer's interest in the role of eating habits in maintaining desirable blood pressure and cholesterol levels. Nutrition education material from the American Heart Association is available at all screening sites. In addition, an "eating out" guide was specifically designed for the New York City police officer by the Hypertension Screening Unit. It lists better food choices when ordering food from delicatessens, bodegas, salad bars and coffee shops. Other print media used to convey a nutrition education message includes articles in the NYPD health newsletter called *Healthbeat* and articles in the NYPD magazine, *Spring 3100*. Workplace activities include nutrition and fitness workshops aimed at department leadership, changes in vending machine food choices at the police academy and police headquarters, and the development and distribution of an NYPD nutrition and fitness poster.

## Program Funding

Funding for the day-to-day operations of the Hypertension Screening Unit comes from the police unions through the Police Relief Fund. The New York City Police Foundation provides additional funding for special projects, such as *Healthbeat*. The Police Foundation was responsible for the start of the Hypertension Screening Unit in 1981, when it demonstrated the need for disease prevention services with a health fair at police headquarters. It has provided support continuously over the past 10 years.

## Similar Programs in Other Law Enforcement Settings

It is possible to provide a work-site wellness program for police department employees in settings where the number of health services staff members is small and the department's resources are limited. When this is the case, a program can be developed by reaching out to experts in the community. The local university or medical center may be able to provide the required professional staff and program expertise. In addition, program participants can be asked to pay a small fee to help defray program costs.

A law enforcement health promotion program was developed by the Austin Police Department (APD) in cooperation with the University of Texas at Austin. The police chief of the APD authorized the formation of a work-site wellness program with a nutrition component. Support from the chief and police department administrators enabled employees to participate in the program on work time. The APD staff physician/health director contacted the faculty at the Division of Graduate Nutrition at the University of Texas and plans were formulated for a 12-month nutrition program. Each program partici-pant was asked to pay $25 to help defray program costs. The goal of the program was to improve police officers' health and appearance. Program objectives were to decrease participants' weight, blood-cholesterol and triglyceride levels and increase HDL cholesterol levels. The program was successful on all counts.

## Summary

Work-site health promotion programs are important in the law enforcement setting. Just as cars and equipment need preventive maintenance, people need programs to prevent disease. Health promotion programs also result in improvements in the health and appearance of the police officer and cost savings for the department. Health benefits include reduced blood pressure and cholesterol levels, weight control and possible prevention of heart disease, stroke, cancer and diabetes. Cost savings include a reduction in days lost due to illness and a decrease in injuries and their attendant cost. Health promotion programs may also result in improvements in staff morale, productivity and job satisfaction. Health promotion programs can be provided by the department's own Health Services Division, or by a local university or hospital.

**Review Questions**

1. List the programs set up by the NYPD to improve the health of its officers.

2. Describe any 2 of the programs established by the NYPD to improve the health of its officers.

3. Identify the benefits of the health programs established by the NYPD.

# A Fireman's (Firefighter's) Heart
*Ann Miller*

Early morning at a fire station is usually a scene of calm and commonplace activity. Routine chores such as drying and stretching the hoses, washing the engines, and restocking supplies are interspersed with reading, eating, watching TV, and sleeping. In addition, most fire stations have a regular schedule of community activities: tours of the station, free blood pressure checks for senior citizens, and home safety inspections.

Yet, woven into the comfortable pattern of daily activity is the certainty that the alarm bell will ring. Shifts may be 24 hours long, and there is never relief from tension or from the need for readiness. Day or night, in any weather, the sound of the alarm may pierce the station house. Within seconds, without protective warm-up exercise, each firefighter's heart gallops to double its normal pace in anticipation of an unknown peril. Miles from the heat and smoke, stress stimulates adrenaline and shocks the heart.

The change of pace and scene is swift—from firehouse to inferno often in only a few minutes. At the end of a brief and bumpy ride, firefighters put on up to 40 pounds of protective clothing and gear. However, the gear that protects them from external danger burdens the heart and lungs with its weight, and the stiff turnout coat stifles the body's normal cooling process of perspiration and evaporation. Facing flames and heat of 500°F and more, climbing ladders or stairs, wielding heavy axes to break barriers, a firefighter's heart is strained to the limit.

## The Heart of the Problem

Since the National Fire Protection Association began a study in 1975, heart attacks have accounted for nearly half of all firefighter deaths each year. Heart attacks, increased incidence of cancer due to toxic gases and smoke, and fire ground injuries make firefighting the most hazardous civilian occupation. High rates of injury and death occur despite rigorous medical screening to select recruits in peak physical condition. The problem, it seems, is maintaining these initial levels of health and physical fitness.

Two major factors insidiously damage vital body systems, particularly the heart and lungs. The first are the toxic gases released by materials as they burn. According to Joseph Kovac, an inspector in the St. Louis city fire department, 120 gases are released in an average burning room "at least 10 of which can kill." Permanent injury can result from even momentary inhalation of superheated toxic gases such as benzene, carbon monoxide, hydrogen cyanide, and acrolein. When plastics and other man-made products burn, smoke is deadlier than flame. Sophisticated breathing gear is essential, yet it is expensive and heavy. Nevertheless, going into a fire without adequate protection does not make sense when the average age of firefighters disabled by cancer and heart disease is 44.

The second factor is the impact of lifestyle and time. Among firefighters, smoking is not usually discouraged, physical fitness slips little by little, the battle of the bulge is often lost, and in most cities, health matters are solely the responsibility of the individual.

Changes are occurring, but with tragic slowness. For those whose hearts and lungs have been crippled by years of exposure to deadly smoke and heat stress, it is too late to undo the damage. The only "protection" now is economic. When health problems result from occupational injury (service-connected disability), firefighters are retired regardless of age at up to three-quarters of active duty pay. In local government budgets, disability pay for firefighters is out of proportion to their numbers.

**Reprinted with permission from the July 1987 issue of *Public Management* magazine (PM), published by the International City/County Management Association, Washington, D.C.**

## The Cities Respond

Local governments across the nation have responded in a variety of ways to improve firefighter safety and health. Recognizing and providing adequate compensation for occupational hazards such as cancer and heart disease is a first step, but prevention needs to be emphasized. Specially trained and outfitted hazardous material handling squads are desirable but expensive, and firefighters note that the presence or type of hazard is not always known. Obtaining improved protective gear, including longer lasting air tanks, is a common goal of fire departments and local government managers.

Dealing with the personal habits of firefighters is more complex. Court cases in several states, including Minnesota, have determined that fire departments may establish policies against hiring smokers, but they may not dismiss firefighters who were hired under different rules. Regular health reviews and fitness programs are probably the most difficult programs to begin and maintain, but they are among the least expensive options available to curtail disability payments.

The city of Los Angeles has the oldest and most comprehensive firefighter fitness program. This "granddaddy" of fitness programs only dates from 1971. Its goal is to decrease heart disease and the incidence of on-duty injuries. Before the mandatory fitness program was instituted, the city force of 3,250 was reviewed for medical fitness, including weight and blood pressure, a physical exam, and heart problems. More than 10 percent, or 394 firefighters did not meet the medical requirements to participate in the beginning level of physical activity. The following year a weight control and nutrition clinic was established, and blood cholesterol measurement was added to the medical examination. Before the fitness program, injuries were growing steadily. Since instituting the program, the city of Los Angeles has decreased the number of injuries.

More typical is St. Louis, where health maintenance is in its infancy. Calisthenics are encouraged at station houses, but physical examinations are only conducted at five-year intervals. According to Inspector Joseph Kovac, "Health-oriented diets are unusual. Firemen are steeped in the old type of cooking with a lot of sugar, salt, and grease," and stops at "McDonald's for a daily allotment of grease" are common. Captain Raymond Cross adds, "The average fireman is not aware of the risk; [he is] stoic, not philosophizing."

Firefighters themselves are reluctant to discuss the dangers of the job. The traditional feeling is that a tough firefighter can overcome the odds and push the human body to extremes.

What should the response to the heart health problem of the firefighter be? Dr. James Barnard, a research cardiologist at the University of California at Los Angeles, recommends that all fire departments have frequent medical exams to identify problems in their early stages. Each fire department should lower risks by instituting a health maintenance program, including physical fitness, weight control, smoking regulation, and education. In support of such programs, Dr. Barnard said, "Good luck to the firemen; they need a lot of it."

**Review Questions**

1. What are the major factors responsible for damaging the heart of firefighters?

2. Discuss the cities' actions to improve the health of fire fighters.

# Firefighters and Heart Disease: Beyond the Statistics

*Mary Jane Dittmar*

One finding stands out when analyzing research related to the factors that have been contributing to firefighter cardiovascular-related line-of-duty deaths (LODDs) over the past decade: Members of the fire service may have more control over their health and these LODD statistics than they realize. These events need not necessarily be accepted as inevitable. With the proper interventions, the number of such deaths and illnesses can be decreased.

"Clogged arteries are a societal disease and heart disease primarily a disease of choice, of lifestyle," says Richard Milani, director of preventive cardiology at the Ochsner Institute in New Orleans. He was commenting on a study headed by Dr. Salim Yusuf, head of the Population Health Research Institute at McMaster University in Hamilton, Canada. Dr. Yusuf and his colleagues identified nine risk factors that "account for 90 percent of the heart disease in every population on earth: smoking, high blood pressure, diabetes, obesity, stress, a desk job (sedentary lifestyle), a diet rich in processed foods and low in fruit and fiber, fats, and 'failure to take a thimbleful of alcohol.' "

"The important issue is that the vast majority of the risk factors outlined in this [the Yusuf] study are modifiable," says Toronto cardiologist Anthony Graham, a spokesman for the Heart and Stroke Foundation of Canada.[1]

Making changes to reduce health hazards demands the same commitment as efforts to overcome safety hazards, as well as a similar approach: Learn, size up, preplan, and prevent. It is also important for firefighters to recognize that their health can be in jeopardy not only when they are fighting fires but also during the considerable down-time between fires, depending on their lifestyle choices.

In its Alert, "Heart Attacks Leading Cause of On-Duty Texas Firefighter Deaths," sent to the state's fire departments, the Texas State Fire Marshal's Office asserted: "Every fire department (paid and volunteer), fire chief, and firefighter must take the initiative in reducing the number of on-duty heart attack deaths." The Texas Fire Marshal's Office has been investigating the state's firefighter LODDs since 2001.

The Alert referred to President Bush's *Healthier U.S. Initiative* (www.whitehouse.gov/infocus/fitness), which identifies the "four keys for a healthier America: Be physically active every day, eat a nutritious diet, get preventive screenings, and make healthy choices."[2]

"Firefighters and their families can take simple, affordable steps to work physical activity, good nutrition, and behavior changes into their daily routine. Your health will improve with modest but regular physical activity and better eating habits," the Alert stated.[3]

## Health is a Safety Issue as Well

Firefighter health status is a safety issue. It is an equal part of the equation for everyone's returning home at the end of the day. "The health of each individual firefighter affects that of all members of the firefighting team," observes Hope McClusky Bilyk, M.S., R.D., L.D., nutrition consultant and clinical instructor.

A firefighter with precarious health, for whatever reason-lack of fitness, dehydration, uncontrolled stress, untreated high blood pressure, undiagnosed cardiovascular disease, or anything that will interfere with job performance can be as much of a hazard for crew members as a hose about to burst during a firefight or a tire about to blow out while en route to a call. A firefighter at less than optimal health can affect crew safety by various means, including a rapid rate of air consumption or the inability to move/carry hose or climb.

**Making Better Health Choices**

Everyone has the ability to make better health choices. The modifications need not be drastic or "depressing." Following are some suggestions based on the resources I have consulted for this article. A majority of them are related to the identified risks for cardiovascular disease. You will be able to come up with some of your own adjustments based on your circumstances and preferences.

1.  **Make use of the standards and guidelines at your disposal; what you don't know can kill you.**

    The Centers for Disease Control and Prevention (CDC) recommends that the fire service adopt and enforce standards covering mandatory medical examinations and fitness. It advocates mandatory preplacement and annual medical evaluations in accordance with National Fire Protection Association (NFPA) 1582, *Standard on Comprehensive Occupational Medical Program for Fire Departments*. This standard also recommends that asymptomatic firefighters with two or more risk factors for coronary artery disease undergo an exercise stress test.[4]

    Such evaluations and tests may make a significant difference when you consider an NFPA study that involved 1,006 on-duty firefighter fatalities over the 10-year period 1995 to 2004. Of these deaths, 440 were caused by sudden cardiac death (an umbrella term that includes heart attacks but not strokes or aneurysms). According to the report, the medical histories, available for 308 of the 440 victims of sudden cardiac death, showed that there had been prior knowledge of their heart-related conditions for 134 (43.5%) of the fatalities. They previously had had heart attacks, bypass surgery, or angioplasty/stent placement. For another 97 (31.5%), there was evidence of arteriosclerotic heart disease (arterial occlusion of at least 50 percent). Although this is a detectable condition, it is not known if the victims were aware of it.[5]

    Another example is a National Institute for Occupational Safety and Health (NIOSH) investigatory report covering the 2004 death of a 28-year-old male volunteer chief who died in his sleep while attending an emergency medical services (EMS) conference in another state. The autopsy identified "accidental multiple drug intoxication" as the cause of death. The chief had been on numerous medications to control severe back pain from an injury suffered on the job in 2001 (he had undergone three back surgeries), insomnia, depression, and anxiety. However, his medical records, dating back to 1993, showed he had had intermittent hypertension and had begun smoking cigarettes in 1994. The autopsy also showed an enlarged heart (which NIOSH said could not be ruled out as a cause of death), mild atherosclerosis, and moderate to marked pulmonary edema. His body mass index (BMI) was 33 kilograms per square meter; 30-39 is considered obese.

    NIOSH noted that the medical history revealed preexisting conditions that could have affected job performance and the firefighter's health/longevity. Although the firefighter's department policy requires that volunteer firefighter applicants complete a job task assessment (physical ability test) and pass a written test related to fire service tasks before selection, it has no preplacement or periodic medical evaluation. Applicants self-report that they are in excellent health and physically fit. No SCBA medical clearance is required, but annual fit tests are performed. There is no required annual physical agility test.

    The NIOSH report pointed out that: "NFPA 1582 was developed to reduce the risk of sudden cardiac arrest or other incapacitating medical conditions among firefighters. The standard considers that ... the use of narcotics or muscle relaxants could prevent a firefighter from safely performing essential job tasks such as firefighting, wearing SCBA, climbing six or more flights of stairs while wearing turnout gear and equipment weighing 50 pounds or more, victim search and rescue, advancing charged hoselines, climbing ladders, and functioning as an integral part of the two-in/two-out team." (The chief did not perform these functions; he had been on light duty since his injury.)

    Among NIOSH's recommendations was that fire departments, although they are not legally required to do so, follow standards and guidance regarding content and frequency of periodic medical evaluations and examinations for structural firefighters as found in NFPA 1582, the International Association of Fire Fighters (IAFF)/International Association of Fire Chiefs (IAFC) Wellness/Fitness Initiative, and the National Volunteer Fire Council (NVFC) Health and Wellness Guide.

The agency also recommended that fire departments phase in a mandatory wellness/fitness program for firefighters, institute an annual physical performance (physical ability) evaluation to ensure firefighters are physically capable of performing the essential job tasks of structural firefighting, and "ensure that firefighters are cleared for duty by a physician knowledgeable about the physical demands of firefighting, the personal protective equipment used by firefighters, and the various components of NFPA 1582." NIOSH proposed that fire departments retain a fire department physician to critically review all medical clearances.[6]

2. **Identify your personal health risks; take steps to modify them.**

Coronary artery disease patients under 55 years old can benefit substantially from cardiac rehabilitation and exercise training programs (CRETP), according to a report in *Archives of Internal Medicine*, Sept. 25, 2006. Dr. Carl J. Lavie, Ochsner Medical Center, New Orleans, Louisiana, found that these patients have "a very abnormal risk profile, characterized by more obesity, dyslipidemia, and much higher psychological distress," which is "markedly improved following formal cardiac rehabilitation."[7]

In addition to the risks for heart disease that apply to the overall population, firefighters are subjected to "job-related" hazards, which must also be factored into the firefighter health-risk assessment. Among those identified by McClusky Bilyk are the following:

1. Exposure to extreme temperatures that range from below freezing to in excess of greater than 570°F, often within minutes of each other.
2. Continuous exposure to various chemical and physical hazards, which includes the "microclimate" created by firefighters' protective gear.
3. Heavy physical labor that can result in heart rates of 88±6 percent of the predicted maximum.
4. The weight of their gear (which approaches 53 pounds), which adds to the problem of generating internal body heat, and the need to transport equipment that can weigh more than 77 pounds while in full gear.
5. Going from a sedentary lifestyle to a sudden, very physical, high-stress situation in which they must lift and hold for extended periods of time pieces of equipment that may weigh in excess of 77 pounds and ascend ladders in full gear while carrying equipment of various weights. (These duties necessitate also strength or muscular endurance.)

   Most scenarios in which the injuries occur cannot be changed, but the procedure on how to prevent each injury can, McClusky Bilyk says. She recommends that firefighters receive training and in-service education in nutrition in areas such as achieving adequate fluid intake for better hydration and reducing daily total caloric and fat intake. Regular exercise that includes aerobic and anaerobic training can be another "precaution," she adds.[8]

   McClusky Bilyk says continuous fluid consumption is important. "Because firefighters never know when they will be called to a fire, it is important that they drink appropriate fluids throughout their entire shift. They should not rely on their thirst mechanism," she advises. "Sporadic fluid intake and a high consumption of caffeine, combined with the high-temperature work environment can result in a life-threatening situation." (8)

   Following are some ways to incorporate physical activity into everyday life. Examples of some fire departments fitness "interventions" are discussed later.
6. Use the stairs instead of the elevator. Start with one flight of stairs; gradually build up to more.
7. Park a few blocks from the station, and walk the rest of the way. If you take public transportation, get off a stop or two early and walk a few blocks.

8. While working, take frequent activity breaks. Get up and stretch, walk around, give your muscles and mind a change of pace.

9. Instead of eating that extra snack, take a brisk stroll around the neighborhood or your building.

10. Do housework, gardening, and yard work at a more vigorous pace.

Exercise burns calories, builds stamina, improves balance, strengthens your lungs, and boosts the way you feel.[9]

3. **Recognize the presence of stress, and work to control it.**

A study headed by Dr. Richard D. Lane, a professor of psychiatry at the University of Arizona in Tucson, showed that survivors of unexplained cardiac arrest likely had been through a highly stressful event the day before or had dealt with a severely or moderately stressful event during the 24 hours before they went into cardiac arrest. In addition, 20 of the cardiac arrest patients said they had been through significant stress in the six months prior to their heart trouble. The researchers noted that some people may have a genetic defect that makes them vulnerable to the heart arrhythmia that could trigger ventricular fibrillation.[10] Mental stress can negatively affect the reflexive (autonomic) control of heart action over which we have no conscious control.[11]

Firefighters face a considerable amount of mental stress, says McClusky Bilyk. "They are always anticipating the alarm. It's similar to being on a roller coaster. Once the alarm sounds, an automatic adrenaline 'rush' causes an increase in their heart rate before they even get to the fire. This emotional stress combined with the health stresses of being overweight and having low cardiovascular fitness and the physical stress of fighting fire add up to a candidate for a heart attack," she explains. (8) A study showed that although a significant minority of patients with heart failure myocardial infarction (MI), or coronary heart disease have psychological distress, only about one-third of them consulted a mental health professional. In analyzing data from the 2002 National Health Interview Survey involving 17,541 U.S. citizens, Dr. Amy K. Ferketich, Ohio State University School of Public Health in Columbus, and Dr. Philip F. Binkley, Ohio State University of Public Health and Medicine, found that the prevalence of psychological distress among patients with heart failure, MI, and coronary heart disease was 10 percent, 6.4 percent, and 4.1 percent, respectively. The estimated rate of psychological distress among individuals without cardiovascular disease was 2.8 percent.[12]

Physicians should address the mental health needs of these patients as well as their cardiac condition, researchers say.

Music was found to modulate stress and induce changes in the cardiovascular and respiratory systems in a study by Luciano Bernardi, MD, University of Pavia in Italy, and colleagues. In previous research, acute MI patients had reductions in heart rate, respiratory rate, and myocardial oxygen demand after music was added to a quiet, restful environment. Tempo appeared to be the most significant factor associated with the changes in cardiorespiratory responses.[13]

4. **Follow the American Heart Association Dietary and Lifestyle Guidelines.**

These guidelines include the following:

1. Consume an overall healthful diet. Eat a wide variety of fruits and vegetables (not fruit juices), especially those that are deeply colored (spinach, carrots, peaches, and berries). Prepare fruits and vegetables with little added saturated or trans fat (partially hydrogenated fats), salt, and sugar. Choose whole-grain, high-fiber foods. Eat two servings of fish, especially those relatively high in omega-3 fatty acids (e.g., salmon, trout, and herring) at least twice weekly. [Follow Food and Drug Administration guideless for avoiding mercury-contaminated fish (shark, swordfish, king mackerel, and tilefish)]. Limit daily sodium intake to no more than 2,300 mg. Middle-aged and older adults, African Americans, and those with hypertension should consume no more than 1,500 mg of sodium daily.

Limit your intake of saturated fat (less than 7% of calories), trans fats (less than 1% of calories), and cholesterol by choosing lean meats, vegetables, and fat-free (skim) and low fat (1%) fat dairy products. Minimize your intake of beverages and foods with added sugars.

2. Increase your awareness of the calorie content of foods for portions you typically consume and of your daily caloric requirements.

3. Avoid tobacco products (see below for more information).

4. Limit alcohol intake to not more than one drink per day for women and two drinks per day for men (one drink = a 12-ounce beer, 4-ounces of wine, 1.5 ounces of 80-proof distilled spirits, or 1 ounce of 100-proof spirits).

5. Maintain a healthy body weight; balance calories consumed with calories burned. Set a goal of at least 30 minutes of physical activity daily.[14]

## 5. Smoking and firefighting: deadly combination.

The recreational use of tobacco in any form exposes smokers to contaminants firefighters might encounter in fire-caused smoke and other calls involving hazardous materials. The question arises: When do "little" continual and "mixed" exposures elevate the potential health threat to the level of definite hazard within an individual?

The NIOSH/OSHA Occupational Health Guidelines for Chemical Hazards state: "Persons with a history of coronary heart disease, anemia, pulmonary heart disease, cerebrovascular disease, thyrotoxicosis, and smokers would be expected to be at increased risk from [chemical] exposure."[15]

A retrospective study of 1,212 tunnel officers exposed to carbon monoxide, resulting in less than 5 percent carboxyhemoglobin, were found to have a significantly elevated risk of dying from arteriosclerotic heart disease.[16] Levels at fires may reach 10 percent, which can raise carboxyhemoglobin levels in active firefighters without respiratory protection to 75 percent within one minute.[17] Heavy cigarette smokers may have carboxyhemoglobin levels as high as 15 to 17 percent.[18]

Nearly 40 percent of patients with moderate to severe carbon monoxide (CO) poisoning will have cardiovascular manifestations, according to Dr. Timothy D. Henry, Minneapolis Heart Institute Foundation. Myocardial injury is common in moderate to severe CO poisoning.[19]

Cigarette smoking can add two to four micrograms of cadmium per pack. Firefighters might be exposed to this heavy metal also through batteries and alloys, pigments, soldering processes, and burning fossil fuels. A direct link between low-dose cadmium exposure and an increased risk of breast cancer was found in studies involving rats, and previous studies in male rats showed changes in the prostate after the administration of cadmium.[20]

Formaldehyde vapors are also present in tobacco smoke, as well as in vehicle exhaust. Consider that these vapors are also present at occupancies that make chemical resins, wrinkleproof fabrics, rubber products, latex paints, dyes, plastics, paper products, and cosmetics and are found in insulation materials, plywood, particleboard, adhesives, glues, paint primers, and fingernail products. If you respond to fires in such occupancies, you can easily be "overexposed" to these vapors. Cal/OSHA and Cal/EPA regulate formaldehyde as a carcinogen.[21]

## Other Factors to Consider

The reserve capacity of the heart is impaired in people with diabetes and high blood pressure, even when the individual doesn't have coronary artery disease. Therefore, it is important to get regularly scheduled checkups to see if you have these conditions and to seek medical treatment if you do.[22]

High blood pressure (140/90) increases the risk of heart attacks, strokes, kidney damage, blindness, and dementia. "The challenge from a clinical point of view is to screen these patients to prevent long-term cardiac complications in this high-risk population," says Dr. Paul Poirier, Hospital Laval, Sainte-Foy, Quebec, Canada.[23]

Losing weight (if needed), increasing physical activity, cutting down on sodium (salt), and eating more fruits and vegetables are the most effective lifestyle changes you can make to lower blood pressure. Most hypertension patients may need medications as well.[24]

Balancing omega-3 fats with other fats in the diets has been shown to reduce substances that stimulate inflammation that may increase the risk for heart disease and related chronic illnesses. Omega-3 fatty acids are found predominantly in cold-water fish and a few vegetable oils (flaxseed, walnuts, and canola). Other food sources of omega-3 include whole grains, legumes, nuts, and green leafy vegetables. These fatty acids are blood thinners and help keep the coronary arteries elastic and flexible, reduce high blood pressure, keep triglyceride levels down, and reduce the risk of blood clots.

The literature stresses that the intake of omega-3 fats and omega-6 fats, found in many vegetable oils, must be balanced. The American diet seems to include a much greater ratio of omega-6 fatty acids. Many of today's chronic diseases are related to the effects of an imbalance in omega-6 and omega-3-fats. Higher levels of omega-6s tend to increase the risk of many inflammatory and autoimmune diseases, or they make these problems harder to treat.

Nutrition experts disagree on the optimal ratio between omega-6 and omega-3 fatty acids. Some recommend consuming equal quantities (a 1:1 ratio); others recommend no more than 10 omega-6s to each omega-3. The current American diet contains roughly 10 to 20 times as much omega-6 as omega-3 fatty acids.

Flaxseed is the best source of omega-3s in the vegetable kingdom. Additional food sources of omega-3 fatty acids include walnuts, Brazil nuts, butternuts, chia seeds, hickory nuts, macadamia nuts, roasted or cooked soybeans, soybean sprouts, beans of various types, peanuts, olives, spirulina, and spinach.[25]

Trans-fats are destructive to health because the body misreads them as omega-3s and omega-6s and uses them for the same purposes. But because the structure of trans fat is straight instead of bent, the part of the cell membrane that needs to be porous becomes tight and rigid, which causes a variety of health problems-including insulin resistance, which can lead to type 2 diabetes.

The U.S. Food and Drug Administration began requiring food labels to list trans fats in January. "Artificial trans fats are very toxic, and they almost surely cause tens of thousands of premature deaths each year," says Dr. Walter Willett, chairman of the Department of Nutrition at the Harvard University School of Public Health. "The federal government should have done this long ago."[26]

Some companies have been working to eliminate trans fats. Wendy's, for example, has switched to a new cooking oil that contains no trans fatty acids. Crisco now sells a shortening that contains zero trans fat. Frito-Lay removed trans fats from its Doritos and Cheetos, Kraft took trans fats out of its Oreos. (26)

Be a more discerning shopper. Read labels. Let food suppliers know you want more healthful foods. Keep asking for them. Purchase foods without trans fats.


**Departments Are Decreasing Health Risks**

Many departments have acted to improve their members' health and decrease their risk of cardio-vascular disease. A few examples follow:


**Arlington County (VA) Fire Department**

The morning shift of platoon firefighters runs two miles every morning. Their philosophy is that fitness is a mental as well as a physical requirement and they have to keep in shape for the job every day.[27]

*(NJ) Fire Department*

The department developed a voluntary dietary cooperative program between labor and management that promotes healthy hearts and bodies. The recently initiated second phase includes hiring a nutritional expert to teach healthful eating habits. Chief Mike Roberts has fresh fruit delivered to firehouses for snacks. During training sessions, they discuss eating habits and cardiovascular health.[28]

## Scottsdale (AZ) Fire Department

Chief Willie McDonald, who understands the importance and benefits of employing healthy and fit firefighters, has made a comprehensive wellness program a high priority, explain Deputy Chief Garret Olson, the program's training and development program director.

Steve Giardini, wellness program coordinator (WPC), is responsible for day-to-day management and is also the liaison between the professional medical services contractor and the fire department.

Program components include an annual firefighter occupational medical certification (OMC) exam, an annual work-related incumbent physical ability test (IPAT), and general health related fitness services (HRFS), the centerpiece of the wellness program, which is offered continuously to help firefighters achieve and maintain a health and fitness level commensurate with the job demands.

A team of peer fitness trainers delivers the services, available to individuals and groups. Participation is voluntary. Group health, fitness, and nutrition (weight management and basic nutrition) open enrollment classes are part of the company training schedule and are also offered at the fire station at the crews' request. Special group wellness services are offered occasionally to promote and stimulate greater participation-for example, a 16-week departmentwide weight loss challenge was held in January 2006. Some 30 department employees (sworn and civilian) participated. Nutrition and behavior modification classes were combined with biweekly weigh-ins. The group lost more than 340 pounds.

Crews may attend a class on-duty with battalion chief approval or individually off-duty Exercise sessions focus on exercise technique; when possible, work-related functional training is incorporated. Work Hardening, a popular firefighter exercise class, combines core strength exercises (push-ups, crunches) and work-related job tasks (climbing stairs with high pack, pulling hose, dragging manne-quins, sledgehammer work, and other tasks). The 30- to 40-minute sessions are designed to improve aerobic capacity and muscular endurance. Firefighters work in pairs and move through the course at their own pace, but continuously.

Individual services include voluntary fitness assessments, personal exercise prescriptions, and weight management consultation. All department personnel have access to fitness facilities. Department health and fitness policy requires sworn personnel to exercise every on-duty shift; captain and battalion chiefs manage this requirement. All firefighters are required to sign a no tobacco use and health and fitness agreement at the time of hire. Health and fitness agreements spell out the annual medical and physical ability test requirements.

The department contracts for a professional medical service, which performs annual comprehensive Occupational Medical Certification exams in accordance with recommended National Fire Protection Association medical standards. Each firefighter must "pass" the medical exam to maintain field operations status. If nonindustrial-related medical problems are identified, the firefighter is referred to his private physician for follow-up. The firefighter must return to the fire department physician for final clearance after the problem is corrected or under control. The annual medical exam also serves to clear firefighters for the required incumbent physical ability test (IPAT), which hired experts are developing.

Testing is expected to begin around January 2007. The goal is a 100 percent pass rate. The timed IPAT is pass or fail. Field operations work status depends on passing this fitness test. IPAT practice sessions including "test out" sessions are conducted well in advance of the scheduled annual IPAT test. Firefighters who fail the test are removed from their field operation position and placed on modified duty. The WPC performs a fitness assessment, establishes personal goals, and writes a personal rehabilitation prescription. Under the direction of the WPC, a peer fitness trainer is assigned to work with the firefighter five days a week. Periodic fitness assessments are repeated and firefighters receive an IPAT retest at specific intervals. For additional information, contact Steve Giardini at SGiardini@ ScottsdaleAz.Gov.

## Southern Nevada Fire Departments and Well eMerica

A partnership of southern Nevada fire departments and nationally known wellness experts from the University of Nevada, Las Vegas' Office of Research and Development for Firefighter Wellness and Fitness (ORDFWF) have worked to develop a comprehensive wellness and fitness program. The program features the Well eMerica© System, an electronic portal designed to improve health, reduce injury risk, and enhance job-related performance of fire service personnel. (Later, target groups will also include fire service retirees and families.) The partnership's genesis (2002) was to formalize and expand North Las Vegas Fire Department's (NLVFD) wellness and fitness program using the International Association of Firefighters/International Association of Fire Chiefs recommendations as the foundation. Las Vegas Fire and Rescue joined the program in 2003–2004, and the Clark County Fire Department in 2004.

The program components include determining current wellness and fitness levels for department members and comparing them with national standards, identifying wellness and fitness goals, and creating a plan for achieving personal goals tailored to the user's needs. Individual wellness and fitness test results are stored in a secured database, which the user can access. Future plans include rehabilitation (physical and psychological) efforts to be coordinated between the fire department's medical staff and the Well eMerica© system.

Dr. Charles Regin and Dr. Jean Henry administer the program. A large percentage of their efforts recently have been directed toward testing and providing recommendations for cadets in 11 academies in three fire departments. The original program was funded by a Federal Emergency Management Agency (FEMA) grant cowritten by Local 1607 (North Las Vegas) leaders and North Las Vegas Fire Department's management representatives.

At press time, partners in the program included kinesiologists, registered dieticians, and graduate and undergraduate student volunteers from the university; a nationally recognized computer software development company; a national computer company; fire departments in southern Nevada (North Las Vegas Fire Department, Las Vegas Fire and Rescue, and Clark County Fire Department), physical therapists and medical doctors; and a fitness club with national sites.

All members of the current partnership have committed to a multiyear timeline. The university is committed to expanding the center for research and development for firefighter wellness and fitness with partnerships developed with additional interested fire service personnel. Information on the program is available at Wellemerica.unlv.edu, or contact Chuck Regin, Ph.D., director, at (702) 895-0856 or by e-mail at charles.regin@univ.edu.

We are all aware of the heart-health initiatives offered through fire service organizations, and many of you are participating in them. These resources are of exceptional benefit. This article is directed more to giving you "empowerment" over your health through daily, conscious decisions that may not be earth shattering in themselves but that continuously and collectively can make a difference, as research is showing, and create a healthier—and safer—fire service. What are you and your department doing to promote heart health? Let us know. E-mail me at maryjd@pennwell.com.

## Endnotes

1   "Nine factors that affect your heart's health," Steve Sternberg, USA TODAY, www.usatoday.com/news/health/2006-01-08-heart-nine-factors_x.htm; The Lancet, Sept. 11, 2006.
2   "Healthier U.S. Initiative," www.whitehous.gov/infocus/fitness.
3   Dept of Insurance, Texas State Fire Marshal's Office, accessed 10/12/06, www.tdi.state.tx.us/fire/fmloddinvesti.html.
4   Morbidity and Mortality Weekly Report, U.S. Centers for Disease Control and Prevention, April 28, 2006.
5   "U.S. Firefighter Fatalities Due to Sudden Cardiac Death, 1995-2004," Rita F. Fahy, Fire Analysis and Research Division, National Fire Protection Association, June 2005.
6   "Fire Chief Suffers Sudden Death during Training-Alabama," NIOSH Fire Fighter Fatality Investigation and Prevention Report, July 21, 2006.
7   "Adverse Risk Profiles Seen in Relatively Young Coronary Artery Disease Patients" Will Boggs, MD, http://www.medscape.com/viewarticle/545476, Oct. 3, 2006.
8   "The Industrial Worker: A New Breed of Athlete," Gatorade Sports Science Institute Roundtable RT#28, Vol. 8 (1997), No. 2, http://are.berkeley.edu/heat/indistworkerathlete.html, accessed 9/22/06.
9   National Heart Lung and Blood Institute, National Institutes of Health.
10  "Stress May Be Behind Unexplained Cardiac Arrest," Psychosomatic Medicine, May/June 2005, www.heartcenteronline.com, accessed June 14, 2005.
11  "Depression, Stress and Heart Disease," http://uimc.discoveryhospital.com accessed 9/22/06 University of Illinois Medical Center at Chicago.
12  "Psychological Distress Common in Cardiovascular Disease Patients," Anthony J. Brown, MD, online Eur Heart J June 9, 2005; target="_new"www.medscape.com/viewarticle/506578_print, June 14, 2005.
13  http://www.medscape.com/viewarticle/513790_print, Online First issue of Heart, Sept 30, 2005.
14  www.medscape.com/viewarticle/536831_print accessed 8/30/06; Rapid Access issue of Circulation. June 19, 2006.
15  Mackison, F.W., R.S. Stricoff, L. J. Partridge, Jr (eds) NIOSH/OSHA Occupational Health Guidelines for Chemical Hazards. DHHS (NIOSH) Publication No. 81-123 (e Vols)., Washington, DC: U.S. Government Printing Office, Jan. 1981, 1; toxnet.nlm.nih.gov.
16  American Conference of Governmental Industrial Hygienists, Inc. Documentation of the Threshold Limit Values and Biological Exposure Indices, 6th ed., Vols. I, II, III, Cincinnati, OH ACGIH, 1991, 229) toxnet.nlm.nih.gov.
17  Ellenhorn, M.J. and D.G. Barceloux, Medical Toxicology-Diagnosis and Treatment of Human Poisoning, New York NY: Elsevier Science Publishing Co., Inc. 1988, 820; toxnet.nlm.nih.gov.
18  WHO; Environ Health Criteria 13: Carbon Monoxide, 74; toxnet.nlm.nih.gov.
19  "Carbon Monoxide Poisoning Often Cardiotoxic," J AM Coll Cardiol 2005;45:1513-1516 www.medscape.com/viewarticle/504738_print, accessed May 18, 2005.
20  Mary Beth Martin, Georgetown University, "Cadmium mimics estrogen, may cause breast disease," Nature Medicine, July 14, 2003.
21  Hazard Evaluation System & Information Service (HESIS), California Dept of Health Services, Jan. 2003.
22  American Journal of Hypertension, August 2006. Dr. Miguel Quintana, Karolinska Institute, Stockholm, Sweden. Sept 7, 2006 http:heart.healthcenersonline.com.
23  "High Blood Pressure, Diabetes, Cut Heart Reserve," http://heart.healthcentersonline.com, Sept 7, 2006.
24  www.msnbc.msn.com/id/14122841/print/1/displaymode/1098, July 31, 2006.
25  "When 'Fatty' is Good: Omega-3 Oils and Fatty Acids," Wyn Snow, managing ed, American Institute for Cancer Research 30 April 2004.
26  "Doughnuts in Danger?" www.msnbc.sn.com/id/15020846, Sept. 27, 2006.
27  Michael Doyle, McClatchy Newspapers, www.realcities.com, Sept. 11, 2006.
28  www.everyonegoeshome.com/newsletter/2006/july/millburn.html, accessed Oct 12, 2006.

**Review Questions**

1. Discuss the Healthy choices you will recommend to a firefighter to promote cardiovascular health.

2. Describe the health and wellness program designed for Scottsdale, Arizona firefighter personnel.

3. List the nine risk factors of cardiovascular disease identified by Dr. Salim Yusul and his colleagues.

4. Discuss five concepts to improve cardiovascular health of firefighters.

# Examining the Cardiovascular Health Issues of Firefighters
*Davidson C. Umeh*

## Introduction

Sudden cardiac death has consistently been the number-one cause of firefighter line-of-duty deaths each year in the United States (Fahy et al. 2010). The cardiovascular fatalities of firefighters occurs either en route to an emergency call or following strenuous activities performed at the scene of the emergency. Spratlin (2011) stated that the line of duty deaths associated with cardiovascular disease often occurred after strenuous duties at emergency scenes. In fact, Kales et al. (2007) specifically identified that firefighters are 12 to 136 times more likely to die of heart disease when putting out a fire; 3 to 14 times more likely to die of heart disease while responding to an alarm; 2 to 10.5 times more likely to die of heart disease while returning from an alarm; 3 to 7 times more likely to die of heart disease during physical training.

The heart is the most important organ in the body because it is responsible for transporting blood containing oxygen, nutrients, and other substances that are necessary for the physiological functions of the body. The heart is a muscle that when at rest beats 60 to 70 times per minute to satisfy the oxygen needs of the body. The number of heartbeats depends on the fitness level of the person. Oldham (2001) stated that cardiovascular fitness is crucial because if the heart cannot pump blood to the body in sufficient quantities to oxygenate the muscles, firefighters will not be able to exert all the strength they require in the line of duty. However, when the arteries (blood vessels) are clogged, the heart muscle is made to work harder (more beats per minute) to accomplish its functions in the body. The firefighter's heart works harder due to the strenuous nature of firefighting.

Firefighters perform a very risky job, which affects their health after several years on the job. The fire department recruits physically fit individuals from society due to the rigorous health and fitness requirements for appointment as a firefighter. But as the years progress, these individuals develop various health problems, particularly cardiovascular health problems. Guilfoil (2010) stated that a firefighter died of a heart attack after helping to fight a multi-alarm fire in a neighboring Tolland over the weekend. It is essential to examine the risk factors that negatively affect the cardiovascular health of firefighters. An expose of these risk factors will encourage or guide fire department administrators to design preventive measures to reduce the health impact of these risk factors for the firefighter personnel.

## Risk Factors

Firefighters are exposed to multiple cardiovascular risk factors during the performance of their duties. The risk factors in the line of duty include the following: smoke and gases produced from burning objects, heat, heavy equipment and clothing, firefighting activities (chopping down doors and breaking windows, carrying victims to safety, carrying and pulling water hose) and fear of the dangers associated with the job and lifestyle issues. The lifestyle issues which affect the cardiovascular health of fire fighters are poor eating habits, physical inactivity, smoking, alcoholism, and personal health problems. Carey and Berg (2010) stated that many factors increase the risk of dying from cardiac arrest by firefighters, including poor dietary habits, the presence of subclinical and clinical heart disease, and most of all, the job's stressful nature. The cumulative effects of these cardiovascular risk factors is the death of 45% of United States firefighters in the line of duty from coronary heart disease (Kales et al. 2003).

## Lifestyle Issues

### Poor Eating Habits

Firefighters are prone to eat food high in fats and cholesterol that are harmful to the cardiovascular system. The fats and cholesterol block the blood vessels. The heart pumps harder to transport blood in the body. Donuts and coffee, which are sometimes eaten on the run, contain caffeine and sugar, which causes an increase in the fat level in the blood. Poor eating habits will, in some circumstances, lead to obesity, which causes severe problems for the cardiovascular system. Spratlin (2011) stated that one cardiovascular disease risk factor among firefighters is obesity, considered to be of "epidemic" proportions in the general population of the United States.

### Physical Inactivity

The jobs of firefighters involve a high level of physical activity. Yet, they do not participate in regular physical activity training to be ready to meet the daily demands of their job. Kales et al. (2007) stated that 70% of fire departments in the United States do not have programs that promote fitness and health for their personnel. The heart muscles will not be able to pump an adequate volume of blood to support the rigorous activities of firefighting.

### Smoking

Smoking is very harmful to the cardiovascular health of firefighters. Yet, many fire fighters smoke on a regular basis. The tar in cigarettes and other tobacco products develops plaque in the arteries. The arteries become hardened and lose their flexibility. Smoking can also affect the respiratory system, which makes it difficult for oxygen to reach the cardiovascular system. Cigarette smoking leads to blood clotting, an increase in blood pressure and heart rate, and a decrease of oxygen to the heart.

### Alcoholism

Consuming alcohol has been identified as harmful to cardiovascular health, yet firefighters and other members of the uniform services consume alcohol as a way to overcome the stress of the job. Caldwell (2008) stated that "alcohol is a scourge in firehouses, too. Last year in Boston, for example, high levels of cocaine and alcohol were found in the blood of two firefighters who died battling a restaurant fire. And in San Francisco, a group of 28 city firefighters sued their department, complaining that on-the-job drinking was 'frequent, open and notorious' and asking a judge to force the department bosses to do something about it." Alcoholic drinks contain carbohydrates, which in great amount in the body is eventually converted to fat that is deposited in the blood vessels. Alcohol calories deposited in the arteries as fat makes blood circulation more difficult resulting to high blood pressure and heart failure.

### Personal Health Issues

Cardiovascular health problems are manifested more easily when a person has personal health problems such as a family history of cardiovascular disease, diabetes, or obesity. Diabetes increases the formation of plaque in the arteries (atherosclerosis) blocking blood vessels and reducing the circulation of blood. Obesity also results to many debilitating diseases such as cancer, high blood pressure, diabetes, stroke and cardiovascular diseases. These health problems affect the ability of the heart to function effectively when the firefighter is in the line of duty or faced with the responsibilities of the job.

### Smoke and Gases

Smoke and gases produced from burning substances significantly affect the cardiovascular health of firefighters. The chemicals in the smoke enter the blood stream from the lungs and causes plaque to form in the arteries, which leads to arteriosclerosis. The devastating effects of the chemicals on the arteries are enhanced if the firefighter also smokes cigarettes. The walls of the arteries harden and lose their flexibility essential for blood transportation.

Different type of gases are produced as byproducts when substances burn. Gases such as carbonmonoxide, hydrogen cyanide, carbon dioxide, nitrous oxide, and benzene are potentially harmful to the cardiovascular and respiratory system. Benzene has the ability to collapse the lungs which makes it difficult for oxygen to reach the cardiovascular system. Carbon monoxide has greater affinity for oxygen than hemoglobin in the blood. Therefore, a lesser amount of oxygen is transported in the blood to the cells for metabolic reactions. The Department of Environmental Protection, Maine stated that carbon monoxide reduces the flow of oxygen in the bloodstream and is particularly dangerous to people with heart disease. The heart muscle works harder under these conditions to perform its functions in the body.

### Heat

The normal body temperature for optimal performance is 98.6 degrees Farenheit. The high heat in a firefighting environment, especially on hot summer days, can be very harmful to the cardiovascular system. The heat in the fire environment increases the temperature of the body. The body tries to cool itself through perspiration and an increase in blood flow. Excessive sweating leads to dehydration, which reduces the volume of blood. The heart is challenged to pump harder to circulate the reduced amount of blood throughout the body. Sweating also depletes other essential substances, sodium, potassium, and other minerals needed for muscle contraction, nerve transmission, and water balance. The heart rate increases to overcome the increased activity in the body of the firefighter. An excessive increase in the body temperature results in heat stress, which affects the function of the cardiovascular muscle.

### Equipment

Firefighters wear different personal protective equipment to assist them during firefighting operations. However, the equipment adds an extra load to be handled by the firefighter while on duty. The oxygen tank, helmet, boots, and clothes present extra work for the heart muscle. It is estimated that the protective equipment weighs about 75 pounds. The cardiovascular system has to provide the needed energy to support the firefighter with carrying the extra load from the equipment.

### Firefighter Activities

It has been found that most of the cardiovascular health problems of firefighters occur after a firefighting operation. Dedman (2011) stated that researchers found the risk of firefighters' deaths from heart attacks nationwide over a decade was highest when the fire fighters are working at a fire scene. The activities performed during firefighting, operations such as chopping down doors and breaking windows, climbing stairs, carrying victims to safety, and carrying or pulling water hoses increase the demands for oxygen to the body. To overcome these challenges, the heart beats faster to satisfy the body's need for an increased level of blood with oxygen and nutrients. We cannot advocate negligence of duty by firefighters, but there is a need to prepare firefighters to be fit and well prepared to meet the challenges posed by their job.

### Fear and Dangers of the Job

The firefighters' natural safety tendencies go into active mode when the alarm rings for a firefighting operation. In fact, heart rates often begin to race at the very beginning of the call, when firefighters are dispatched, as a result of an activation of the sympathetic nervous system and continues throughout the remainder of the call because of increased exertion (National Institute of Occupational Safety and Health, 2007). The physiological changes in the body at this time results in the following activities: increase in heartbeat, increase in respiration, increase in sugar and fat in the circulatory system and increase of water in the circulatory system. These changes are essential to facilitate the movement of blood to different parts of the body to overcome the stress incurred by the dangers that may arise from the fire alarm. Adverse reaction to fire alarms over the years will enhance the deposition of the by-products of the stress reactions (fat) in the arteries making blood circulation more difficult for the heart muscle.

**Prevention**

The job of a firefighter is risky and dangerous, but administrators cannot fold their hands and leave them to die from cardiovascular health problems. It is the responsibilities of administrators to design programs to assist the staff to improve their health, while meeting the responsibilities required by the job. Preventive measures will be effective if the fire department develop and implement a health and wellness program for its personnel. The administrator should appoint a peer coordinator to implement the program. The administrators and the workers union must provide financial support and personal commitment to the success of the program.

The following units should form the basis of the health and wellness program to reduce/prevent the risk factors of cardiovascular health problems of fire fighters:

*Exercise Programs*
*Smoking and Alcohol Cessation*
*Nutrition Education*
*Regular medical examination and screening*

### *Exercise Programs*

The job of firefighting is very physically demanding on the body. It is essential for fire fighters to participate in regular physical activity to prepare themselves for the challenges of the job. Participation in a regular exercise program improves the strength, flexibility and endurance of the cardiovascular muscles and enhances its ability to supply adequate oxygen and nutrients during firefighting activities. The department should establish fitness centers in the firehouses or provide memberships for its personnel in private fitness centers which are conveniently located to the firefighter's duty station or home. It is also necessary to hire an exercise instructor to assist and monitor the progress of firefighters engaged in the exercise program.

Firefighters who participate should apply the following principles to obtain the necessary benefits from exercise. That is, exercise should be performed at least three times a week. Exercise sessions should also be at least 30 minutes long and each exercise session should be intense enough to work the heart rate beyond the threshold level.

To begin an exercise program, the firefighter should first warm up. Warm up is essential to warm and stretch the muscles in readiness for more rigorous activity. After warm up, the firefighter performs the rigorous activity, for example, aerobic activity such as running, jogging, or bicycling which are necessary for developing cardiovascular fitness. The exercise session should end with a cool down activity. Cool down activities help to normalize the heart rate and blood pressure throughout the body after a rigorous activity.

### *Smoking and Alcohol Cessation*

The fire department has to develop a smoking cessation program to help those who smoke. Smokers should be directed to consult with counselors who can assist them, in the effort to stop smoking and drinking alcohol. Administrators should address the stressful issues on the job that make firefighters susceptible to smoking or drinking alcohol. Peer and professional counselors should be made available to firefighters and counseling services should be confidential.

### *Nutrition Education*

Nutrition education on how to prepare balanced diets should be provided to firefighters. Education on nutrition can be addressed at individual and department levels. Individual nutrition education can be accomplished by organizing workshops on how to prepare a balanced diet. Literature on various recipes can also be distributed to the staff during the workshops.

Nutrition education at the department level can be provided by displaying only foods that conform to a proper diet in vending machines. Posters with foods comprising balanced diets can be displayed at strategic places in the department.

### Regular Medical Exams and Screening

Firefighters are exposed to different toxic substances and gases in the line of duty. They are more susceptible to acquire a health problem due to the circumstances of their job. Regular medical examinations will enable the identification of any health problems before they become more serious. The department should mandate annual physical check-ups for every firefighter. Firefighters who are identified to have any health problems due to screening results should be referred to a specialist for further investigation. There should also be a follow up on the results of the investigation before the firefighter returns to duty. Kales et al. (2003) stated that improved fitness promotion, medical screening, and medical management could prevent premature death of firefighters.

### Personal Responsibility

The maintenance of good cardiovascular fitness lies mainly with the firefighter. The firefighter must commit to take the necessary actions that will promote and enhance cardiovascular fitness. Individual commitment to take positive action will lead to behavior change. Rhea (2010) stated that behavior change requires a change in one's environment, a change in one's thought patterns, and a goal to better oneself. Firefighters can commit to change the following behaviors to improve their cardiovascular health: exercise on a regular basis, eat a balanced diet, avoid unnecessary stress, learn strategies to manage stress, join a social group, for example, church/choir, create time to socialize with family, and be aware of the stressful situations on the job.

### Conclusion

Firefighting is a very dangerous job that is prone to many situations that can harm the health of the firefighting personnel. But, careful effort should be made to reduce these harmful situations through implementing programs that will enhance the health of firefighters. Administrators of fire departments must commit to policies that will protect the health of their staff. Healthy firefighting personnel will be very beneficial in service to the community.

### References

Caldwell, B. (2008). Firefighters grapple with alcohol abuse. http://www.oregonlive.com. Retrieved 2/15/2012.

Carey, R. E. and Berg, S. (Feb. 2010). A burning need—Preventing heart disease among firefighters. *Today's Dietician Magazine*, Vol. 12. No. 2 p. 44.

Dedman, B. (2011). Firefighters' heart attack risk soars at the scene. http://www.msnbc.msn.com. Retrieved 11/3/2011.

Department of Environmental Protection, Maine (2011). Effects of vehicle pollution. http://www.maine.gov/dep/air/lev4me/effects.htm. Retrieved 12/13/2011.

Fahy, R. F.; LeBlanc, P. R.; Molis, J. L. (2010). Firefighter fatalities in the United States—2009 and US fire service fatalities in structure fires, 1977–2009. Retrieved from National Fire Protection Association Website: http://www.nfpa.org/assests/files/PDF/osfff.pdf/

Guilfoil, J. M. (July 26, 2010). Otis firefighter, 70, collapses and dies after fire. *Boston Globe*.

Kales, S. N.; Soteriades, E. S.; Christophi, C. A. and Christiani, D. C. (2007). Emergency duties and death from heart disease among firefighters in the United States. *New England Journal of Medicine*. 356 (12): pp. 1207–1215.

Kales, S. N.; Soteriades, E. S.; Christophi, C. A.; and Christiani, D. C. (2003). Firefighters and on-duty deaths from coronary heart disease: A case control study. Environmental Health, Vol. 4, p. 14. Retrieved on line 11/27/12.

National Institute for Occupational Safety and Health. (2007). Preventing fire fighter fatalities due to heart attacks and other sudden cardiovascular events. Publication No. 2007-133, Cincinnati, OH.

Oldham, S. (June 2001). Physical fitness training for police officers. *Law and Order Magazine,* Vol. 49, Issue 6, pp 75–78.

Rhea, D. J. (March 2010). Back to the basics: Eat right and get active. *Journal of Physical Education, Recreation and Dance.* Vol. 81, No. 3, pp. 4, 5 & 56.

Spratlin, K (2011). Firefighter obesity: A public safety risk. *Fire Engineering Magazine*, Vol. 164, Issue 1, pp. 20–28.

## Review Questions

1. Discuss the risk factors that affect the health of a firefighter.

2. Discuss the prevention strategies to reduce the health risk experienced by firefighters on the job.

# PART TWO
# Drugs and Alcohol Issues

## Anabolic Steroid Abuse Among Law Enforcement Officers

*Roland C. Dart, III and Dale A. Ferranto*

Because police officers are selected from society's mainstream, they are bound to reflect the changes in society's social and moral fabric—both the positive *and* the negative.

Substance abuse problems among law enforcement personnel have traditionally centered around those drugs most commonly encountered while enforcing the law—marijuana, cocaine, and methamphetamine. More recently, however, a new problem substance has appeared in the police workplace—anabolic steroids.

First synthesized prior to World War II and used primarily for a wide range of growth and sub-fertility disorders, steroids are widely manufactured by pharmaceutical companies worldwide. Anabolic steroids are a synthetic version of the male hormone testosterone, used to enhance muscle development either for body building or sports competition.

Although the medical community was once skeptical, sports physicians and medical researchers have discovered that muscle mass can be increased when steroids are coupled with a very high-protein diet and rigorous exercise.

Indeed, it is the bodybuilding aspect of steroid abuse that law enforcement administrators are most likely to encounter among their personnel. As officers become more concerned about their ability to adequately protect themselves on the job, the incidence of abuse will probably increase. In their pursuit of increased fitness, some officers are innocently introduced to steroids at gymnasiums where body builders—who may also be steroid abusers—work out. Others may turn directly to steroids to give them the physical edge they fear they lack.

When nontherapeutic amounts of anabolic steroids are taken by abusers, it is usually in megadoses that "supersaturate" the body with testosterone, resulting in adverse psychological and physiological effects.[1,2,3] In most cases, the abuser will experience heightened levels of anxiety and aggression, known as "roid rages." With very little provocation, he can become violent and uncontrollable. Perhaps most significant among the physical dangers associated with anabolic steroid abuse are highly elevated cholesterol and blood pressure, which can lead to the early onset of heart disease.

Various states have enacted controls on the illegal distribution and abuse of anabolic steroids. In California, the Uniform Controlled Substances Act schedules steroids and human chorionic gonadotropin (another synthetic substance used by steroid abusers to stimulate muscle development) in Schedule III, provides criminal penalties for possession, possession for sale and sale of steroids, and restricts the administration, dispensing and prescription of anabolic steroids to medical purposes only. Nationally, the Anabolic Steroids control Act, which took effect February 27, 1991, added anabolic steroids to Schedule III of the *federal* Controlled Substances Act.

Law enforcement administrators must adopt a multidimensional approach to successfully combat the phenomenon of steroid abuse among their officers: drug screening should be expanded to include steroids; in-service training should be provided on the legal and medical dangers of steroid abuse; supervisors should be taught to recognize the symptoms of steroid abuse, as well as what administrative action is appropriate when a "reasonable suspicion" of abuse is present. With regard to pre-employment screening and internal investigations, agencies should apply the standards of abuse adopted by the

International Olympic Committee, including a maximum ratio of 6:1 for serum testosterone to its isomer epitestosterone.

There is no way to completely escape the internal personnel problems associated with illegal drug use. But by making effective use of our strategic and administrative skills, we can do much to minimize the damage.

## References

[1]William M. Taylor, M.D., *Hormonal Manipulation* (Jefferson: McFarland & Co., 1985), p. 27.

[2]Eugene F. Luckstead, M.D., and Stephen G. Taylor, M.D., "Medical Concerns for the Adolescent Athlete," *Iowa Medicine,* September 1987, p. 436.

[3]Herbert A. Haupt, M.D., and George D. Rovere, M.D., "Anabolic Steroids: A Review of the Literature," *The American Journal of Sports Medicine, 1984,* vol. 12, no. 6, p. 475.

## Review Questions

1. State the reasons why law enforcement officers abuse steroids.

2. What strategies can be adopted to help officers stop the use of steroids?

# DRUGS
# Alcohol Abuse In Policing: Prevention Strategies
*John M. Violanti*

Alcohol abuse represents an important issue in police work. Estimates shows that alcohol abuse among police officers in the United States is approximately double that of the general population where 1 in 10 adults abuses alcohol.[1] While the social use of alcohol may be accepted in most professions, excessive use can impair an individual's ability to function properly at work and at home. This can prove particularly dangerous for police officers.

Researchers find the occupational and personal losses associated with alcohol abuse among police officers difficult to determine, and deficits in job performance due to alcohol abuse cannot always be easily detected. Because alcohol use often is considered part of the police lifestyle, officers who have a problem seldom get approached by their peers.

Ultimately, officers who abuse alcohol get noticed by their organizations and sometimes by the public. Their drinking problems may lead to an automobile accident, a domestic violence situation, or a citizen's complaint. To deal with such situations, many police agencies adopt a strategy of getting help for abusers only after they discover a problem. Help may include a referral to an employee assistance program or alcohol rehabilitation clinic. Agencies often use a late-stage treatment strategy because police managers sometimes lack faith in early detection approaches and view them as ineffective. Yet, if agencies intervene before officers get into trouble, they can help officers onto the road to recovery, avoiding damage to both their personal and professional lives.

## The Case for Early Intervention

Prevention approaches view the causes of alcohol abuse to be based on the behavior of the officer, as well as being influenced by the officer's social network. The police social network has similar risk factors for alcohol abuse as other high-stress occupations. Police officers may endure stress, experience peer pressure, and be subjected to isolation-all within a culture that approves alcohol use.[2] Oftentimes, police officers gather at a local bar after their shifts to relax over a few drinks with their peers and reinforce their own values. Furthermore, because of the close-knit police culture, officers may feel reluctant to report colleagues for alcohol-related difficulties. Many officers may go to great lengths to protect fellow officers in trouble.

If a police department hopes to effectively reduce alcohol abuse, it should intervene early into the very network that reinforces such behavior in the first place-the police culture.[3] Agencies should get involved as early as the police academy stage and follow up with periodic in-service interventions.

Departments can use numerous strategies for early intervention. For example, they can help to improve the fitness and well-being of officers; provide education on lifestyle rather than on alcohol itself; Initiate stress management programs; and shift the responsibility of detection to individuals other than the affected officer.[4]

## Prevention Strategies:

### *Improve Physical and Mental Fitness*

Improving physical and mental fitness represents an important first step in alcohol abuse prevention. Experts believe that individuals who live unhealthy lives increase their risk of becoming excessive drinkers. Fitness protects against developing destructive habits, which, over time, can lead to health problems. For example, a physically fit individual generally does not smoke and drinks only at a low risk level. Thus, poor physical health may prove compatible with excessive drinking because officers may not perceive drinking as worse than other aspects of an unhealthy lifestyle. In this sense, the appropriate target for alcohol prevention becomes the unhealthy lifestyle of the officer rather than the drinking behavior itself.[5]

### *Provide Lifestyle Education*

Education serves as another part of an alcohol abuse prevention strategy. Individuals unaware of the effects of alcohol risk the development of alcohol-related problems. Although the use of such knowledge likely can be affected by values and beliefs, experts argue that the presence of such knowledge reduces the likelihood of alcohol abuse. Contrary to common belief, lectures on alcoholism remain one of the least effective methods of educational prevention. Providing information about how to identify and explore lifestyle factors that support alcohol abuse proves more beneficial. For example, smoking cessation clinics identify cues that trigger cravings for smokers and teach them new responses to avoid those cues. The point of an alcohol education program should be that change in alcohol abuse behavior is unlikely to occur unless factors in the officer's lifestyle are identified and changed.[6]

### *Reduce Stress*

Minimizing stress in the workplace also can help to prevent alcohol abuse. Research has shown that people who experience high stress remain more at risk for alcohol abuse. Stress can exist on both the organizational and individual levels in police work. Within the organization, managers should identify and minimize sources of stress as much as possible, particularly stress that serves no legitimate organizational goal. On the individual level, officers should be taught how to deal with the effects of stress from inside and outside the workplace. For such occupations as policing, where inordinate stress exists, something should be done before alcohol abuse becomes a problem.[7]

Officers' sense of control over the environment represents another factor in the amount of stress they experience and in turn whether they abuse alcohol. Officers who feel more in control of their lives generally feel less stress. A feeling of participation in important decisions that affect their work can increase their sense of control, instill confidence, decrease stress, and make them less likely to abuse alcohol. Moreover, allowing officers to participate in important workplace decisions can help them maintain the self-regulating mechanisms necessary to control alcohol use under stressful conditions.

Increasing an individual's control of work situations remains a long-standing problem in military structures similar to policing. A good starting point can be small, self-reinforcing changes that make officers feel more in control and better about themselves. First-line supervisors are important in instilling these feelings.[8] They can accomplish this by emphasizing the officers' positive achievements and recognizing superior work performance.

### *Encourage Early Detection*

Some common signals of alcohol abuse may be increased absenteeism, a change in personality, or possibly memory lapses such as forgetting work assignments. Detecting these early signs of alcohol abuse can limit its devastating effects and illustrates another factor in prevention. A significant difficulty for those individuals abusing alcohol remains their reluctance to admit the problem; therefore, it becomes necessary for others to intervene.

In this regard, first-line supervisors become invaluable. Supervisors should monitor the performance and activities of their workers and should recognize when problems arise. Complaints from other workers may focus the supervisor's attention on a particular employee. The supervisor can provide constructive advice on alcohol abuse, which can help guide the officer toward treatment and possibly even prevent an officer from becoming an alcohol abuser. Supervisors should become more familiar with their officers by getting to know them both professionally and personally. Becoming acquainted with the officers in this way may help supervisors to discover issues that may later develop into problems. Thus, supervisors, through education and policy, can become aware of the signs of alcohol abuse and responsible for detecting them in the workplace.[9]

Finally, an officer's family remains an additional source of detection. The officer's family may suffer as a result of alcohol abuse, which provides motivation for members of the family to seek help for the troubled officer. However, police families, much like fellow officers, may be reluctant to report alcohol-related problems. Departments should inform families of known problems police officers often have with alcohol abuse and emphasize the importance of the rehabilitation process for the officers and their families. Departments also should provide information to the family regarding the help available for officers and their families.[10]

**Conclusion**

A preventive approach has the long range potential to reduce alcohol abuse. Police departments should note that proactive prevention strategies designed to prevent alcohol abuse are more economical and practical than curing those who abuse alcohol.

Based on the prevention strategies of wellness, lifestyle education, and stress reduction, police administrators should set two goals for dealing with alcohol abuse. First, they should seek to lower alcohol consumption levels among all personnel but especially in those who already manifest high intake levels. They should encourage officers to decrease alcohol consumption while making other changes in their lives that would sustain that practice. Second, administrators should encourage the minimization of factors, such as stress, that may lead to alcohol abuse. Stress management programs, similar to alcohol related programs, remain essential in a comprehensive approach to mental well-being at work.

When police managers implement such strategies early on, they can reduce the likelihood of alcohol abuse within their departments. When officers get the help they need from the onset, both the officers and their agencies benefit.

**Endnotes**

1   E. Kirschman, *I Love A Cop* (New York: Guilford Press, 1997), 158.

2   Ibid., 163.

3   M. Braverman, Beyond Profiling: An Integrated Multidisciplinary Approach to Preventing Workplace Violence, symposium conducted at Work, Health, and Stress 95 Conference, Washington, DC, 1995.

4   C. McNeece and M. DiNitto, *Chemical Dependency: A Systems Approach* (Englewood Cliffs, NJ: Prentice Hall, 1994), 25–56; and B.L. Schecter, "It's More Than Testing, It's Wellness," resource paper, Prevention Associates. Oakland, CA, 1991.

5   Ideas for Action on Substance Abuse Prevention: Healthy Lifestyles, Mandatory Health Programs and Services (Toronto, Ontario, Canada: 1991), 25–35.

6   M.A. DiBernardo, Drug Abuse in the Workplace: Employer's Guide to Prevention, U.S. Chamber of Commerce (Washington, DC, 1988), 12–19.

7   J.M. Violanti, J. Marshall, and B. Howe, "Police, Alcohol, and Coping: The Police Connection," *Journal of Police Science and Administration* 13 (1984): 106–110.

8   U.S. Department of Labor, *An Employer's Guide to Dealing with Substance Abuse* (Rockville, MD, 1990), 12.

9   Ibid.

10  Supra note 1, 12.

**Review Questions**

1. Discuss the early intervention strategies to prevent alcohol abuse for law enforcement officers

# Police Trauma and Addiction: Coping with the Dangers of the Job

*Chad L Cross and Larry Ashley*

Law enforcement officers face traumatic incidents daily. These events, typically unexpected and sudden, fall well beyond the bounds of normal experience;[1] hence, they can have profound physical, emotional, and psychological impacts-even for the best-trained, experienced, and seasoned officers.

The ability to cope with stressful incidents is a personal journey that depends on an officer's past experiences with trauma; appropriate development of coping strategies for stress; availability of support networks (e.g., family, friends, and colleagues); and recognition of the dangers of ignoring signs and symptoms of post-incident stress, which is a normal response to abnormal circumstances.[2] Regardless of an officer's personal experiences with traumatic incidents, avoiding, ignoring, or burying the emotional aftermath of a traumatic event can lead to serious short- and long-term consequences. Sadly, however, some officers believe that substance use and abuse may offer the best way to cope with their otherwise unbearable feelings.

Certainly, not every officer deals with stress and trauma by abusing chemicals, and not every officer who chooses to abuse chemicals does so to numb the effects of trauma. However, overwhelming evidence suggests that the two factors often are linked, particularly in the high-stress environment of police work. Therefore, law enforcement administrators need to understand the responses to trauma and stress, the link between trauma and substance abuse, and the strategies for intervention and treatment needed to help their officers survive the rigors of their chosen profession.

## Understanding Trauma and Stress Responses

Critical incidents experienced by law enforcement officers are broad and far-ranging. A retired officer turned counselor, who survived a serious assault early in his career, has suggested that "any situation in which an officer's expectations of personal infallibility suddenly become tempered by imperfection and crude reality can be a critical incident."[3] Examples could include an officer-involved shooting, the death of a coworker, serious injury while on duty, life-threatening incidents, hostage situations or negotiations, exposure to intense crime scenes, a police suicide, or any situation that falls outside the realm of normal experience.

Stress responses and the symptoms resulting from such incidents can be cognitive (confusion, difficulty concentrating, or intrusive thoughts), physical (fatigue, headaches, or changes in appetite or sleep patterns), behavioral (withdrawal, acting out, or substance use), or emotional (anxiety or fear, depression, anger or guilt, or feelings of helplessness).[4] Most often, a combination of these symptoms emerges—frequently worsening and compounding as multiple traumas occur over time. If officers do not develop or take advantage of avenues for coping with stress appropriately, physical, mental, and emotional exhaustion ("burnout") can result.

## Diagnosis of Psychological Stress Responses

Similar to military combat veterans, law enforcement officers experience a plethora of treacherous, violent stresses on a daily basis.[5]

The psychological aftermath of such experiences can be either acute or chronic and can emerge or reoccur across broad temporal scales. While on active duty and upon returning to civilian life, military personnel—and, likewise, law enforcement officers—carry this stress-laden emotional baggage, which can produce multitudinous residual effects that, all too often, lead to substance use and abuse.

Post-traumatic stress disorder (PTSD) is associated most often with critical incidents experienced by law enforcement officers,[6] but many other diagnostic criteria could be linked to stressful incidents, including such disorders as adjustment, mood, anxiety, impulse-control, and substance abuse/dependence. PTSD includes symptoms that develop owing to experiencing intense fear, helplessness, or horror, which, in turn, often can lead to reexperiencing the traumatic event, avoiding situations associated with it (even if not experienced at the time the event occurred), and "numbing" of the arousal response. These symptoms cause impairment or distress in social or occupational functioning. If the symptoms persist for more than 1 month or appear for the first time 6 months after the event, then possible PTSD would need to be investigated. If the symptoms appear and subsequently disappear within a 1-month time frame, then acute stress disorder should be investigated.[7] Of note, subclinical individuals may chronically develop PTSD symptoms indistinguishable from those formally diagnosed with the disorder if they remain untreated.[8]

## Impacts of Trauma

The impact of traumatic experiences differs for every individual; however, beginning with the studies of combat fatigue after World War II, similarities across individuals have led to a generalized conceptualization of expected stress reactions, particularly those that might lead to career burnout. If or when this occurs, law enforcement organizations and other first-responder public safety agencies may find themselves understaffed, unable to perform expected duties, and faced with increased apathy, suicide rates, and substance abuse.[9]

Generally speaking, stress responses begin with anxiety and panic reactions, which often lead to difficulties in concentration and feelings of being overwhelmed or out of control. This can progress to physical symptoms, such as tachycardia, gastrointestinal distress, and hypertension. If intervention does not occur, then worker apathy tends to increase, leading to absenteeism, lateness, procrastination, and increased use of chemical substances (e.g., tobacco, caffeine, alcohol, pain killers, or sleeping pills). If officers continue along this path, then major depressive symptoms begin to increase, feelings of hopelessness and helplessness abound, suicidal ideation and rates increase, and, all too often, substance abuse to dull these feelings leads to addiction and dependence.[10]

## Linking Trauma and Substance Abuse

Substance use and abuse among law enforcement officers represent widespread, albeit somewhat under-reported, phenomena. Alcohol and other drug abuse are maladaptive behaviors associated with stress and trauma, and when these behaviors emerge in law enforcement, the profession must afford them special attention.[11]

## Alcohol Use and Abuse

Studies have indicated that nearly one-quarter of law enforcement officers are alcohol dependent as a result of on-the-job stress; however, researchers believe that this estimate falls well below the true number due to incomplete reporting.[12] A study of 852 police officers in New South Wales, Australia, for example, found that nearly 50 percent of male and 40 percent of female officers consumed excessive amounts of alcohol (defined as more than 8 drinks per week at least twice a month or over 28 drinks a month for males and more than 6 drinks per week at least twice a month or 14 drinks a month for females) and that nearly 90 percent of all officers consumed alcohol to some degree.[13]

The unique subculture of the law enforcement profession often makes alcohol use appear as an accepted practice to promote camaraderie and social interaction among officers.[14] What starts as an occasional socializing activity, however, later can become a dangerous addiction as alcohol use evolves into a coping mechanism to camouflage the stress and trauma experienced by officers on a daily basis.[15] When the effects of the alcohol wear off, however, the stress or trauma that led to the drinking episode still exists.

In addition, researchers have identified four occupational demands that can trigger alcohol use by law enforcement officers, namely depersonalization (reacting unemotionally to the everyday stresses of the job), authoritarianism (officers' behavior governed by a set of regulations, making them feel as if they are not in control), organizational protection (the structure in place to protect law enforcement agencies from criticism), and danger preparation (the stress related to officers knowing that their lives potentially are in constant danger).[16] Some may argue, then, that alcohol use among officers serves both as a personal coping mechanism related to socialization and presumed stress/trauma reduction and also as a reaction to the internal stresses created by law enforcement agencies themselves.

## Drug Use and Abuse

Other drug use also is on the rise in law enforcement agencies.[17] This increasing problem has led to the establishment and maintenance of drug-testing programs. Though this has caused numerous challenges within the legal system, an ever growing movement toward maintaining a drug-free workplace exists throughout law enforcement agencies.[18]

Sadly, those officers, clinically diagnosed or not, facing the aftermath of traumatic experiences may feel that drugs can help numb their pain, if only temporarily. Additionally, law enforcement officers maintain a role that may make them more susceptible to abusing drugs. For example, they have ample opportunities to obtain drugs because they often come in close contact with illegal substances and the individuals who use or deal in them; they learn how, why, when, and where to obtain and use drugs and the rationalizations for such use from drug offenders; and they may find that drugs offer a way to help them cope with the constant stress on the job and the ever-present traumatic incidents that they encounter.[19]

## Impacts of Substance Use and Abuse

Both the acute and chronic impacts of substance use and abuse often lead to profound negative consequences. Not limited to the individual user, these consequences can extend to loved ones, colleagues, the employing agency, and the citizens who depend on law enforcement personnel. In other words, substance abuse by law enforcement officers is not a personal journey because they always must be prepared to conscientiously and continually react, respond, serve, and protect. Such high expectations can prove difficult to meet when sober, let alone when impaired by alcohol and other drugs or while recovering from using such substances.

Alcohol and other drug use and abuse have both overt and covert social and economic costs, including lost productivity and wages; increased family problems, including risks of domestic violence; and rising costs to the criminal justice system to respond to, house, or adjudicate substance abusers.[20] When substance abusers are members of the public safety sector, the problems multiply—employees can become unable to perform their sworn duties, administrators can find themselves increasingly over-burdened trying to deal with a problem that can result in negative perceptions of their agencies, and the public can lose faith and trust in the system.

Substance use may lead to a number of problems for law enforcement officers and their agencies. When officers deal with stress or trauma using alcohol and other drugs, they may find that they simply cannot perform their duties adequately. They often become agitated, hypervigilant, and aggressive. They feel tired and overwhelmed and have difficulty concentrating on their work. Family problems mount, and officers become isolated. Accelerated substance use leads to occasional and then progressive lateness and absenteeism. Continued use may result in the inability to perform the job at all and intensified feelings of worthlessness and apathy, causing officers to become more and more depressed and confused. Ultimately, the end result is a tremendous increase in the risk of suicidal ideation, which studies have linked strongly to alcohol and other drug use among law enforcement officers.[21]

## Breaking the Cycle of Trauma and Substance Abuse

Substance use often begins with the best intentions—a means of social interaction. However, when the mind-numbing qualities of alcohol and other drugs become a means of coping, albeit a shortsighted one, substance use then may progress into abuse and dependence because officers see no other avenue of reducing stress. More stress often means more chemical use, and, before long, officers may find themselves in a dangerous cycle. Unfortunately, however, this means that the officers never dealt with the real problem or issue in a satisfactory way; it remains an open wound that often cannot heal on its own, despite the best efforts of self-medication.

Where and when, then, does the cycle of trauma/stress and substance use/abuse end? If appropriate intervention does not occur, tragedy may result. But, agencies do not have to wait for tragedy to occur; they can act beforehand to save their officers.

## Intervention Strategies

Traditional trauma/stress intervention involves some type or form of critical incident stress management or debriefing;[22] however, recent researchers have questioned the ability of these techniques to reduce the symptoms stemming from trauma.[23] These techniques may prove useful for some, but reactions to traumatic events and the stresses inherent in police work make a more individualized model more appropriate in many circumstances.[24] Situations may indicate individual and group mental health treatment, along with professional or peer counselors, as a necessary part of the intervention. However, treating law enforcement officers can pose some challenges to mental health personnel.

Traditionally, law enforcement officers have viewed the mental health profession with some skepticism because they often did not feel that counselors understood what it meant to do police work. To combat this mind-set and deal effectively with officers, counselors must receive some unique training. They also must have—

- a grounding in policing;
- a localized knowledge of the agency and administrations within which their clients reside;
- a unique comprehension of the trauma and stresses inherent in police work;
- an understanding of the dark humor often used by officers to vent stress-induced anger and frustration; and
- an ability to build rapport by establishing a trusting, respectful atmosphere wherein they can assure officers of complete confidentiality.[25]

A unique field, substance abuse counseling requires specialized training to appropriately and legally administer assessments and treatments. The first intervention for substance abuse should occur at the earliest possible time-before recruits become law enforcement officers. Police academies should contain didactic training in substance use and abuse and the inappropriateness of such behavior in police work. Increasing awareness at this stage of professional development not only puts useful and necessary information into the hands of future officers but also raises their awareness of the many potential problems, both personally and professionally, that substance use can cause. Additionally, training at this stage reaffirms that the law enforcement agency administration understands the pressures inherent in police work that may lead to substance use and abuse. Further, instruction by senior officers during the training phase provides appropriate models of behavior and sends the message to young recruits that they need not resort to substance use as a means of coping with the trauma and stress of the law enforcement profession.

Many brief interventions exist for initial stages of substance abuse, and most have focused on group interventions where members discuss the pros and cons of binge drinking and alcoholism. These discussions often focus on the health effects of alcohol and other drug use, an understanding of societal norms as a baseline to compare an individual's personal consumption, and the cognitive-behavioral interventions to change the thinking patterns associated with substance use.[26] Long-term, heavy drinkers, on the other hand, may need detoxification and a period of recovery before introducing psychoeducational intervention.[27] Providing a supportive intradepartmental atmosphere for officers in need of this level of intervention is a necessary component.

## Integrated Treatment Approach

It seems clear that treating trauma/stress and substance use/ abuse should occur in complement. After all, police trauma and stress will not disappear nor will substance use and abuse within the ranks. What can change, however, is the atmosphere within those law enforcement administrations that may tend to downplay, rationalize, or deny addictions. To help effect this change and to save time, money, and, most important, lives, law enforcement agencies can invest in an integrated model of awareness and treatment. To help agencies, the authors offer some considerations in developing such a model.

### *Support Services*

- Law enforcement agencies should have mental health professionals trained and certified in addictions counseling on staff for consultations, interventions, and referrals. They should offer police counselors trained in policing who have knowledge of police infrastructure, programming, and administration.
- Agencies should have trauma teams that include mental health professionals on call for consultations and interventions when needed.
- They should make employee assistance professionals available to provide confidential services outside the agency.
- Agencies should institute peer counseling programs.[28] Ideally, these peer counselors would have experiences in both trauma and addictions or would work in teams to develop integrated programs. Officers are more likely to respect the experiences of fellow officers over outside professionals, and the models of positive behavior that such peer support groups offer may be a key component of successful intervention.

### *Training and Research*

- Young recruits should receive training in recognizing stress, dealing with traumatic incidents, and understanding the negative effects of substance use and abuse.
- Law enforcement agencies should make critical incident trauma management training available to all officers on an ongoing basis. Officers often receive training in such programs for the treatment of the citizens they protect. But, a strong effort also needs to focus internally within law enforcement agencies, specifically aimed at the traumatic incidents most often encountered in police work.
- Agencies should provide ongoing training to continually educate their officers on the effects of alcohol and other drug use. Agencies frequently serve their communities by supporting alcohol and other drug prevention programs, yet, all too often, they neglect the problems of their own personnel.
- Law enforcement agencies need to learn the value of early intervention programs over treatment programs and how to provide a supportive atmosphere that acknowledges trauma and addiction intervention efforts within their organizations. Further, upper-level officers and administrators need to exhibit empathy toward their officers, provide services when necessary, and encourage open communication about addiction problems in their ranks.
- Researchers, mental health professionals, and law enforcement experts need to further examine the role that trauma, stress, and addiction plays in the lives of all first-responding public safety personnel and find new methods of intervention and treatment to help these dedicated men and women deal with the tremendous pressure of their profession.

## Conclusion

All members of the law enforcement community have an important role to play when it comes to evaluating, intervening, and treating trauma and addiction. When officers suffer the aftermath of trauma, they are not alone. Many may tout their "tough guy" image, see themselves as weak or abnormal if they seek help, and believe that admitting psychological or emotional pain will result in disciplinary action and, perhaps, job dismissal. Unfortunately, however, severe anxiety reactions, workplace apathy, absenteeism, and depressive symptoms have far-reaching impacts, not only on the officers suffering the trauma but, importantly, on their colleagues, the families they love, and the public they have sworn to protect and serve. Adding substance abuse to this already tragic scenario tremendously increases the potentially harmful impact—because when chemical substances enter the picture, everyone loses.

## Endnotes

1   J.T. Mitchell and O.S. Everly, Jr., *The Basic Critical Incident Stress Management Course: Basic Group Crisis Intervention,* 3rd ed. (Baltimore, MD: International Critical Incident Stress Foundation, Inc., 2001).

2   Ibid.

3   A.W. Kureczka, "Critical Incident Stress in Law Enforcement," *FBI Law Enforcement Bulletin,* February/March 1996, 10–16; and A.W. Kureczka, "Surviving Assaults: After the Physical Battle Ends, the Psychological Battle Begins," *FBI Law Enforcement Bulletin,* January 2002, 18–21.

4   Ibid, and supra note 1.

5   J.M. Violanti, "Residuals of Police Occupational Trauma," *The Australian Journal of Disaster and Trauma Studies* 3 (1997); and J.M. Violanti and D. Paton, *Police Trauma: Psychological Aftermath of Civilian Combat* (Springfield, IL: Charles C. Thomas, 1999).

6   J.M. Violanti, Police Psychological Trauma, Law Enforcement Wellness Association, Inc.; retrieved on August 5, 2003, from http://www.cophealth.com/ articles/articles _psychtrauma.html.

7   *Diagnostic and Statistical Manual of Mental Disorders,* 4th ed., text revision (Washington, DC: American Psychiatric Association, 2000).

8   D.S. Weiss, C.R. Marmar, W.E. Schlenger, J.A. Fairbank, K. Jordan, R.L. Hough, and R.A. JCulka, "The Prevalence of Lifetime and Partial Post-Traumatic Stress Disorder in Vietnam Veterans," *Journal of Traumatic Stress* 5 (1992): 365–376.

9   J.M. Violanti, *Police Suicide: Epidemic in Blue* (Springfield, IL: Charles C. Thomas, 1996); and supra note 5.

10  Supra note 1.

11  B.A. Arrigo and K. Garsky, "Police Suicide: A Glimpse Behind the Badge," in *Critical Issues in Policing: Contemporary Readings,* 3rd ed., eds. R.G. Dunham and G.P. Alpert (Prospect Heights, IL: Waveland Press, 1997), 609–626.

12  J.M. Violanti, Dying from the Job: The Mortality Risk for Police Officers, Law Enforcement Wellness Association, Inc.; retrieved on August 5, 2003, from http://www. cophealth. Com/articles/ articles_dying_a.html.

13  R.L. Richmond, A.K. Wodak, and L. Heather, "Research Report: How Healthy Are the Police? A Survey of Lifestyle Factors," Addiction 93 (1998): 1729–1737.

14  Supra note 11; and H.W. Stege, "Drug Abuse by Police Officers," *Police Chief* 53 (1986): 53–83.

15  Supra note 11.

16  J. Dietrich and J. Smith, "Nonmedical Use of Drugs and Alcohol by Police," *Journal of Police Science and Administration* 14(1987): 300–306.

17  R.G. Dunham, L. Lewis, and G.P. Alpert, "Testing the Police for Drugs," *Criminal Law Bulletin* 24 (1998): 155–166.

18  TJ. Hickey and S.T. Reid, "Testing Police and Corrections Officers for Drug Use After Skinner and Von Raab," *Public Administration Quarterly* 19 (1995): 26–41.

19  Supra note 17, 155.

20  Alcohol and Drug Services: Impacts of Alcohol, Health Services, San Diego County Web site; retrieved on August 12, 2003, from http://www.co/san-diego.ca.us/ cnty/cntydepts/health/services/ads/ aclimpctl05.html.

21  M. Wagner and RJ. Brzeczek, "Alcoholism and Suicide: A Fatal Connection," *FBI Law Enforcement Bulletin,* August 1983, 8–15; and supra notes 9 and 11, 620.

22  Supra note 1.

23  I.V.E. Carlier and B.P.R. Gersons, "Brief Prevention Programs After Trauma" and R. Gist and J. Woodall, "There Are No Simple Solutions to Complex Problems," in *Post-Traumatic Stress Intervention: Challenges, Issues, and Perspectives,* eds. J.M. Violanti, D. Paton, and C. Dunning (Springfield, IL: Charles C. Thomas, 2000), 65-80 and 81-96.

24  J.M. Violanti, D. Paton, and C. Dunning, eds. *Post-Traumatic Stress Intervention: Challenges, Issues, and Perspectives* (Springfield, IL: Charles C. Thomas, 2000).

25  Supra note 3.

26  R.L. Richmond, L.H. Kehoe, S. Wodak, and A. Uebel-Yan, "Quantitative and Qualitative Evaluations of Brief Interventions to Change Excessive Drinking, Smoking, and Stress in the Police Force," *Addiction* 94 (1999): 1509–2140.

27  Psychological education designed to help clients access the facts about a particular mental health issue.

28  J.M. Madonna, Jr. and R.E. Kelly, eds. *Treating Police Stress: The Work and the Words of Peer Counselors* (Springfield, IL: Charles C. Thomas, 2002).

## Review Questions

1.  Discuss the intervention strategies to prevent substance abuse for police officers.

2.  Explain the impacts of substance use and abuse.

# PART THREE
# Infectious and Non-Infectious Disease Issues

## Blood Borne Diseases: Developing a Training Curriculum

*Jerry D. Stewart*

Every day, law enforcement personnel around the Nation respond to thousands of situations ill-equipped and poorly prepared. Even worse, many department administrators remain unaware of how to train their officers to protect themselves adequately in these situations.

To what new foe has the law enforcement community been so slow to respond? Unfortunately, it is not new at all but one that has assumed a drastically more dangerous character within the past decade—blood borne diseases (BBD).

The increasing spread of AIDS, as well as various strains of hepatitis and other blood borne diseases, presents the public safety community with a formidable enemy. Furthermore, two dangerous allies—ignorance and unsubstantiated fear—often accompany this adversary.

Accurate information and effective precautionary procedures represent the best response strategies for law enforcement. However, increasingly frequent media stories and a recent survey indicate that the public safety community as a whole may not be reacting quickly enough to this threat.

The results of inaction could be devastating—unnecessary threats to law enforcement personnel, lawsuits, and a loss of credibility within communities. These factors, combined with emerging Federal regulation, make it imperative that agency administrators work to develop effective training programs that address the transmission of blood borne diseases.

### Survey

An informal survey of 70 law enforcement administrators, managers, and trainers conducted during a recent session of the FBI National Academy revealed some rather startling statistics.[1] Of the 70 supervisors questioned:

- 43 did not have a comprehensive departmental policy in place regarding blood borne diseases.
- 42 state that their departments had not provided at least 4 hours of BBD training to each employee within the past 4 years.
- 50 were unaware of recent Occupational Safety and Health Administration (OSHA) regulations that require employers to provide all vulnerable employees with protective equipment (such as gloves) and to offer free hepatitis B vaccinations to those who desire them.
- 50 were not aware that the Centers for Disease Control (CDC) designed a curriculum guide to address the training and education needs of public safety workers who may be exposed to hepatitis B and the human immunodeficiency virus (HIV)—the virus that causes AIDS.

Although admittedly limited in scope, this survey indicates that despite new OSHA health precaution rules, urging by Federal agencies, and readily available information resources, many law enforcement agencies fail to address blood borne diseases adequately from policy and training standpoints. This failure reinforces a warning issued by policy researchers nearly 5 years ago, "Too many organizations simply have not prepared for the consequences of a case or many cases of AIDS among their workforce, and many of these organizations will regret their unpreparedness."[2]

How should law enforcement agencies prepare? The ideal approach is to establish training curriculums and operating procedures that reduce the threat to officers, thereby helping to limit agency liability.

Each department should develop its own blood borne disease training program—one designed to accommodate the needs of each individual workforce. In addition, a written policy directive should be the cornerstone of frequent, ongoing training. Because research continues to uncover important information, education in this area should be considered a process, not merely a one-time event.

## Developing a Curriculum

In 1989, the Centers for Disease Control prepared a curriculum guide to meet the training and educational needs of public safety workers who may be exposed to blood borne pathogens on the job. "A Curriculum Guide for Public Safety and Emergency Response Workers" is based on Federal guidelines for preventing occupational transmission of HIV and HBV (the hepatitis B virus).[3]

This curriculum serves as a model that any public safety agency can adopt. The course covers:

- Means of HIV and HBV transmission
- Suggested personal prevention practices
- Universal precaution strategies
- Protective equipment
- Specific workplace prevention practices
- Exposure management procedures

Individual agencies may choose to modify the contents of the curriculum or design one that addresses departmental needs. Agencies that include these elements in some form, however, will provide employees with a comprehensive training program.

## Special Training Considerations

A successful training program must also incorporate a sensitive, yet direct, approach to providing information. To that end, program planners should stress special considerations to keep in mind when addressing this issue.

## Emotions and Attitudes

Certain diseases—particularly those with controversial methods of transmission—arouse intense emotions in people. Therefore, it is important that training in this area not only convey factual information but also address emotional responses.

When discussing AIDS, program instructors should focus on the facts and should not attempt to change individuals' basic attitudes concerning morality or cultural values. At the same time, instruction should stress the importance of distinguishing personal beliefs from professional responsibilities.[4] Through proper training, individuals should come to accept AIDS as a dangerous disease without any religious or moralistic overtones.

## Goals and Objectives

To guarantee that training accomplishes its stated purpose, program administrators should first establish overall training goals. Then, trainers should establish specific instructional objectives to ensure that the goals are met. The following sample objectives are adapted from the CDC curriculum guide. Employees who complete this program should be able to:

\* Define HIV, HBV, and AIDS

\* Identify high-risk workplace situations, exposure protection/management measures, and decontamination procedures

\* Know and understand laws and departmental polices governing treatment, testing, confidentiality, and reporting procedures.[5]

While these objectives may be adapted to fit the needs of individual agencies, all performance-based objectives should reflect the established general goals set by administrators.

### Definitions

To clarify how blood borne diseases are transmitted, instructors should provide definitions of certain key terms. The following basic definitions provide a basis for discussing these issues as they relate to law enforcement.

**HIV *and* AIDS**: the human immunodeficiency virus (HIV) causes the acquired immunodeficiency syndrome (AIDS). AIDS results from the progressive destruction of an individual's immune system—the body's defense against disease. The virus that causes AIDS is transmitted through sexual contact, exposure to infected blood (or blood components), and perinatally from mother to neonate. Epidemiologic evidence implicates only blood, semen, vaginal secretions, and possibly, breast milk as a means of transmission.

***Hepatitis* B**: Hepatitis B is caused by the hepatitis B virus (HBV). This disease results in liver damage, which may range in severity from mild or even unapparent to severe or fatal. HBV is transmitted through blood, semen, vaginal secretions, and saliva.

### High-Risk Exposure Situations

Training should describe work-place situations and address issues that relate to public safety workers. This training should be tailored to the learning group in order to make the curriculum relevant. To increase the impact of the training, instructors should introduce hypothetical case studies, coupled with discussions of actual situations. Copies of these case studies should be distributed to each class member, and discussion questions should be prepared in advance to promote group interaction.

Scenarios used in case studies may include traffic accidents with injuries, drug raids, demonstrations and rallies, autopsies, and evidence handling, among many others. Instructors may use this opportunity to provide specific information relating to viral transmission, departmental procedures, and applicable laws.

### Exposure Protection

In the medical sense, the "universal precautions" concept assumes all patients to be infected with blood borne pathogens. For law enforcement, training should emphasize that when personnel encounter body fluids under uncontrolled, emergency circumstances, they should treat all body fluids as potentially hazardous.

During training, standard personal protective equipment (PPE) should be displayed and its use demonstrated. Trainers should provide detailed instruction regarding disposable gloves, masks, protective eye wear, gowns, and resuscitation equipment. However, trainers should stress that PPE is not limited to these items. In situations where gross contamination can be reasonably anticipated—during an autopsy or the processing of an extremely contaminated crime scene—additional protective equipment, such as shoe coverings, would be required.

## Decontamination Methods

Training programs should also discuss specific decontamination processes, including disinfection procedures and disposal equipment. Instructors should present current information on needle disposal, hand washing, sterilization methods, cleaning and decontaminating blood spills, packaging evidence, handling infective waste, and laundering processes for protective clothing.

## Managing Exposures

Trainers should explain that exposure results from contact with blood or potentially infectious body fluids through various means, including needle sticks, contacting blood or blood-contaminated body fluids with chapped skin, open wounds or mucous membranes, and saliva. Training should stress that any incident involving contact with blood or body fluids should be treated as an exposure.

The curriculum should then address procedures for treating exposed workers, including referral to proper medical authorities, counseling, and preventive treatment. Instructors should also discuss internal procedures for reporting and documenting cases in detail.

## Ethical Issues

Each year, State and Federal legislators review over 1,000 AIDS-related bills. Numerous jurisdictions have enacted ordinances preventing discrimination against persons infected with AIDS.

This makes it imperative that blood borne diseases training address ethical issues. These include:

* Discrimination
* Duty to provide care
* HIV testing and confidentiality
* Prevention of occupational exposure
* Treatment after exposure

While criminal justice personnel may have legitimate concerns when providing care to those they suspect have a contagious disease, these workers also have a professional responsibility to perform their jobs. Generally, public safety employees cannot refuse to render assistance to persons in need.

Any legal claim supporting officers' refusal to perform duties based on fear of contracting a blood borne disease would be difficult to sustain on two grounds. First, research points to the unlikelihood of viral transmission through the types of contacts likely to be experienced by police officers, assuming officers take standard precautions. Second, officers assume certain risks in accepting their positions.[6]

## Health Precautions

The training curriculum should also address new health precaution rules and their impact on law enforcement agencies. Federal regulations were recently developed to protect against occupational exposure to infectious blood borne agents.

OSHA compels certain employers to provide protective equipment and to institute other precautions to safeguard public safety workers and the public.[7] OSHA also mandates that agencies make a copy of the 1992 standard available to all affected or potentially affected employees, along with information regarding:

• Epidemiology and symptoms of blood borne diseases
• Transmission modes of blood borne diseases
• Employers' exposure control plan
• Signs, labels, and color-coding associated with blood borne diseases
• Methods for recognizing tasks/activities that may involve exposure to blood borne pathogens
• Comprehensive guidelines for the use and disposal of personal protective equipment

- Procedures to follow when exposure occurs.

The OSHA standard further requires these employers to make available hepatitis B vaccinations and related information to those employees who desire them.

## Resources

The Centers for Disease Control curriculum guide contains 22 pages of resources. In addition to general information on HIV, AIDS, and HBV, the guide includes resources specially tailored to law enforcement officers, correctional personnel, emergency medical technicians/paramedics, and firefighters.

Among the most referenced resources is AIDS *and the Law Enforcement Officer: Concerns and Policy Responses.* This book specifies 13 relevant subjects that should be addressed in AIDS education programs and suggests 7 key elements for providing effective training.[8]

## Evaluation

After training sessions, instructors and attendees should be allowed to evaluate the content and quality of the instruction provided. Because proper evaluation forms the basis for improving future training, it represents a valuable component of the process.

Evaluations should determine if the course attained its stated objectives. Attendees should also comment on the physical environment, audiovisual equipment, and amount of time allocated and make specific suggestions for improving course content and presentation.

Instructors may also want to use pre- and post-tests to evaluate attendees learning. When examinations are used, written measurable objectives should determine what constitutes acceptable levels of performance.

The training unit manager should maintain all relevant written material on file. This information provides a record of class attendance, course content, and test results. This documentation may prove invaluable during litigation should an agency need to produce evidence of training.

## Conclusion

Blood borne diseases represent increasingly serious health problems in this Nation. As with today's health care workers, law enforcement officers are constantly exposed to deadly diseases. Despite this fact, many agencies have yet to develop training policies in this area.

However, rising rates of infection among the general population clearly point to the need for blood borne disease training in all public safety agencies. Administrators who have not acted on Federal recommendations in this area delay at the peril of their employees, agencies, and communities. But those who develop effective training programs reduce the threats to officers, limit agency liability, and constructively address a potentially divisive issue within their communities. In this case, the choice is clear.

**Endnotes**

1   Study conducted during the 169th Session of the FBI National Academy, Quantico, Virginia, May 1992.
2   Sam B. Pucket and Alan R. Emery, Managing AIDS in the Workplace (Reading, Massachusetts: Addison-Wesley, 1988), 13.
3   *A Curriculum Guide for Public-Safety and Emergency-Response Workers* (Atlanta, Georgia: Centers for Disease Control, 1989).
4   Supra note 2, 114–115.
5   Robert F. Mager, *Preparing Instructional Objectives* (Belmont, California: Fearson/Lear Siegler, Inc.).
6   Theodore Hammett, AIDS and the Law Enforcement Officer: Concern and Policy Responses, *National Institute of Justice—Issues and Practices* 1987, 31.
7   OSHA 1910.1030, Blood borne Pathogens.
8   Supra note 6.

**Review Questions**

1.  Discuss the area that should be covered in a curriculum for blood borne pathogen education.

2.  Briefly describe HIV/AIDS and Hepatitis B diseases.

# Bloodborne Pathogens Training Is a Lifesaver for Correctional Staff
*Lisette Hilton*

Donny R. Giles, training manager at the Metro-Davidson County Detention Facility in Nashville, Tenn., knows that by taking simple steps every day at his job, he protects himself from blood borne-pathogens transmission. The transmission of microorganisms in human blood that can cause such diseases as human immunodeficiency virus (HIV) and hepatitis is a real threat for those working in correctional institutions because inmates are known to have a higher prevalence of blood borne diseases than the general population. "I want to protect myself and make sure that when I go home I'm just as safe and healthy as when I came in," Giles said.

According to Giles, much has changed since he joined the detention facility 14 years ago. In the past, he says, bloodborne-pathogens transmission prevention was, at best, hit or miss—sometimes, based on widely held misconceptions and myths. Today, every one of Metro-Davidson's 235 employees go through bloodborne pathogens training in their orientations, then, annually in in-service training.

"Outside of our medical department, we practice universal precautions, using personal protective equipment, handwashing, etc. We let [staff] know what bloodborne pathogens are; how they're contracted; and how to protect themselves," Giles said. "The concept of 'universal precautions' is to treat blood and certain body fluids as if they are infected and protect yourself, so the potential for infection is minimal."

## Why the Concern?

Bloodborne pathogens may be present in blood and other materials, such as body fluids containing visible blood; semen and vaginal secretions; and injured or loose skin, according to Louis Gonzales, chair of the American Heart Association's Emergency Cardiovascular Care First Aid subcommittee. AHA recently launched the Heartsaver Bloodborne Pathogens (BBP) course, a one-hour, on-the-job training program for employees who are not in the medical field but who must receive the training for their jobs as required by the Occupational Safety and Health Administration (OSHA).

"Bloodborne pathogens can cause infection by entering the body in a variety of ways, including through open cuts, skin abrasions and mucous membranes of the mouth, eyes or nose," Gonzales said. "There are many different bloodborne pathogens including malaria and hepatitis C, but hepatitis B (HBV) and the HIV are the two diseases specifically addressed by the OSHA Bloodborne Pathogen Standard."

Government statistics suggest that both of these diseases are more prevalent among incarcerated populations than the general population. In each year from 1999 to 2006, the prevalence of confirmed AIDS in the prison population was between 2.7 and 4.8 times higher than in the general U.S. population, according to U.S. Centers for Disease Control and Prevention (CDC) data for incarcerated populations at midyear 2007.

And, according to information updated by the CDC in June 2008, hepatitis B (HBV) vaccination is recommended for adults in correctional institutions because of their increased infection risk inside and outside of prisons and jails.

Correctional staff are among groups at potential risk for occupationally acquired infections with bloodborne pathogens, CDC reports. "Correctional employees have reported injuries from human bites, needles, and other sharp instruments, as well as skin and mucous membrane exposures to blood and body fluids. ... Limited data from correctional workers have indicated 21 percent reported blood contact with intact skin, and 7 percent reported a percutaneous exposure (including needle stick, cut with a contaminated object, or bite) or mucus membrane exposure," according to CDC's June 24, 2003, Morbidity and Mortality Weekly Report.

It is no surprise that inmates have higher rates of these diseases, according to Giles. Bloodborne pathogens are commonly transmitted among high risk populations, through sex and intravenous drug use. People who work in prisons and jails come into contact with those who could be infected in many ways. "Obviously our staff members have to touch these people to search them and we want them to be prepared. Our correctional staff members are involved in inmate and housing area searches. Even our support staff, are coming into contact with these people," he said.

The basics of prevention involve creating barriers between one's skin and other people's blood and body fluids. "When you are in a situation where maybe someone has injured themselves or someone has come in from the street with injuries, you have to be very careful what you touch, including clothing and bedding," Giles said.

### Knowledge Protects

Protection from bloodborne pathogens transmission means more than putting on a pair of gloves. And that's where the need for formal training comes in, according to Giles. Safety practices range from frequent handwashing to use of barrier gloves, eye guards and clothing; proper cleaning and disposal of anything that might be contaminated; and a systematic approach to getting prompt medical care for staff members who have come into contact with another's body fluid. "If you're doing a search and the individual has a razorblade or has a hypodermic needle that they've hidden and you injure yourself with that, the staff member would immediately contact his or her immediate supervisor," Giles said. "We would have that person relieved, so that staff member could go to our medical department to receive a prophylaxis kit, before going to the local hospital emergency department. The doctors would make the determination if exposure was likely or not likely and make recommendations."

Standardized BBP training for nonhealth care personnel should focus on more than prevention but also swift action in the case of a potential exposure, according to Gonzales. "The American Heart Association's BBP course is based on the PACT concept: P, for protect; A, for act; C, for clean; and T, for tell," he says. "Through the Heartsaver BBP Course, students learn how to protect themselves from exposure to bloodborne pathogens; how to act when a workplace bloodborne-pathogens exposure occurs; how to clean themselves and the area when a workplace bloodborne-pathogens exposure occurs; and how to report any blood-borne pathogens exposures."

### Training Puts It All Together

Sporadic communication about prevention is not enough, experts say. Facilities need to consider formal bloodborne pathogens training for anyone on staff who may come into contact with blood or body fluids. Many organizations, including AHA, offer a wide range of training options - from traditional classroom instruction to online courses.

Giles says optimal training involves students and does not just focus on a lecture. "I like to encourage students to talk and ask questions," he said. "If you don't allow folks that feedback, you might think you've done a good job putting the information out there. But if they don't know how to apply universal precautions when they get to the job, they're not going to be successful."

Corrections is among the many settings targeted by OSHA and other industry organizations to protect people at work. "Potential on-the-job hazards are a reality for many people," Gonzales said. "People should be able to go to work knowing their health and safety are valued, and they must have the skills and tools to protect themselves and others."

### Review Questions

1. Explain the reasons why it is essential to educate correctional officers about bloodborne pathogens.

2. Develop a lesson plan for a bloodborne training program on Hepatitis B virus or HIV for corrections officers.

# Hepatitis Not Just Corrections' Problem
*Robert D. Jones*

Many correctional employees probably have learned more about hepatitis C than was ever taught in medical school decades ago. Twenty-five years ago, hepatitis C was known as non-A, non-B hepatitis and there was no effective treatment. Physicians have since learned it is a virus primarily spread through intravenous drug use.

Because of the lack of effective treatments, medical doctors became familiar with the natural course of the disease and know that in some people it will lead to cirrhosis (marked scarring and destruction) of the liver after 20 to 30 years. Less than 20 percent of infected people will develop end-stage liver disease and die. More than 80 percent of individuals will die of some other disease process, but they can still spread the virus to others through sharing needles and, in a few cases, through sexual intercourse. The hepatitis C virus is also associated with liver cancer—especially in those who have the disease and continue to consume any alcohol. Hepatitis C is the leading cause of liver failure and will lead to death unless a liver transplant is undertaken.

## Risks and Symptoms

One can explain the risk to inmates in the terms of "odds"—just like gambling. If an inmate contracts the disease, his or her odds of developing a chronic form of it is four out of five. However, the odds of developing cirrhosis and liver failure are very much in the inmate's favor as only one in five go on to this point. The best thing an inmate can do is not infect others and never drink alcohol.

Unfortunately, this is not a disease that causes many symptoms. When first infected, approximately 75 percent of individuals have no symptoms at all. When symptoms do occur, they are not specific and are often ignored by the individual. The virus seems to be very clever in dealing with the immune system as only one person in five actually clears the initial infection. The remaining 80 percent will have minimal symptoms (fatigue is most common) and will not be aware that they are carrying the infection in their blood and liver.

The virus causes inflammation and destruction of the liver cells. When this happens, certain chemicals are released into the bloodstream in higher than normal amounts. The most common enzyme followed is referred to as ALT (alanine aminotransferase). These levels fluctuate during the course of the illness. Occasionally, they can be normal even when there is liver cell inflammation and also in the later stages of the disease when much of the liver has been destroyed. An ALT blood test is used to follow the course of the disease and, by the most recent recommendation, has come back into favor as a way to "track" the course of the disease.

The only way to know if a person has hepatitis C is to perform a blood test, which probably should be done with all individuals who have ever engaged in high-risk behaviors. Individuals who have injected illicit drugs; received a blood transfusion or organ transplant before 1992; received clotting factors prior to 1987; are undergoing chronic hemodialysis (used to treat renal failure); had percutaneous (break in the skin) exposure to hepatitis C virus-positive blood; have a history of tattoos or body piercings, especially when in jail or prison; or have a history of multiple sexual partners (five in one year or 10 in a lifetime) are considered high risk.

## Treating Inmates

The hepatitis C virus, like HIV, has many different types of subsets or "cousins." These types are usually numbered and may have a subtype represented by a letter. The most common types in the United

**Reprinted from** *Corrections Today Magazine,* **October 2003, pp. 78–84 with permission of the American Correctional Association, Lanham, MD.**

States are type 1a and 1b, which make up approximately 70 percent of those infected. The type of hepatitis C virus becomes important when an individual is being considered for antiviral treatment.

All of this would just be for intellectual curiosity if it were not for the fact that there is now a treatment. As with most new medications, it is not inexpensive, requires both pills and injections, and must be taken for 24 to 48 weeks. There are also a number of reasons why one should not be treated, such as requirements that women do not become pregnant during and for six months after, and that men do not produce children during the same time period. While it is a treatment, it is not the best option, and there are some promising drugs on the horizon. In types 2 or 3, current treatment guidelines are effective in 70 percent to 80 percent of the cases. Unfortunately, for the most common types of hepatitis C in U.S. prisons and jails, it is effective in less than half of the cases.

In some correctional systems, 15 percent to even 40 percent of inmates within the facilities are infected with hepatitis C—the average probably being closer to 25 percent to 30 percent. It seems that this fact has recently been "discovered" by the media, who are quick to blame corrections for this problem. While there may be some transmission during incarceration, it is clear that the majority of these individuals, particularly those who share needles for drug use, have gotten infected "on the streets." If every infected inmate in a given state's correctional system were to be treated, the cost would probably consume the state's entire health care budget for a full year, but this would be a waste of valuable and limited resources.

Though not everyone should be treated with antiviral therapy, all offenders should be educated about the disease and how not to contract or spread it. Those who have engaged in high-risk behavior should be screened for hepatitis C and, if positive, should be followed to determine the course of the disease—which usually means following their ALTs. If they never have been immunized for hepatitis A and/or B, this would be a valuable use of resources. It is unfortunate that Congress has not provided a "vaccines to inmates" program much as they have for children. Immunization is simply good public health policy, especially when it is possible to target the most at-risk populations. There is not, however, a vaccine currently available to prevent hepatitis C, and it will probably be years before there will be one.

Often, it is forgotten that antiviral treatment is not the only treatment—avoiding alcohol and other illicit drugs, good nutrition, rest and exercise are important considerations. Quitting smoking is also a good consideration, along with limiting the amount of medications and other chemicals that the liver has to break down, which is its normal function. Making lifestyle changes is difficult but should be encouraged. Consideration for substance abuse treatment must also be a component if inmates are to avoid getting reinfected.

The ultimate question is, "Do I have to treat, and how much money is it going to take?" A number of systems have some experience with this process, Rhode Island having led the way in taking on this challenge by creating and implementing a treatment protocol and beginning to evaluate inmates and start treatments. The important thing to remember is that the more correctional staff and health care providers know about this disease and are able to teach inmates, the better the decision to treat or not to treat will be. Protocols that rigidly exclude individuals are much more likely to be legally challenged. By contrast, following guidelines that take into consideration the multitude of factors of why and when a person is or is not ready to be treated is a much more reasonable approach, although time consuming.

The readiness for treatment requires an assessment of motivation, current health status, possible contraindications and need for substance abuse treatment. Readiness also requires the health provider to assess how likely an inmate may return to high-risk behaviors. The health care provider must know enough about the inmate to make this clinical determination. It requires the development of trust and mutual respect of the individuals involved in the process—a task that is not always easy in corrections. This process cannot be determined by a single visit, and additional information can be gained and shared with each contact. Much teaching could be accomplished through handouts and videos but is probably best accomplished by the peer education process—especially when the peer educators understand the guidelines being used.

Valuable resources will be wasted if someone is treated and engages in high-risk behavior again. The treatment with antivirals will make most people feel like they have a bad case of the flu for the 24 to 48 weeks of treatment required. (The length of treatment is determined by the type of hepatitis C.) It is not the purpose of this article to provide a detailed guideline of clinically treating the disease. If a particular system does not currently have one, a good starting point is the recent Centers for Disease Control and Prevention publication, Prevention and Control of Infections With Hepatitis Viruses in Correctional Settings. For offenders who have normal ALTs (over time) and are early in their clinical course—especially if they have type 1a or 1b—they probably should be encouraged to wait for more effective treatments, which are currently being developed and tested. Even with today's treatments, it is probably cost-effective to treat those who will not relapse and become reinfected.

Correctional systems will need to develop methods of tracking and follow-up to assist with the management and documentation that will be necessary to longitudinally follow large portions of their overall offender population. There will need to be central review to provide consistency in how each individual is treated.

Administratively, a course of treatment should not be started if it cannot be completed. While this takes jails a bit "off the hook," they will need to continue treatment of individuals entering their facilities or who are clinically determined to be "ready" for treatment and have time to complete it. Initial evaluation takes six to 12 months to work up an individual for treatment, which is usually longer than most sentences. Jails, however, should not ignore those who revolve through their system and have clinical indicators of a need for evaluation. Those who qualify for Meclicaid or veterans' benefits should be encouraged to avoid any alcohol consumption and have their ALTs monitored to help determine if and when treatment with antivirals should begin.

Politically, correctional administrators must make certain that the public and governmental bodies are also aware that this is not just a corrections problem. Correctional administrators and medical directors need to partner with public health and other community-based organizations to accomplish this educational process. Since treatment is difficult and only partially effective, prevention is the most important consideration. Experience has shown that "just saying no" does not work for many individuals. They must know how to reduce their risks and, if infected, how to avoid spreading it to others. While not popular, harm-reduction techniques have proved effective. Ultimately, if corrections and public health do not help individuals prevent becoming infected, everyone, not just corrections, will be feeling the burden of this disease. Correctional and health care staff need to be trained on standard precautions and have their questions answered through regular training. Scarlett O'Hara's approach, to "worry about that tomorrow," cannot be taken in regard to hepatitis C. It is here today and demands attention now.

**Review Questions**

1. List the symptoms of hepatitis C.

2. Discuss the strategies to prevent correction officers from contracting hepatitis C.

# Danger in the Station: Drug-resistant Infections

*Derek Williams*

As fire and emergency services workers, we are constantly reminded of the inherent dangers of our jobs. We accept these dangers as manageable risks to protect lives and property. We do this out of a sense of duty and try to eliminate as many of the risk factors as we can. As the world changes, so do the hazards of our jobs. We must recognize these new hazards and manage them with a proactive approach rather than from a reactive crisis management standpoint.

An emerging new hazard to our ranks is *Methicillin-Resistant Staphylococcus Aureaus* (MRSA) (photo 1).

MRSA is a type of staph infection that is resistant to antibiotics called "Beta-Lactams," which include methicillin and other more common antibiotics such as oxacillin, penicillin, and amoxicillin.[2] Because these bacteria are unique in that they remain unaffected by all but the highest concentrations of antibiotics, they are extremely difficult to treat, especially if allowed to remain untreated inside the body over time while gaining strength.

MRSA is commonly found on the skin and in the nose of healthy people. It is estimated that approximately 25 to 30 percent of the population is colonized with staph, approximately one percent being colonized with MRSA. The truly serious nature of MRSA arises when it finds its way from *on the body* to *inside the body*. This may occur from even the tiniest cut, scrape, or abrasion.

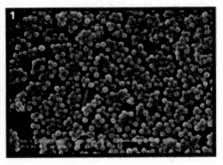

(1) Electron micrograph of MRSA. (Photo courtesy of Wikipedia free encyclopedia.[1])

## Classifications

There are two classifications of MRSA. The first is Hospital Based MRSA. MRSA occurs most frequently among persons in hospitals and health-care facilities (such as nursing homes and dialysis centers) who have weakened immune systems.

The second classification is Community Associated MRSA, more commonly referred to as CA-MRSA. These infections are acquired by persons who *have not* been recently hospitalized (within the past year) or have not had a medical procedure such as dialysis, surgery, and catheters. Staph or CA-MRSA infections in the community are usually manifested as skin infections such as pimples and boils and occur in otherwise healthy people.

## Transmission and Characteristics

CA-MRSA most commonly can be encountered in the following places or ways:

- ☐ Communal living areas [fire stations, locker rooms, jails, and social services housing (halfway houses), for example].
- ☐ Shared personal items such as bedding, towels, razors, and bar soap.
- ☐ Shared personal hygiene areas such as sinks, showers, and toilets.
- ☐ Equipment such as cardio equipment, weight rooms, sports "pads"/protective equipment, firefighting turnouts, and EMS/CPR manikins.

MRSA is transmitted *most frequently* by direct skin-to-skin contact, referred to as "direct transmission." MRSA can live on surfaces (especially warm, moist surfaces) for extended periods of time, the exact length of which has not been specifically identified. Its ability to live on surfaces such as gurneys, bedding, and bar soap can lead to "indirect transmission" of MRSA to emergency services personnel.[3] Factors that have been associated with the spread of MRSA skin infections include close skin-to-skin contact, openings in the skin such as cuts or abrasions, contaminated items and surfaces, crowded living conditions, and poor hygiene.

Staph bacteria, including MRSA, can cause skin infections that may look like a pimple, boil, or spider bite (a very common misdiagnosis) and can be red, swollen, and painful with pus or other drainage (photos 2–5). MRSA infections are usually asymptomatic in healthy individuals and may last from a few weeks to many years. More serious infections may cause pneumonia, bloodstream infections, surgical wound infections, and even death. Symptoms include fever, lesions, shortness of breath, high fever and chills, wound drainage, or increased white blood cell count. *Infection warrants treatment.*

### Colonization

As discussed, asymptomatic individuals may have MRSA but not show any signs or symptoms. This coupled with the bacteria's ability to live on inanimate surfaces may lead to what is referred as "colonization." With colonization, MRSA is present in or on a body site; no clinical signs or symptoms of illness or infection are present. Colonization may not warrant treatment, but a colonized patient may transmit MRSA to others.

Colonization may be found in "pods" or "clusters." This occurs when a number of people from the same social or work group test positive for MRSA. The Centers for Disease Control and Prevention (CDC) has investigated clusters of CA-MRSA skin infections among athletes, military recruits, and prisoners.[4] Clusters of MRSA in locker rooms have been a hot topic of discussion among athletic trainers and coaches for almost a decade.

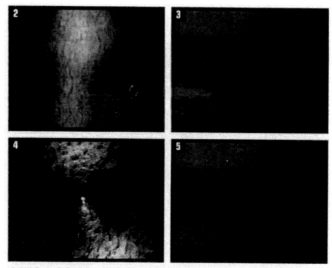

(2-5) "Typical" MRSA manifestations. [Photos courtesy of Phoenix (AZ) Fire Wellness Office/MRSA Power Point®.]

### Effects on Emergency Services Workers

How do MRSA and CA-MRSA affect emergency services workers? We are a particularly high-risk group. We contact patients with MRSA not only in medical settings such as nursing homes and dialysis centers but also patients with CA-MRSA in group homes, shelters, jails, and so on. We are a high-risk group for CA-MRSA just by the very nature of our jobs. We, for the most part, live a "communal" lifestyle at the fire stations, sharing close quarters and personal hygiene areas/items.

MRSA has already touched the fire service. The following are examples of MRSA infections and cases of "clusters" of MRSA found in several fire departments.

The Phoenix (AZ) Fire Department (PFD) and the City of Los Angeles (CA) Fire Department (LAFD) were valuable resources, because they have been actively tracking MRSA infections. Because of this, the LAFD as well as the PFD were able to collect data regarding the number of MRSA and CA-MRSA exposures. Tracking of MRSA among fire department members has proven difficult because MRSA either was not identified as the initial cause of injury and reported to infection control officers or members simply treated the infection with the help of their primary care physician and the use of sick time. The Mesa (AZ) Fire Department has recognized this as a significant threat to our membership and now is actively tracking MRSA and CA-MRSA infections among our members.

## The Los Angeles (CA) Fire Department

Since April 2003, the LAFD has had 136 claims for possible MRSA infection. Of these, 50 were confirmed MRSA cases, five of which required hospitalization of the members for aggressive antibiotic treatment. The LAFD also found "clusters" of MRSA at certain fire stations where several crews on several shifts contracted MRSA despite no known source patient contact.[5] It was found that the MRSA in these cases was CA-MRSA (community-based MRSA) transmitted to the members by surface contact of unclean work areas such as the workout rooms, bathrooms, and kitchens.

Since then, the LAFD has issued new strict guidelines/standard operating procedures related to station cleaning procedures, personal hygiene, and personal protective equipment during patient contact as well as proper decontamination (hand washing with liquid soap) after every medical call. Since these procedures have been put into place, the LAFD has seen a dramatic reduction in MRSA-related industrial injuries.[6]

## The Phoenix (AZ) Fire Department

During the years 2004 through 2006, the PFD had 29 cases of MRSA infections. Eleven members required some level of hospitalization for treatment. Since then, with the help of the department's infection control physician, Dr. Sem Jou, Phoenix has instituted procedures to protect its membership.

Dr. Jou has educated the members relative to the benefits of cleanliness, hygiene, proper diet, rest, and the risks of neglecting these areas. Phoenix has also installed antibacterial hand cleaner dispensers in various areas of the stations, including the entryways, bathrooms, and kitchen. Dr. Jou and the PFD have emphasized prevention and education. The result has been a marked decrease in the instance of MRSA infections among members.[7]

## The Mesa (AZ) Fire Department

Mesa Fire has already had MRSA cases within our ranks. More members may have been infected with MRSA; most likely, some cases went unreported or were not diagnosed. Although we have an extensive Wellness Program, only until recently have we recognized the potential of MRSA and CA-MRSA to affect our members. Here are just two cases of MRSA affecting our members.

## Case 1 — Mesa Fire Department Engineer/EMT:

In September 2001, a Mesa firefighter/engineer from Station 10 went to fourth-quarter training and participated in rescue drills crawling in full turnouts. At 11 a.m., he noticed a small red bump, similar to an ingrown hair, on his knee. By 3 p.m., the firefighter had a fever, and his knee was hot to the touch and was swollen and painful to move. He went to a local emergency room and was given his first dose of oral antibiotics at 9 p.m.; he then went home to rest.

The next day, the firefighter went to his primary care physician and was given a shot of concentrated antibiotics and instructed to increase his oral dose. Two days after noticing the bump, the firefighter went to see an orthopedic physician (associated with Mesa Fire for member injury treatment) because the pain was increasing and he believed that he had an orthopedic injury. The physician recognized it as aggressive MRSA and admitted the firefighter to a local hospital, where he was on IV antibiotics for four days.

This case illustrates not only that MRSA can be easily misdiagnosed but also that not all physicians know that MRSA should be considered in their diagnoses. For this reason, it is important for health care providers to keep abreast of changing patterns of infection in their local communities to properly diagnose and treat these cases.[8]

**Case 2 — Mesa Fire Department Captain/Paramedic:**

One afternoon in April 2006, a Mesa fire captain on duty at Station 6 noticed an irritation on top of his foot. By 9 p.m., the irritation had formed a small bump, similar to an ingrown hair, with redness and swelling around it. The captain went to his primary care physician two days later. The doctor examined the bump but did not identify it as MRSA. The captain was given a shot of antibiotics and a script for oral antibiotics.

After five days, the foot was painful to touch, hot, red, and swollen. On the sixth day, the captain went back to his primary care physician. When consulted, another doctor in that office, who had been involved in treating military personnel in the past (one of the other high-risk groups), recognized it as aggressive MRSA. The captain spent the next three weeks on high-dose antibiotics. Only after two weeks did the captain see any improvement to his foot. The captain told the Mesa Fire Wellness Office captain that during this process he began to wonder, "Will I be able to do my job with a prosthetic limb?" That's how bad it got! He was sure he would lose his foot (photos 6–8).

**IAFF: "Serious Hazard for Firefighters"**

The International Association of Fire Fighters (IAFF) recognizes this as a serious hazard to firefighters. The following quotes are from the IAFF's main Web site at www.iaff.org/safe/content/MRSA/MRSA.html regarding firefighters' health and MRSA:[9]

(6) The wound after the first doctor appointment. (Stock photos of member injury. Used with permission of injured member.

(7) The wound at its worst. The captain already had been given antibiotics by injection and mouth for several days.

(8) The wound started to heal after he had been on antibiotics for two weeks.

☐ "Firefighters, by nature of their contact with the public, are in constant danger of exposure to many infectious diseases. MRSA is a serious, potentially life-threatening infection."

☐ "The primary concern for firefighters is the switch from hospital-acquired to community-acquired infections."

☐ After reviewing this issue and recent events, IAFF General President Harold A. Schaitberger stated, "Following universal precautions with every patient contact, including hand washing, is very important—regardless of whether or not the patient's disease status is known. What you can't see may kill you."

**Protecting Against MRSA**

So how do we protect our membership from MRSA infection? There are several things we need to do to stop the spread of MRSA and protect fire and emergency workers:

1. Wear personal protective equipment (PPE) on all medical calls.
2. Use personal hygiene before and after calls/decontamination.
3. Clean the station and follow personal hygiene protocols.
4. Clean workout rooms and equipment.
5. Clean turnout/PPE.

Placing a barrier between you and the patient greatly decreases your chances for MRSA infection. Current PPE guidelines and techniques create a very effective barrier. Continually wear gloves during patient contact; remove them whenever you must access equipment. Don a fresh pair of gloves when patient contact is resumed. But as stated before, MRSA can live on surfaces. You must use PPE during the entire call, including during decontamination procedures afterward. Before and after decontaminating equipment, wash your hands thoroughly. In addition, always consider the following when it comes to protecting yourself from MRSA:

☐ Have you touched unprotected areas of the scene-did you kneel on the floor with shorts (if they are part of your uniform) or handle items/equipment on-scene with contaminated gloves?
☐ Are you bringing MRSA, along with other contaminates, back to the station or your home and family on your boots or clothes?

After a call, make every effort to wash your hands and any unprotected area that may have contacted the patient or equipment. The CDC recommends using an alcohol-based hand cleaner as a first-line decontamination agent if hands are not visibly contaminated. If hands are visibly contaminated, wash hands with liquid soap (do not use bar soap—MRSA lives on bar soap) immediately after a call; then use a disinfectant hand cleaner. Hand washing alone is inferior to alcohol-based hand cleaners for the purpose of decontamination unless the hands are visibly contaminated. Antibacterial/alcohol-based hand cleaners that do not require water for use should be kept on all apparatus for this purpose. At the Mesa Fire Department, we have issued a Medical Personal Protective Equipment Pack to our entire membership. This PPE pack consists of a fanny pack holding such items as glasses, gloves, medical protective sleeves, TB-masks, and antibacterial hand cleaner. This pack can be carried on members during every medical call to provide initial PPE as well as backup PPE to replace soiled/contaminated equipment. The PPE pack has been used very successfully within our department (photo 9).

## Cleaning Protocol

Decontaminating all equipment, *including the med boxes*, after each call is essential. If equipment is thoroughly and properly decontaminated after each call, it eliminates the potential of contacting MRSA and other contaminants on equipment surfaces. Many times, medical equipment is given detailed decontamination attention after a call. However, the boxes/bags in which the equipment is carried are often neglected. Often, boxes/bags containing medical supplies are placed on unclean surfaces during the course of medical treatment. If

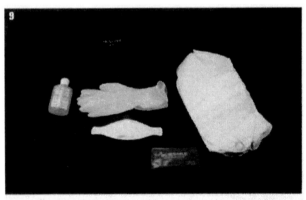

[9] Mesa Fire Department PPE Pack. [Photo courtesy of Mesa [AZ] FD.]

not properly decontaminated, they could potentially expose members to MRSA and other biohazards during normal equipment handling at a later time. A disinfectant or bleach concentration can be very effective in decontaminating such equipment. Spray the box/bag with a disinfectant, and *do not wipe off.* Allow the disinfectant to sit on the equipment and air dry. This is the only way to kill MRSA effectively.

Even if you do not run medical calls or are exposed to patients on a regular basis, the danger of CA-MRSA still exists at fire stations. Proper hygiene and cleanliness are the only ways to combat CA-MRSA clusters at fire stations. We need to take a "back to basics" approach to cleaning the stations and equipment. This must be done each day with particular attention to detail on our Saturday station detailing/cleaning routines (if that is part of your department's culture). Disinfect surfaces, paying close attention to common areas. Saturate the area to be cleaned, and let the surface air-dry. Wash bed covers, blankets, and other linens commonly used routinely. Pay particular attention to the kitchens, bathrooms, workout areas, and equipment each day; give them a thorough disinfecting at least once a week.

A cleaning schedule for EMS and community training equipment, such as CPR manikins, should be devised to ensure that all pieces are cleaned on a regular basis following manufacturer guidelines. This is especially important for equipment used by multiple providers and students. Don't forget the areas of the apparatus that should be disinfected, such as door handles, headsets, and the steering wheel.

MRSA stays on warm/moist surfaces for unknown/extended periods of time. Each time you use exercise equipment, disinfect it for the next person. Not only is this common courtesy, but cleaning equipment after each use has been proven to help halt the spread of CA-MRSA. (4)

Keeping firefighting PPE/turnouts clean is another essential step to limiting MRSA and CA-MRSA infections. Departments should institute a turnout cleaning procedure following guidelines set forth in NFPA 1500, *Standard on Fire Department Occupational Safety and Health Program*, Jan 31, 2002; NFPA 1971, *Standard on Protective Ensembles for Structural Fire Fighting and Proximity Fire Fighting*, Feb. 7, 2005; and NFPA 1581, *Standard on Fire Department Infection Control Program*, Nov. 12, 2003, for protective clothing and equipment; Occupational Safety and Health Administration (OSHA) standards regarding infection-control programs; and manufacturer guidelines.[10]

Mesa Fire's system for turnout washing combines an in-house cleaning program with dedicated washers and specialty dryers for turnouts and a private contractor certified by the manufacturer for turnout repair and cleaning (photo 10). We have had great success with this system, scheduling regular turnout cleaning through our battalions as well as having an emergency cleaning repair system in place. This system is supported by Saturday PPE inspections by the company officers. The department is also considering issuing two sets of turnouts to all members. This would allow a member to have a clean set of turnouts on hand at all times should one be contaminated. This also allows members to schedule routine cleaning of their turnouts and still be available for shifts and overtime. A system that ensures PPE cleanliness and repair not only greatly decreases the chance for exposure to MRSA and other biohazards but also ensures that the turnouts are in good operational condition at all times.

### Education: The Five Cs

The best way to prevent MRSA and CA-MRSA is education. The CDC has distilled the educational components down to "The five Cs": close contact, contaminated items, crowding, cleanliness, and compromised skin.[11]

(10) Mesa Fire Department turnout washing area. (Photo courtesy of Mesa (AZ) Fire Department.)

1. **Close Contact (skin-to-skin):** We must continue to encourage the use of PPE on medical calls and whenever there is close contact with customers in the field. We must continue to evaluate the adequacy of current PPE and challenge paradigms regarding equipment and procedures. We must continue to change as the world does, to allow our procedures to reflect current threats to our membership.

2. **Contaminated Items:** We must continue to emphasize proper decontamination of equipment (including turnouts) and provide procedures, develop guidelines, and provide properly equipped areas/facilities to support contamination.

3. **Crowding:** The CDC regarded this as a high priority primarily for areas such as jails, social service housing, and the like. However, we must understand that the very concepts of camaraderie and

family that we instill in our membership and take pride in also predispose us to CA-MRSA clusters. By this, I mean that we enjoy one another's company (for the most part) and do not mind living in close quarters with one another. We, as a population, must respect one another by maintaining our personal hygiene, engaging in the common courtesy of cleaning equipment and areas after use, and understanding that the closeness we enjoy at our fire stations must not be taken for granted.

4. **Cleanliness:** We must continue the tradition of keeping our equipment and stations clean. We must instill this trait as a source of pride among our younger members and take a back-to-basics approach with established members, reminding them of the importance of cleanliness in station life.

5. **Compromised Skin:** Any time you or a member of your crew has a compromised skin area, you must protect that area from exposure. Proper bandaging and the use of suitable duty uniform when needed (long pants or long-sleeve shirts) provide protection from exposure during medical calls and protect the area from possible infiltration of MRSA. Remember, MRSA on skin is common and not a problem. It is when it finds a route inside the body that its truly dangerous potential is unleashed.

MRSA and CA-MRSA infections are on the rise. I hope that this article helps you to recognize these new and serious hazards for firefighters and emergency services workers. I encourage you to use the Internet as a resource to continue your education and awareness regarding this subject. Many Web sites have valuable information on MRSA and CA-MRSA. The CDC has a wealth of information on this and many other subjects affecting our members.

### Endnotes

1    Photos 1-5. "Methicillin-resistant Staphylococcus aureus," Wikipedia, The Free Encyclopedia, http://en.wikipedia.org/w/index.php?title=Methicillin-resistant_Staphylococcus_aureus&oldid=62042460 (accessed July 5, 2006).

2    Centers for Disease Control and Prevention, "Methicillin-resistant Staphylococcus aureus, information bulletin," www.cdc.gov/ncidod/aip/research/mrsa.html (accessed July 5, 2006).

3    Jeffery R. Lejeune and David M. Berkowitz, "Bad Bugs. What You Need To Know About VRE/MRSA," *Journal of Emergency Medical Systems* (JEMS), Dec. 2000.

4    *The New England Journal of Medicine*, "A Clone of Methicillin-Resistant Staphylococcus Aureus Among Professional Football Players," http://content.nejm.org/cgi/content/short/352/5/468 (accessed July 5, 2006).

5    Phone conversations regarding MRSA among LAFD members with City of Los Angeles Fire Department Captain Chadwick Spargo and Captain Vance Boos, LAFD Medical Liaison Unit/Wellness Office, July 2006.

6    Safety Bulletin 04-14 (Addendum) "CA-MRSA," Safety Bulletin (Addendum) 05-05 "MRSA Prevention and Treatment Guidelines," and Department Memorandum "MRSA, Addendum to Bulletin 04-14, Captain Randy Yslas, Medical Liaison Unit, City of Los Angeles Fire Department (internal), Feb. 22, 2006.

7    MRSA Power Point® educational piece. Capt. Clarence "T-Baby" Tucker, Phoenix (AZ) Fire Department Health Center, 2006.

8    Mike McEvoy, Ph.D, REMT-P, RN, CCRN, editor *fireEMS* and consultant *Fire Engineering*, clinical associate professor pulmonary and critical care medicine at Albany Medical College in Albany, N.Y.: Proofreading and MRSA technical advice on first draft.

9    "Educational Project: MRSA," International Association of Fire Fighters, http://www.iaff.org/safe/content/MRSA/MRSA.html (accessed July 10, 2006)

10   National Fire Protection Association, Quincy, Mass.

11   Lisa Schnirring, "MRSA Infection, Physicians Expect to See More Cases in Athletes," *The Physician and Sports Medicine*, 3:10, Oct. 2004.

### Review Questions

1.  State the locations where firefighters are susceptible to contract MRSA infections.

2.  Discuss the protective measures to be taken by firefighters to prevent MRSA infection.

3.  Discuss the CDC 5C education program for the prevention of MRSA infection.

# "Checking Up" on Staff Health Education

*Carol Ahrens*

In Wisconsin, as in the rest of the United States, federal and state agencies have implemented mandatory exposure plans for blood borne pathogens and tuberculosis. An exposure control plan is required of employers who have an employee with occupational exposure in an effort to eliminate or minimize employee exposure. Under these plans, several steps must be taken, including educating staff with yearly update about blood borne pathogens.

Some states, such as Minnesota, allow each institution to decide how to train staff on these important issues. Other states use the purchased-package approach to meet the needs of diversified staff. There has been a proliferation of programs developed by various training companies, media groups and publication entities which generally consist of a video produced for mass audiences and sometimes contain a workbook or study guide. While these programs can be adapted to specific situations, it is important to remember that the Office of Safety and Health Administration (OSHA) directive requires someone to be available for questions and answers during and after the program. A video alone will not suffice.

Wisconsin's Department of Corrections chose to hire a full-time public health educator in August 1993 to design a program to meet the needs of its nearly 6,000 employees throughout the state's 10 major institutions, minimum security camps and field agencies. The department funds its staff health education programs with its budget for the Bureau of Health Services, through which public health educators operate their own budgets. The program is not funded through project money. It is a permanent position with ongoing state funding.

Educators work in conjunction with public health agencies, AIDS service organizations, community-based groups, medical personnel and other correctional agencies to prepare the training program. Valuable information is exchanged among all the agencies and organizations involved. Because of this ongoing collaborative effort to understand each other's concerns, cooperation among the many governmental and private agencies involved in health care has increased.

In addition to the necessary funding and cooperation among key groups, top-level administrators need to be committed to employee health education programs for them to be successful. For example, in February 1994, the secretary of the Wisconsin Department of Corrections issued a memo directing all of his staff to receive training on blood borne pathogens.

This kind of support and training helps accomplish the following:

- improved employee morale;
- improved employee decision-making; and
- improved work atmosphere.

Training in communicable diseases is offered yearly to all staff at one of the three state correctional training centers on site. Training also is offered through orientation and education for new officers.

To reach everyone, various training setups are used. On-site training is provided at institutions, training centers and unit meetings of Probation and Parole and the Division of Intensive Sanctions.

Through newly installed interactive television networks, training programs are able to reach most major institutions.

The department's educational programs focus on the hepatitis B virus (HBV), human immuno-deficiency virus (HIV) and tuberculosis (TB). Ideal conditions must be present for the spread of HIV, HBV and TB. By educating staff to recognize these conditions, headway is made in eliminating or controlling these diseases. This is all part of the education program.

**Reprinted from *Corrections Today Magazine*, October 1996, pp. 102–103 with permission of the American Correctional Association, Lanham, MD.**

Emerging pathogens have challenged societies throughout history. With few exceptions, public concern regarding these threats is not warranted. However, the media tend to sensationalize these new threats, and fear becomes one of the most prevalent plagues. As one health educator likes to remind her classes, "We are dealing with two epidemics here—one is AIDS and the other is AFRAIDS."

Helping staff learn more about their health has been one of the key duties of public health educators. Since the early 1900s health educators have used concise and accurate printed materials to educate their students. Today, interactive sessions are considered the best way to disseminate information on current disease concerns.

In the past year, there has been increasing concern among some staff about the transmission of hepatitis B, as well as confusion about the distinction between hepatitis B and hepatitis A. The public health educator does not assume that everyone knows what hepatitis is or how many types of hepatitis viruses have been identified. The educator begins with the basics: explaining the difference between virus and bacteria and why people with bacterial infections can be cured with antibiotics but cannot be cured of viral infections. The different types of hepatitis then are discussed.

To provide the best possible health education training program, a comprehensive curriculum guide has been developed. The curriculum includes outlines for lessons on TB, HBV, HIV and exposure plans. This guide allows anyone appointed by the public health educator to present a program that disseminates information accurately and consistently. This is particularly important because such a widespread audience requires occasional use of outside instructors.

The curriculum guide begins with 11 performance objectives that state what participants should be able to do at the end of the module. There are two evaluation procedures: (1) monitoring participants' correct or incorrect responses to questions asked by the instructor and (2) pre- and post-test exams. Next are lesson plans for tuberculosis, hepatitis, HIV/AIDS and exposure plans. A resource list also is included.

The lesson plans clearly outline what is to be covered. Issues such as transmission, disease progression, symptom, treatment and testing are detailed. For example, the lesson plan for tuberculosis covers these items, as well as medical conditions that increase the risk of developing TB, increased risk of TB, and the TB and HIV connection.

Incorporating variety and humor into any educational program is important, too and so it is with health education. Lecturing on heavy topics, such as blood borne and airborne pathogens, can be overwhelming even for health professionals, let alone for lay audiences. Trainers and educators often use humor, games, multimedia activities and flip charts to lighten the discussion.

The game that is particularly effective involves scrambling words used in training, such as "blood borne," "exposure," "virus," and so on, and giving participants 10 minutes to unscramble the words. This activity allows them to interact as they search for answers, and lightens up the presentation.

Although the basic material is covered consistently and accurately, how it is presented is as varied as the audience and presenters themselves.

An important part of any educational program is evaluation. Evaluation means different things to different people. For some, evaluation means statistics and computers; for others, it means reflecting on past practices. For the Wisconsin Department of Corrections, evaluation means a little of both. Written evaluations from program participants are standard components of each program. This feedback provides insights into which program components work well, which need strengthening and which need to be added or deleted.

To allow staff to continue the learning process at their own speeds, a leading library of videos is being developed and a supply of informational brochures is kept on hand.

Health education programs provide accurate information on health issues and safe sex and condoms, and address the psychological and emotional aspects of each issue. Staff who go through this training tend to feel more comfortable with the workplace, notice improved communication among supervisors and staff, and experience increased awareness of health and safety issues. Has such a program worked in Wisconsin? With the program less than three years old, the answer so far is, "Yes."

Instructors no longer receive questions about the possibility of being infected with HIV through a mosquito bite. People are better educated about certain health issues than they were three years ago. They are more concerned about getting the facts straight and recognizing the real risks in their jobs. This is what the program helps them do: to know the facts, protect themselves and recognize risks. Program evaluations indicate that the program has accomplished its goals.

**Review Question**

1. Describe the Wisconsin Department of Corrections training program for blood borne pathogens.

# AIDS Education in Law Enforcement

*Titus Aaron*

A high percentage of police officers are concerned about AIDS and many professionals agree that officers should receive training related to AIDS. Some claim that training officers will reduce the fear they have of contracting AIDS while on-duty.

Evidence suggests that many officers have incorrect information about AIDS. One study of 728 officers from a large urban police department published in 1989 reflected that the majority of the officers (62.2%) reported their primary information source on AIDS as newspapers or magazines; 167 (22.9%), listed health professionals as their primary source; and 86 (11.8%) reported other officers as their sources.

In August 1989 publication of the National Institute of Justice stated that "media coverage of the disease is sometimes misleading and may foster unnecessary fear." Police administrators can use training programs in an attempt to combat the fear of AIDS by developing programs for both recruit training and in-service training.

One study conducted in a large urban police department found that "AIDS training sessions did indeed reduce participants' perceptions of risks for infection. Analyses of responses about individual risk items showed that only for two plausible or known risks of transmission—being stuck with a hypodermic needle and providing first aid to a bleeding person—were there no significant reductions of anxiety."

Another reason to train officers about AIDS is that police regularly come into contact with people at high risk of contracting AIDS (prostitutes and drug users are examples). Also, police officers are in a unique position to convey important health resource information to those most in need of it.

The "dark figure of AIDS" is yet another reason law enforcement managers should implement AIDS-related training programs. The number of people who actually carry the HIV virus or who have ARC or AIDS is unknown. It was not until the summer of 1981 that the first cases of AIDS were diagnosed in the United States. The first test for the presence of the HIV virus was not licensed by the FDA until March 2, 1985. Some feared how the public would react if AIDS was more common than previously estimated. Many states enacted laws prohibiting employers from testing employees or prospective employees for the presence of the HIV virus.

On July 26, 1990, President Bush signed into law the Americans with Disabilities Act of 1990 (ADA). The ADA applies to most state and private employers of more than 25 employees beginning July 26, 1992 and will cover most state and private employers employing more than 15 employees after July 26, 1994.

The ADA allows employers to test employees for the presence of the HIV virus between the time an offer of employment is made and the time the employee actually begins working. The ADA will have the effect of invalidating state laws to the contrary. If the testing of employees increases, the numbers of documented/diagnosed cases of AIDS is certain to increase even if the number of people who actually carry the HIV virus remains the same

The increase in the number of diagnosed cases in employees of police agencies can create inter-agency personnel problems. An increase in the number of diagnosed cases in the population at large may create a public panic, as has increases in the number of officially reported crimes. The enactment into law of the ADA creates an additional reason for law enforcement officials to immediately implement AIDS-related education programs.

Once commitment to an AIDS-related training and education program has been made, the substance of the training must be identified. A Red Cross program entitled "Emergency Service workers and the AIDS Epidemic" appears to be the most commonly used basic program in California law enforcement

**Reprinted from *Law and Order*, March 1991, pp. 35–36 with permission of *Law and Order Magazine*.**

agencies. This program includes: history and epidemiology of AIDS; definitions of AIDS, ARC and HIV; how the human immune system works; how HIV is transmitted; who is at risk; symptoms of AIDS and ARC; risk reduction and prevention; what to do if you are exposed; AIDS and the law; and additional resources about AIDS.

The more successful California programs supplemented the basic Red Cross program with practical information such as the proper procedures for conducting searches; the utility of wearing gloves and masks; the proper procedures for handling clothing soiled with blood or bodily wastes; the proper procedures to decontaminate resuscitation equipment; and safety tips in the provision of CPR.

Theodore Hammett (1989:2) argues that once basic medical information has been presented, "AIDS training programs should be related specifically to criminal justice and law enforcement situations and concerns." Hammett recommends the following topics be covered in police AIDS training and education programs:

- Means of HIV transmission;
- Methods of preventing transmission;

Staff participation can counteract possible suspicion that departmental management may not be forthcoming with all information. The inclusion of line-staff in developing a training program can also make management aware of the specific concerns of line-staff, and those concerns can be addressed in the training program.

Initial training should be supplemented with periodic updates. New information should be made available as soon as possible. Law enforcement may well have a fight in sight, a fight against a fear of AIDS, but the more the officers know about the enemy, the more effective they are likely to be.

It is imperative that law enforcement managers immediately enact meaningful AIDS-related training and education programs for all police officers.

### References

Forst, M., Moore, M. and Crowe, G. (Dec. 1989). AIDS education for California law enforcement. *The Police Chief*, pp. 25–28.

Hammett, T. M. (Aug. 1989). *AIDS bulletin, AIDS and HIV training and education in Criminal Justice agencies*. US Department of Justice, Office of Justice Programs. National Institute of Justice. NCJ 115904.

Sheridan, K., Lyons, J.S. Fitzgibbon, M., Sheridan, E.P. and McCarty, M.J. (Sept./Oct. 1989). Effects of AIDS education on police officers perceptions of risk. Public Health Reports, Vol. 104, No. 5, pp. 521–522.

### Review Questions

1. Why is it necessary to educate law enforcement officers about HIV/AIDS?

2. Discuss the topics to be covered in police AIDS training and education programs.

# PART FOUR
# Stress Issues

---

## Dispatcher Stress
*Tod W. Burke*

During the past decade, the law enforcement community and individual researchers have devoted considerable attention to the issue of police stress. Much of this research has focused on finding better ways to manage those specific factors that cause stress for law enforcement officers.

Today, as a direct result of this research, it is common to find police officers attending stress management seminars, lectures, and workshops as part of academy and in-service training programs. Unfortunately, this increased attention to police stress has failed to reach other components of the law enforcement community that also experience high stress levels.

This article focuses on the specific factors that may contribute to stress and burnout among an often forgotten segment of the law enforcement population—police dispatchers. In particular, it examines the relationship between dispatcher stress and job satisfaction, social support, and control. The article then discusses the findings of a recent survey of civilian dispatchers in New Jersey. It also offers recommendations for agency administrators to enhance not only the conditions under which police dispatchers work but also the ability of dispatchers to serve their agencies and their communities.

### The Dispatcher's Role

Dispatchers perform a complex and stressful function. Unfortunately, the critical role they play often is misunderstood by administrators, officers, and citizens. Dispatchers must be able to handle incoming calls, dispatch officers, transfer calls to appropriate agencies, coordinate multiple units for emergency calls, record computer requests by field units, and in some cases, process written reports. Frequently, they must provide immediate emergency care instructions to panicked, distressed, and highly emotional callers. They must perform all of these functions while remaining calm and reassuring. Additionally, dispatchers often play a vital role in ensuring the safety of others, not only callers but also officers on the street.

Those who most rely on dispatchers—hurried officers who demand immediate attention to their requests and citizens who expect instant resolutions to their problems—often fail to appreciate the diversity of roles performed by dispatchers. Likewise, supervisors and administrators often overlook the many different functions that dispatchers perform.

### Factors Contributing To Stress and Burnout

Many individuals in law enforcement regularly refer to the terms "stress" and "burnout" without possessing a clear understanding of their meanings. For the purposes of the research presented in this article, stress is defined as "the non-specific response of the body to any demand."[1] By contrast, burnout is defined as "the result of constant or repeated emotional pressure associated with an intense involvement with people over long periods of time." [2] "It is the painful realization that (individuals) no longer can help people in need; that they have nothing left in them to give."[3]

Reprinted with permission from *FBI Law Enforcement Bulletin*, October 1995, pp. 1–6, Courtesy of *FBI Law Enforcement Bulletin*.

While many occupational settings are stressful, dispatchers experience specific stress unique to their position. Past studies identified aspects of the dispatcher's job that contribute to stress and burnout.[4] They include: being relegated to a low position within the departmental hierarchy; insufficient training; lack of support and positive reinforcement from officers, supervisors, and managers; shift work; lack of control; antiquated equipment; confinement and lack of interpersonal communication; lack of breaks; negative citizen contacts; lack of personal development; and insufficient pay.

Although many of these stressors have been cited in informal interviews, more formal studies that fully examine the relationship between dispatcher stress and independent stressors have been lacking. The New Jersey study marks the first formal effort to examine the relationship between stress and burnout among dispatchers, with particular attention devoted to job satisfaction, social support, and supervisory control.[5]

## Method of Research

For this study, researchers randomly selected civilian dispatchers from various police agencies throughout southern New Jersey. The research focused only on civilian dispatchers and thus excluded status issues pertaining to sworn officers who performed dispatcher duties. Further, the counties of southern New Jersey were selected because they included urban, suburban, and rural agencies, thereby permitting greater application of the survey results.

After securing approval from the heads of the selected agencies, researchers mailed survey forms to the departments' dispatchers. Of the 411 surveys distributed, 254 completed responses were received, for a return rate of 62 percent.

## Results of The Study

### Job Satisfaction

The researchers predicted that police dispatchers who were dissatisfied with their job, lacked social support, and perceived little control over their working environment would experience the greatest amount of occupational stress and burnout. Job satisfaction was defined as the totality of the dispatchers' feelings about various aspects of their occupation. These aspects included the work itself, pay, promotional opportunities, coworker support, and supervisory support.[6]

Results indicated that perceived job satisfaction was a major factor in police dispatcher stress and occupational burnout. Specifically, those dispatchers who were dissatisfied with their current position experienced significant stress. Dispatchers who were dissatisfied with their current pay and lack of promotional opportunities also reported elevated levels of stress and burnout.

Additionally, dispatchers reported a high level of role conflict and confused sense of loyalty in the workplace. In other words, as the dispatcher's role became more complex, the level of stress increased. While a lack of supervisory support was a major stressor, dispatchers who had the support of coworkers reported less psychological stress and burnout. Thus, those dispatchers who perceived that they were being treated as second-class citizens, lacked pay and promotional opportunities, experienced conflicting role demands, or lacked supervisory support reported higher levels of job stress and burnout.

The study defined social support as a network of communication offering guidance and feedback about individuals' behavior that validate their self-concept.[7] Results indicated that lack of social support plays a vital role in dispatcher stress. Those dispatchers who indicated the *least* amount of job stress and burnout possessed the following characteristics: Intimate contacts with close friends outside of the workplace; a sense of belonging to some type of social network; a close working relationship with colleagues; belief that family members could be counted on for assistance in an emergency; and belief that they could count on colleagues for advice, guidance, and expertise in certain areas. In other words, those dispatchers who perceived that they had a network of support—both within and outside the workplace—reported the least amount of job stress and burnout.

## Focus of Control

Focus of control refers to the level of control individuals exert over their environment. Specifically, internal locus of control refers to those events that are contingent upon one's own behavior. External locus of control suggests those events that are not contingent upon one's own actions, but rather upon luck, chance, fate, or other outside factors.[8] Survey results indicated that dispatchers who perceived a lack of control over their working environment experienced greater occupational stress and burnout.

Those dispatchers who perceived that they had control over their work setting also reported a greater sense of personal achievement and responsibility on the job, while those dispatchers who perceived a lack of control within their agency reported feeling emotionally exhausted and overextended by their work. This lack of control accounted for dispatchers' reporting an impersonal and uncaring attitude toward the citizens they served. A majority of dispatchers also reported that their training, education, skills, and experience were inadequate for the demands of the job. In essence, many dispatchers perceived a negative work setting.

## Unique Aspects of Dispatcher Stress

While respondents indicated an extensive list of stressors, three particular aspects of their work emerged as particularly stress-inducing. These included their low status within the department's hierarchy, the high level of responsibility they felt toward others, and the lack of training provided to them.

## Low Status

One of the stressors that most affected job satisfaction among dispatchers was their perception of low status. Dispatchers commonly reported hearing disparaging remarks such as "What do you expect? They are only dispatchers," from department personnel or callers. Their civilian status within a sworn organization and their physical isolation from other personnel reinforced this perception of being second-class citizens. This degradation came not only from line officers but also from supervisors and other civilian employees who participated in "dispatcher bashing."

## Responsibility to Others

The high level of responsibility that dispatchers feel toward others represented another unique source of stress. Dispatchers truly act as "lifelines" to fellow workers and citizens. Thus, when someone calls for assistance, the dispatcher must initiate the response and monitor the progress. For example, when a police officer calls for backup, it is the dispatcher's responsibility to identify the problem and send available units to the scene, while at the same time remaining calm and handling other incoming emergencies.

## Lack of Formal Training

Dispatchers cited the lack of formal training as another significant source of stress and burnout. While many occupations require advanced education degrees and provide formal training to employees, dispatchers often learn their trade on the job. Although their high level of responsibility would suggest proper training, this is rarely the case. Academy and ongoing in-service training programs for dispatchers are extremely rare. The training programs and workshops that do exist often are conducted by private organizations not associated with the agency.

Should individual dispatchers decide to attend an outside training program, it is unlikely that their departments will sponsor or reimburse them for expenses. Yet, dispatchers know that few police administrators would hesitate to sponsor or reimburse a sworn officer who attends a training program.

**Stressors Cited by Dispatchers**

The following factors contribute to stress among police dispatchers:

- Dissatisfaction with job
- Dissatisfaction with position
- Dissatisfaction with pay
- Dissatisfaction with promotional opportunities
- High level of role conflict
- Lack of loyalties in the workplace
- Lack of close friends (outside of the workplace)
- Poor working relationship with colleagues/officers
- Inability to count on family members for support
- Inability to count on colleagues for advice, guidance and expertise
- Low status
- Lack of supervisory support
- Lack of control over the work setting
- Lack of training
- Lack of education/skills/experience for job demands

**Recommendations**

Administrators can use the results of this study to re-examine the support networks within their agencies in order to alleviate the high level of occupational stress inherent in *all* aspects of policing. Simple steps may prove quite effective. For example, by making sure that dispatchers are included in after-hours gatherings, supervisors can go a long way toward integrating them into an agency's sense of esprit de corps. Such seemingly modest moves afford dispatchers a chance to socialize with officers and other members of their department and gives them an ideal opportunity to establish peer support.

In addition, professional or peer counseling should be made available to any dispatcher experiencing high levels of job-related stress. Counseling may prove invaluable not only in terms of the health of individual employees but also in terms of job performance. Administrators should consider support networks and seminars as part of an in-service training program. For example, spouse/companion programs could be implemented to give spouses and significant others a better understanding of the complex role dispatchers play in an agency and the anticipated stress that may accompany that role.

Communication and understanding between dispatchers and line officers also foster a sense of support. Supervisors should strongly encourage that dispatchers ride along with field officers to observe the actual scenarios officers encounter. In turn, officers, as part of their in-service and academy training, should observe dispatchers within their particular work setting. Administrators also must avoid assigning officers to the dispatch center as a form of punishment for ineffective field performance. The dispatch center should *not* become a dumping ground for officers with poor attitudes.

Police executives must recognize the importance of job satisfaction among all employees, including dispatchers. Therefore, they should re-examine promotional opportunities, particularly for those dispatchers who perceive themselves as lower status employees.

While salary and benefits do not guarantee job satisfaction, adequate compensation does affirm an agency's commitment to its employees. Improved salary and benefits are a tangible way to show dispatchers that management understands their difficult role.

The complex role performed by dispatchers can be simplified through proper training sessions so that the training, education, and skills of dispatchers correspond adequately to the job demands. These sessions should be similar to academy and in-service classes provided to officers but should be modified to meet the specific needs of dispatchers. Like in-service training designed for officers, they also should be tuition-free.

Additionally, "dispatcher reference guides" should be made available to assist each dispatcher. These guides should contain details and procedures focusing on: Obtaining vital information; performing call analysis; protecting callers, victims, and officers; learning apprehension/custody processes; and preserving evidence. Departments can obtain these guides from a commercial dispatcher training provider and modify them to meet specific agency needs and demands.

Further, police managers need to create a work environment that allows dispatchers some degree of control over their actions. This can be accomplished by permitting dispatchers to provide input during any decision making process affecting the communications section. Examples include operational policy and communications center hiring procedures.

Finally, if dispatchers are to be perceived as team players, they must receive supervisory support, as well as support from other members of the department. Supervisory support includes not only positive reinforcement but also the necessary resources to accomplish assigned tasks.

## Conclusion

The findings of this formal research project indicate that dispatchers report job stress and burnout primarily as a result of job dissatisfaction, a lack of social support, and a perceived lack of control. Fortunately, police managers can take fairly simple steps to address these factors and thus foster a better work environment for dispatchers.

As the role of law enforcement officers continues to grow more complex, so too do the role and responsibilities of police dispatchers. Administrators who treat dispatchers as second-class citizens do more than contribute to stress and burnout among a vital component of their agency's workforce. They jeopardize the ability of their agency to respond effectively to criminal activity and emergency situations.

## Endnotes

1   H. Seyle, *Stress without distress* (revised) New York: McGraw Hill, 1978.
2   A.M. Pines, E. Aronson, and D. Kafry, *Burnout: From tedium to personal growth,* New York: Free Press, 1981.
3   Ibid
4   J. D. Sewell, and L. Crew, "The forgotten victims: Stress and the police dispatcher." *FBI Law Enforcement Bulletin,* 53, No. 3, 1984.; T. Guthery, and J. Guthery, "Dispatchers: The vital link." *Police Product News,* Dec, 1984; T. W. Burke, "The relationship between dispatcher stress and social support, job satisfaction and locus of control." Ph.D. dissertation, City University of New York, 1991, *Dissertation Abstracts International* 52/05-A, 1903.
5   The study included subjects who were exclusively police dispatchers ; exclusively fire/ambulance dispatchers; those who dispatched both police and fire/ambulance personnel; or those who served as civilian clerks within a law enforcement institution. However, for the purpose of this article, only those who were exclusively police dispatchers are discussed.
6   C. L. Hulin, P. C. Smith, L. M. Kendall, and E. A. Locke, *Cornell studies of job satisfaction: Model and methods of measuring job satisfaction.* Ithaca, New York: Cornell University, 1963.
7   G. Caplan, and M. Killilea, *Support systems and mutual help: Multidisciplinary explorations,* New York: Grune and Stratton, 1976.
8   H. M. Lefcourt, *Locus of control: Current trends in theory and research,* New Jersey: Erlbaum, 1976; J. B. Rotter, "Generalized expectancies for internal versus external control of reinforcement." *Psychological Monographs,* 80, no. 1, 1966.
9   H. Seyle, *Stress without distress* (revised) New York: McGraw Hill, 1978, A. M. Pines, E. Aronson, and D. Kafry, *Burnout: From tedium to persona growth,* New York: Free Press 1981.

## Review Questions

1a. Discuss the factors that contribute to stress for dispatcher personnel.

1b. Identify approaches for reducing stress for dispatcher personnel.

# The Police Supervisor and Stress
*Steven R. Standfest*

The puzzled young police commander had long envied his superiors' seemingly stress-free positions, but since his promotion, he has been experiencing chronic symptoms that rarely affected him in all of his years on patrol. His stomach pains feel like an ulcer, he frequently cannot sleep, and all too often, he turns to alcohol for relief. Last week, chest pains sent him to the emergency room, where the doctor diagnosed his problem—stress.

Many police managers experience health problems, both physiological and emotional, and have difficulty understanding the cause. As patrol officers, they might have believed that a promotion would alleviate the stress they faced every day. Soon after taking command, however, many find that they must contend with a variety of new stressor, in addition to the ones experienced by the patrol officers they lead.

Police commanders must cope with stressors similar to those faced by their private-industry counterparts such as office politics, deadlines, budget constraints, performance appraisals, and grievances, to name a few. But police commanders, unlike private industry executives, also must respond to death scenes, family disturbances, or accidents in which people have been seriously injured or killed. The combination of leadership stressor and the unique stressor faced by the police can be a recipe for a health catastrophe.

Stress affects the performance of individual supervisors and commanders and, consequently, the performance of the police department as a whole. Municipal authorities and police executives first should learn about the causes and consequences of stress and then take steps to help management personnel reduce its influence and effects.

## The Effects of Stress

Limited amounts of stress can have positive results. Spectators pay money to experience the exhilaration of a boxing match, a hockey game, or an auto race. The tension of competition drives participants to excel in these events and often enhances their performance. Yet, other stressors inhibit performance and can cause health problems. According to some doctors, as much as 70 to 90 percent of all illnesses have stress as the root cause.[1]

Stress occurs in three stages within the human body: Alarm reaction, resistance, and exhaustion.[2] The alarm reaction produces physiological changes, known collectively as "fight-or-flight" syndrome, in response to an emergency. Heart rate, blood pressure, and muscle tone increase. The secretion of adrenaline heightens awareness, a crucial survival factor for police officers confronted with life-or-death situations.

Prolonged exposure to a stressful situation eventually causes the resistance stage to set in. In many cases, such as hostage situations, or drawn-out domestic disturbance calls, even though the stress-inducing danger still might be present, an officer's body adjusts to the situation and tries to return to normal. The resistance phase is characterized by more control and a greater ability to withstand the effects of stress while maintaining performance levels.

However, when the resistance stage persists, exhaustion overcomes an individual's coping mechanisms. The responses initially experienced during the alarm reaction stage might reappear.

Physiological and psychological problems, such as chronic fatigue or depression, feelings of alienation, and irritability, can develop. The body continues to respond in a fight-or-flight mode and keeps producing high levels of adrenaline. The heart becomes overworked, blood-cholesterol levels increase, and actual tissue damage can occur, producing common illnesses such as heart disease, gastric disorders, arthritis, allergies, and kidney disease.[3]

**Reprinted with permission from *FBI Law Enforcement Bulletin,* May 1996, pp. 7–10, Courtesy of *FBI Law Enforcement Bulletin.***

Not all stress-inducing situations involve a responding to calls for service. In fact, the daily stressors associated with management of the department, such as responding to personnel shortages, dealing with budget constraints, and taking disciplinary action, can produce the same kinds of stress reactions among supervisors and managers as a domestic disturbance call might provoke among line officers. These effects of stress debilitate police managers, which in turn inhibits the effectiveness of their departments. What now becomes critical to the well-being of both is to identify the causes of stress and the means to alleviate them.

## High Anxiety

Patrol officers often seem to believe that only they experience job stress. Some of the limited research on the topic of law enforcement executive stress shows, however, that police managers indeed suffer from the adverse side effects of stress as often or even more often than other police officers.

A 1974 study identified several causes of stress among administrators and field supervisors in the Cincinnati, Ohio Police Department. Eighteen of 30 supervisors identified excessive bureaucratic red tape as a major stressor. Others pointed to their lack of input into administration of the department, poor equipment or the scarcity of it, personnel shortages, and lack of consideration by the courts in scheduling patrol officers for court appearances.[4]

Perhaps the study's most interesting result was the identification of two stressors unique to the supervisory role. The survey found that taking disciplinary action against a subordinate and making amends with the public because of a subordinate's mistake cause supervisors the most stress.[5]

Much of the stress experienced by supervisory or administrative police officers stems from their location in the department's hierarchy. People on all sides—bosses, subordinates, members of the public, and even municipal officials—make constant demands on them.

In a more recent study of supervisory law enforcement officers' stress levels, respondents concurred, citing such stress factors as a poorly defined role within the department, insufficient support from administrators, little or no input into departmental policy, and authority incommensurate with responsibilities. It also found that the normal supervisory activities of meting out discipline, motivating employees, building morale, appraising performance, identifying personal problems in subordinates and making appropriate interventions, and communicating effectively with subordinates caused stress among the law enforcement supervisors studied.[6]

Fortunately, stress levels do not have to reach the point of causing physiological and emotional illness among supervisory personnel. City leaders, police executives, and the individual supervisors themselves can take steps to manage stress effectively.

## Steps To Alleviate Stress

To begin, agencies might want to be certain that city leaders understand the negative effects of stress in order to garner their support for stress management and stress reduction initiatives. Stress can lead to physical diseases, such as cancer and heart disease, which in turn hurts the organization by preventing employees from contributing their full measure to the agency. Heart attacks and strokes kill more people, including managers, than all other diseases combined.[7] Once city leaders realize this, they often are more willing to support agency initiatives to reduce the stress of supervisors in the workplace.

Working with city managers, police executives can employ a practical four-step plan to reduce stress levels among supervisory personnel. Notably, many of the techniques that help supervisors cope with stress and avoid its debilitating effects also improve the quality of life in the entire police department, and thus reduce the inherent stress both in the office and for those officers working patrol and other areas. The four steps—assessment, planning, action, and follow-through—ensure that executives address the appropriate problems, develop and implement workable solutions, and then monitor progress and make adjustments as necessary.[8]

**Step 1: Assessment**

First, police executives must determine exactly what problems affect the managers and supervisors in the departments. By listening to these employees, an accurate diagnosis can be made.

Do supervisors consistently point to a particular policy or practice within the department that causes stress? Does some aspect of the department's physical space, such as poor lighting or temperature control, inadequate storage space, or insufficient prisoner holding areas, cause problems?

Administrators also should consult recent research on stress to obtain ideas about possible causes of stress and potential problem areas. For example, studies conducted at the FBI National Academy showed that as the education level of officers increased, stress levels decreased.[9] This information, coupled with input from employees, could lead administrators to recognize that managers' educational levels might be a factor impacting on their stress levels. Stressors in one department might not be the same as in other departments, so administrators must carefully assess their own situation.

**Step 2: Planning**

Once they have identified specific stress factors, administrators must continue to work with managers and supervisors to find ways to improve the situation. Solutions need not be expensive or complex to be effective. For example, repairing problems with the station house, equipment, or vehicles could go a long way to reducing stress levels among managers and line officers alike. City leaders might sanction a program to reimburse those who take management or career development classes at local colleges and/or department leaders might institute a policy of flexible scheduling to accommodate course schedules. Any action taken must show a good faith effort on the part of the agency and the city to address the problems faced by managers and supervisors.

**Step 3: Action**

Whatever solution is chosen must be implemented fully. Studying problems and talking about solutions have no effect, or worse, have a negative effect when administrators fail to implement the planned actions. If supervisors are encouraged to seek higher education, the department should make it easier for them to do so immediately. Administrators must put the key elements in place as promised or morale will suffer, and the stressors of the job will continue to inflict their debilitating effects on supervisory personnel.

**Step 4: Follow-through**

Just as important as implementing the planned course of action is monitoring the success of those actions. Administrators should go back to the managers and supervisors to find out whether the situation has improved, if they feel better about the situation, and if stress levels have declined. Based on this input, programs should be fine-tuned or replaced. Helping managers and supervisors deal with stress is a continuous process, not a one-shot remedy.

**Personal Responsibility**

Supervisory police officers must realize that they too experience stress. True, they might not deal with the difficult human relations problems that street officers face daily; yet, every job brings stressors of its own. Police managers need to learn ways to deal with the stressor that affects them in addition to taking advantage of programs offered by their department. Ultimately, individuals must take responsibility for their own personal health.

Command personnel should learn to put things into perspective. For example, in the studies cited earlier, disciplining subordinates proved to be one of the biggest stress producers. When confronted with situations that require disciplinary action, supervisors should look at the big picture. Will the world collapse if an unproductive subordinate must be reprimanded? Ten years from now, will anyone really remember the reprimand? Probably not. Of course, I do not recommend taking any of the prescribed supervisory duties lightly; however, officers do not need to agonize over them 24 hours a day.

One of the best ways to circumvent the effects of stress simply is to get out of the office and leave work at work. Managers and supervisors should spend more time with their families, take up golf, go fishing, or get involved in church activities or with a social group.

Law enforcement personnel tend to socialize with their co-workers. When groups of officers get together they naturally talk shop, which, far from being relaxing, merely brings home the stress from work. Instead, it is important to make an effort to socialize with people not connected to law enforcement. Having outside interests and social contacts helps command personnel maintain a healthy perspective and not get caught up in the constant pressures of the station house.

## Conclusion

Stress does not end when a patrol officer assumes an administrative or supervisory role in the department. In fact, it often multiplies. Realizing this, agency executives and city leaders can take steps to relieve stress within the department and help supervisory personnel cope with it better. Through their actions, law enforcement executives can lead by example, showing supervisors within the ranks how to deal productively with their stressful positions.

It is up to each one of us, however, to learn to handle stress well. We do not need to take the job home with us; we do not need to suffer from the ill effects of stress reactions. With education and a little effort, stress can be controlled and be used to our best advantage at work and at home. By learning to identify and deal with stressful work situations, our careers can form a rich and rewarding part of a healthy and well-balanced life.

## Endnotes

1   John G. Stratton, Ph.D. Police Passages, Manhattan Beach, CA: Glennon, 1984, 104.
2   Ibid., 106.
3   Ibid., 106–109.
4   William M. Kroes, Joseph J. Hurrel, Jr. and Bruce Margolis. "Job Stress in Police Administrators." *Journal of Police Science and Administration*, vol. 2, no. 4, 1974: 381–387.
5   Ibid.
6   Nancy Norvell, Dale Belles and Holly Hills, "Perceived Stress Levels and Physical Symptoms in Supervisory Law Enforcement Personnel," *Journal of Police Science and Administration*, vol. 16, no. 2, 1988:75.
7   Karl Albrecht, *Stress and The Manager—Making it Work for You* (New York: Simon & Schuster, 1986), 292.
8   Ibid., 305–309.
9   Hillary M. Robinette, *Burnout in Blue* (New York: Praeger Publishers, 1987), 151.

## Review Questions

1. Describe the steps for overcoming stress experienced by supervisors.

2. Explain the stages in stress reaction.

3. Discuss the factors responsible for supervisors stress on the job.

# Retiring from the "Thin Blue Line": A Need for Formal Pre-retirement Training

*Carl B. Caudill and Kenneth J. Peak*

Law enforcement agencies typically use a variety of approaches to ensure that they employ only the most competent and psychologically stable people in the applicant pool. To be deemed worthy of acceptance into this vocation, candidates must usually navigate a "hurdle process" of written, physical, and psychological tests; multiple interviews; and in-depth background investigations. Then, neophyte officers face several months of intensive academy and field training, all to prepare them for any type of incident that they may confront in their role as society's protectors. This protracted period of training serves to underscore that wearing a badge carries grave responsibilities, poses serious challenges, and is a daunting task.

Also inculcated into recruits is that law enforcement is not just a 9-to-5 job; rather, it is a calling. Moreover, those who answer this call possess the ability to exercise discretionary authority, including the mandate to judiciously apply force as necessary to resolve societal issues and critical incidents. During their careers, officers must continue a training regimen designed to ensure that they have the skills necessary to perform their duties efficiently, effectively, and equitably. Owing to this training and the dependence on fellow officers for the accomplishment of their work and the social ties that bind sworn personnel together, policing has developed its own subculture wherein officers often maintain a level of camaraderie that constitutes a surrogate family.

In stark contrast to this continual training and support while in active-duty status, officers contemplating retirement and the transition back into civilian life usually find little in the way of organized preparation and planning. The authors assert that this situation demands attention and correction because with the end of their careers looming, officers face one of the most stressful, debilitating, and consequential events of their lives.[1] After all, retirement is not an event; it is a process. Therefore, the authors propose the creation of a formal approach to this major aspect of policing and call on law enforcement administrators to take a hands-on, proactive role in assisting their personnel during this significant life change.

## Retirement in General

The recent economic downturns likely will affect normal retirement trends for years to come. What will not change, however, is that people are, and increasingly expect to continue, working beyond the usual retirement ages of 62 and 65. A contributing factor might be that those in today's labor force are generally living longer after retirement. Currently, men average an additional 17 years and women 20 years of life expectancy beyond what most consider as the typical retirement age, several years longer than half a century ago. Although retirement rates always have risen steeply at ages 62 and 65 (since the advent of Social Security), many older people remain in the work force, either part or full time.[2] Indeed, an increasing proportion of baby boomers expect to work beyond age 65.[3]

## Making the Decision

Several possible factors have a bearing on why people do or do not retire early. Health status can strongly influence the decision. Financial variables also can weigh heavily; changes in retirement incentives within the Social Security program and in private pension plans have reversed the trend toward early retirement. In addition, the labor force has come to rely increasingly on technological and interpersonal skills in a growing service economy, and computer users are 25 percent more likely to remain in the labor force.[4] Moreover, people are less likely to retire if their spouses still work.

Employees with defined-benefit pension coverage tend to retire a few years earlier than those without,[5] and early retirement incentive programs, particularly those involving a cash bonus, are accepted by about one-third of those given the option.[6] Health insurance costs appear to only modestly discourage retirement. Additional reasons why people wish to retire early include spending more time with family (33 percent), wanting to do other things (30 percent), and not liking their work (10 percent).[7] Finally, job-induced stress also can impact the decision to retire, with 61 percent of workers ages 55 to 59 reporting that their jobs involve "a lot of stress."[8]

### Understanding the Consequences

According to one survey, about half of today's retirees are miserable in their postretirement lives.[9] Retiring early may seem like a status symbol, signaling financial success, but it may not be the right action to take. People are not ready to retire until they have decided what they are going to do for an "encore."[10] And, many fail to realize that what pleases them during a 10-day vacation may not necessarily provide them with what they want from a retirement that lasts 30 years. An unforeseen potential problem also can exist when people ponder a postretirement career in the field of consulting, a road rife with aspirants and, therefore, filled with competition.[11]

People fare better in retirement if they have planned for the event and have received support from their employer. Research has found that employee preretirement programs can give participants a feeling of well-being and generate enthusiasm toward their respective organizations,[12] as well as result in greater satisfaction while still working and after retirement.[13] One retirement preparation study concluded that the program significantly enhanced attendee knowledge in the areas of finance, lifestyle, health care, and social activities; it further empowered them to handle their financial and health affairs and, within the organization, promoted the potential for increased productivity and morale among current workers.[14] Furthermore, retirees who felt their employers still cared about their well-being tended to have improved health, better social interactions, and a sense of belonging.[15]

Many potentially negative factors may occur upon approaching retirement from any occupation. Some involve mentally separating from the job; forming new social circles; coping with leisure time; losing status, self-esteem, and social networks and roles established over time; and entering a world where social adjustments are based on previous social backgrounds.[16]

Research also has suggested that psychological and physical problems incurred during their careers can impact how people adapt to retirement. Individuals who, prior to retiring, exhibit poor self-actualization, have not planned for the event, face financial challenges, or are in ill health appear to have more anxieties.[17] Irrational thoughts on getting older, stressful life events, poor health, and job status also may increase postretirement stress.[18]

### Retirement for Police

By virtue of union-negotiated changes in retirement benefits, law enforcement officers today often retire earlier and under far different circumstances than their civilian counterparts. Many who have worked the minimum number of years needed to retire suddenly realize that having a guaranteed pension means continuing to work in their agency for pennies on the dollar (i.e., their regular paychecks as compared with what they could earn in retirement income). Or, they may simply wish to do something different, perhaps less demanding and mentally and physically challenging.

### Unique Considerations

While several valid reasons can exist for opting to retire, separating from a career in law enforcement carries the potential for being much more psychologically debilitating than for other members of society who leave a regular "job." For example, a strong bond typically has developed between officers and their coworkers. They have shared the dangers, successes, and frustrations inherent in the work, as well as the prestige, authority, and status that society accords its police officers.

Furthermore, when officers retire, they also lose important trappings and symbols of the position—the badge; the uniform; and the specialized knowledge, skills, abilities, and insights for which the community has sought out and compensated them—that loomed so large in their lives for many years.

Retirement, therefore, can prove distinctly difficult for officers and can obviously foment a loss of identity and feelings of helplessness, along with instability and depression.[19] Some may view leaving the agency as abandoning the "thin blue line," a significant contributor to why severing the ties can prove highly stressful and have maladaptive psychological and physical consequences.

To compound their problems as they enter the retirement phase, officers also may have to come to tenus with the fact that they have little to offer the labor force beyond their knowledge of policing. They may be unprepared to transition into a second career or to even enjoy their newfound leisure time. This rummaging about for ways to keep occupied in retirement also can exacerbate their stress levels, heightening their feelings of isolation and withdrawal and the loss of identity, fraternity, structure, and internal control.[20]

## Mental and Physical Health Issues

Retirement can become problematic from the standpoint of mental and physical health, especially if not addressed before officers leave the job. Studies have suggested that like their civilian counterparts, officers also have similar maladaptive associations with retirement.

Some research has found that due to inherent stress factors, officers are different in their psychosocial stages of maturation, which supports the need for retirement training and more flexible retirement programs.[21] In studying the relationship between experiences during the police career and satisfaction in retirement, other research has suggested that successful adaptation to retirement was predicated on the level of satisfaction during the career.[22] In other words, those who viewed police work as "just a job" fared better in retirement than those who attached high emotional value to their police role, did not prepare well enough financially, adopted casual thoughts about the event, or ignored psychological and social considerations of what would substitute for a lifetime involvement in policing.[23]

Contemporary research also has indicated that as with their civilian counterparts, officers can encounter a number of adverse complications with retirement, such as loss of identity and self-esteem, marital problems, and boredom.[24] Police work provides a type of personal security that when given up, can generate, hopelessness, chaos, anxiety, and a loss of purpose.[25]

Research in other countries has supported the assertion that officers may experience retirement difficulties. For example, a survey of 174 retired members of the Royal Ulster Constabulary in Northern Ireland (now the Police Service of Northern Ireland) found that officers who retired on medical grounds exhibited more psychopathology and ill health than those who did under normal circumstances. They perceived themselves as financially deprived and believed that gratifying psychological and physical health held the key to future life satisfaction.[26] In addition, a study of 1,300 retired Scottish officers revealed that early retirement posed a risk for anxiety and depression and recommended that such officers be targeted for screening and intervention. Furthermore, subjects in this study were found to become increasingly prone to depression from the mid-50s upward, a time when many officers enter the retirement phase.[27]

## Trauma and Mortality Factors

Law enforcement officers experience varying forms of job-incurred trauma throughout their careers; residual effects can eventually create trauma during retirement. Officers may develop symptoms of post-traumatic stress disorder (PTSD) from carrying accumulated emotional baggage into their retirement years.[28] Their age plays a significant role in how they respond to the stress of trauma. Researchers have found that the incidence of PTSD and depression increased for officers between the ages of 40 to 49, a period when many begin to think about retirement.[29]

Mortality is another topic of research in police retirement. An extensive study of more than 2,000 officers in Buffalo, New York, found that the age-mortality rate for officers was, on average, 12 years lower than their civilian counterparts; health issues, such as cancer and heart disease, increased as officers drew closer to retirement; and the average life expectancy after retiring was 5.05 years less than that of people in other occupations.[30] This research also revealed that officer suicides were three times higher and appeared to occur more often just before retirement, a possible indicator of the stress of retirement at a time period when maladaptive factors can form.[31]

Not all studies of police retirements have concluded that the event itself is problematic. For example, some have found that retired officers appeared to live as long as other retired state employees[32] and that officers in good health upon entering retirement had no more adverse psychological health issues than the surrounding civilian community as a whole.[33] Previous lifestyle also may contribute to post-retirement difficulties, with alcohol consumption, tobacco use, irregular sleeping habits, lack of exercise, and poor diet being specifically problematic.[34]

Some research has suggested that active-duty officers have more stress dealing with administrative issues, such as work schedules and clashes with superiors, rather than from negative contacts with the public, exposure to dangers of the job, anguish caused by human suffering, and other such mental traumas.[35] Studies on police suicide are mixed as well; not all conclusions point to a definitive link with either the nature of the work or the retirement process.

## Conclusion

Those who answer the vocational call to the law enforcement profession often face their most difficult challenge at the end of their careers when they must retire from the "thin blue line." The authors contend that retirement for officers—not unlike the nature of their work and its inherent stressors - -can prove quite different from that of their civilian counterparts. Because of this occupational stress, the vagaries of retirement itself, and the fact that officers typically retire at a relatively young age, the road into and through this phase of their lives can be highly daunting and even fraught with peril. Part two of this article will focus on developing a preretirement program.

## Footnotes

1   John M. Violanti, Police Retirement: The Impact of Change (Springfield, IL: Charles C. Thomas. 1992) and Police Suicide: Epidemic in Blue (Springfield. IL: Charles C. Thomas. 1996): Bill Rehm. "Retirement: A New Chapter. Not the End of the Story." FBI Law Enforcement Bulletin. September 1996. 6–11: Michael J. McCormick. "Resolving Retirement Issues for Police Officers," Criminal Justice Institute, University of Arkansas System, retrieved on December 1 0, 2008. from http://\vww. cji.edu/papers/Resolving%20Retirement%20/ssues%20fbr%20Potice%20Officers.pdf, and Jim Ruiz and Erin Morrow. "Retiring the Old Centurion: Life After a Career in Policing. An Exploratory Study," International Journal of Public Administration 28, no. 13/14 (2005): 1151–1186.

2   U.S. Department of Health and Human Services, National Institute of Health, National Institute on Aging, Health and Retirement Study (March 2007), 40. retrieved on March 1 6. 2009, from http://hrson/ine.isr.umich.edu/intro/sho uinfo.php?lrf\le=oven,ie\v_histoiy&xtyp:=2.

3   Ibid., 49.

4   Ibid., 45.

5   Ibid., 51.

6   Ibid., 50.

7   Ibid., 47.

8   Ibid.

9   Suzanne McGee. "7 Common Retirement Mistakes to Avoid," retrieved on January 5, 2009. from http://articles. moneycentral.msn.com/lnvesting/StockInves/ingTrading/7CommonRetirementTrapsToAvoid.aspxripageTop Anchor.

10  Ibid.

11  Ibid.

12  Sylvia Odenwald. "Preretirement Planning Gathers Steam." Training and Development Journal 40. no. 2 (1986): 62–63.

13   Anita L. Kamouri and John C. Cavanaugh. "The Impact of Preretirement Education Programs on Workers' Preretirement Socialization," Journal of Occupational Behavior 7. no. 3 (1986): 245–256.

14   Emily T. Heath. "Do Retirement Preparation Programs Improve the Retirement Experience?" Benefits Quarterly 1 2, no. 2 (1996): 40–46.

15   Louis Yen. Alyssa B. Schultz. Timothy McDonald. Laura Champagne, and Dee W. Edington. "Participation in Employer-Sponsored Wellness Programs Before and After Retirement." American Journal of Health Behavior 30. no. I (2006): 27–38.

16   Fiorella Marcellini, Cristiana Sensoli. Norma Barbini, and Paola Fioravanti. "Preparation for Retirement: Problems and Suggestions of Retirees," Educational Gerontology 23. no. 4 (1997): 377–388; Marlene M. Rosenkoetter and John M. Garrís. "Psychosocial Changes Following Retirement." Journal of Advanced Nursing 27. no. 5 (1998): 966–976: and Donald C. Reitzes and Elizabeth J. Mutran. "Lingering Identities in Retirement." Sociological Quarterly 47. no. 2 (2006): 333–359.

17   Bruce Fretz. Nancy Kluge. Shelly Ossna, and Sharon Jones. "Intervention Targets for Reducing Preretirement Anxiety and Depression." Journal of Counseling Psychology 36, no. 3 (1989): 301–307.

18   Dani Jakubowski. "The Initial Impact of Retirement on Mental Health and Social Adjustment: A Prospective Study" (PhD diss.. University of Iowa, 1985).

19   Ruiz and Morrow, 1152.

20   McCormick.

21   M. Michael Fagan and Kenneth Ayers. "The Life of a Police Officer." Criminal Justice and Behavior 9. no. 3 (1992): 283–275.

22   Dennis Forcese and Joseph Cooper. "Police Retirement: Career Succession or Obsolescence?" Canadian Police College Journal 9, no. 4 (1985): 413–424.

23   Ibid.

24   Daniel A. Goldfarb. "An Instrument for Predicting Retirement Satisfaction in Police Officers: A Pilot Study," (Paper presented at the Society for Criminal and Police Psychology, Madison. WI, 1994).

25   McCormick; and Nnamdi Pole. Madhur Kulkarni. Adam Bernstein, and Gary Kaufmann. "Resilience in Retired Police Officers," 1 Traumatology 12. no. 3 (2006): 207–216.

26   Michael C. Patterson. A. Desmond Poole, Karen J. Trew. and Nicola Harkin, "The Psychological and Physical Health of Police Officers Retired Recently from the Royal Ulster Constabulary," Irish Journal of Psychology 22. no. I (2001): 1–27.

27   Alan Tuohy, Christina Knussen. and Michael J. Wrennall. "Effects of Age on Symptoms of Anxiety and Depression in a Sample of Retired Police Officers," Psychology and Aging 20. no. 2 (2005): 202–210.

28   John M. Violanti, "Residuals of Police Occupational Trauma," The Australasian Journal of Disaster and Trauma Studies 3 (1997): 1–8.

29   Tahera Darensburg, Michael E.Andrew, Tara A. Hartley, Cecil M. Burchfiel. Desta Fekedulegn, and John M. Violanti, "Gender and Age Differences in Posttraumatic Stress Disorder and Depression Among Buffalo Police Officers." Traumatology 12, no. 3 (2006): 220–228.

30   John M. Violanti, John Vena, and J. Marshall, "Disease Risk and Mortality Among Police Officers: New Evidence and Contributing Factors," Journal of Police Science and Administration 14, no. 1 (1986): 17–23.

31   Ibid.

32   Richard Raub, "Police Officer Retirement: The Beginning of a Long Life," retrieved on December 10, 2008, from http:// www.ncjrs.gov/pdffiles l/pr/l 09485.pdf.

33   Patterson, et. at.. 22.

34   Violanti, Police Retirement: The Impact of Change; and Ruiz and Morrow, 1 1 54.

35   Jerome E. Storch and Robert Panzarella. "Police Stress: State-Trait Anxiety in Relation to Occupational and Personal Stressors," Journal of Criminal Justice 24, no. 2 (1996): 99–107: and Deborah W. Newman and M. LeeAnne Rucker-Reed. "Police Stress, State—Trait Anxiety, and Stressors Among U.S. Marshals," Journal of Criminal Justice 32 (2004): 631–641.

## Review Questions

1.   Discuss the factors that negatively affect the health of Police Officer after retirement.

# Correctional Employee Stress & Strain
*Shannon Black*

Stress and strain are critical yet often ignored safety factors for everyone. Work-related stress has been the object of considerable research during the last 20 years. Stress has been described as a "perception of imbalance between resources and demand."[1] Strain is defined as "an immediate, short-term emotional response" to the imbalance between resources and demands, which is "characterized by feelings of anxiety, tension, fatigue and exhaustion."[2] The symptoms of strain associated with stress can create problems for both employees and employers.[3]

The potential effects of work-related stress include increased absenteeism, employee turnover, illness, marital problems, and alcohol or drug use.[4, 5, 6,] Systematic research about stress and strain in corrections has increased during the last 15 years and cannot be ignored without significant costs to employers and employees.

## Sources of Stress

There is considerable evidence that work in the corrections field can be stressful.[7] Several different sources of stress among correctional officers have been identified. One such source is role ambiguity, which is defined as the uncertainty employees feel regarding the expectations, responsibilities and priorities of their jobs.[8] For example, employees may have been told not to leave their posts but later are reprimanded for not responding to an emergency in another part of the institution.

Another potential source of stress is role conflict. Consistently, officers are trained to follow rules "to the letter," rather than to use discretion and judgment to enforce rules while preventing the escalation of certain situations. This creates problems because not all possible situations are described in the rules. Novel situations require employees to use their own judgment. Whenever an atypical situation is encountered and handled, it is possible that an inmate will report staff for showing favoritism. Because of their jobs and these types of situations, correctional employees may experience difficulty appeasing both administrators and inmates without feeling caught in the middle of a no-win situation.

Contact with inmates also has been identified as a source of stress, i.e., continual supervision of and frequent interactions with inmates. The perceived lack of authority over inmates also has been found as a potential source of stress.[9] This lack of authority has been described as the officers' informal daily influence on inmate activity and behavior. A related factor is the employees' perception of a lack of "institutional control" over inmates.[10] "Institutional control" refers to the administrative, centralized policy and procedures. Prison reform and legal regulations have restricted the procedures prison administrators may use to control inmate behavior. These restrictions can be perceived by correctional employees as limiting staff authority and seemingly increasing inmate rights and authority. Carroll M. Brodsky of the University of California has suggested two key factors associated with reported levels of stress: competition with peers for attractive work assignments, and lack of support from co-workers and supervisors.[11]

## Stress Variations

Prior research on stress and strain in corrections has given little attention to examining differences across such variables as job assignment, rank, gender and ethnicity. Presumably, uniformed male lieutenants are exposed to somewhat different stressors than corporals, female sergeants or non-uniformed unit management staff. The experiences of strain also may differ. Several authors note that female staff tend to report co-worker and supervisor issues as major sources of stress" and that these factors may be

**Reprinted from *Corrections Today Magazine,* Oct. 2001, pp. 82–87 with permission of the American Correctional Association, Lanham, MD.**

more frequent sources of stress for females than for males. It has been speculated that these issues would be more stressful for females because corrections traditionally has been viewed as a "man's job."[12]

In a 1992 preliminary study of one Midwestern state correctional system, interviews were conducted with 60 male and 22 female correctional staff members employed at all-male correctional facilities at various security levels. Staff were divided into uniformed and non-uniformed personnel and into positions of lieutenant, sergeant, corporal, officer, unit manager, unit case manager and unit caseworker. Staff were asked about their experiences and that of their co-workers regarding stress, symptoms of strain and coping strategies. Seven categories of stress were identified: inmate-related matters, administrative issues, supervisor issues, co-worker issues, policy and procedures, work in corrections and crisis/emergency situations.

A follow-up study in 1994 included 201 male and 71 female employees from seven maximum-security prisons in three Midwestern states. They were divided into two categories: 178 uniformed and 94 non-uniformed staff. The uniformed staff included 42 lieutenants, 47 sergeants, 19 corporals and 70 officers, while the non-uniformed sample included 26 unit managers, 25 unit case managers and 43 unit caseworkers. Responses to a 101-item questionnaire developed from the preliminary study asked subjects to rate how frequently a particular event occurred and how stressful they perceived it to be.

The results of the study indicate that staff as a whole identified inmate-related matters and work in corrections as the most frequently occurring category of stress. The most frequent inmate-related matters reported were: "Inmates make demands or requests of you" and "Inmates complain to you." In terms of work in corrections, the most frequently reported events were: "Staff are outnumbered within specific areas, such as the dining hall or the visiting room," "There are staff shortages where and when you work" and "You are aware that inmates have weapons even though you don't know for sure who or where."

The categories identified as the most stressful for staff overall were emergencies, administrative issues, work in corrections and policy and procedures. Ironically, emergencies were noted as the least frequently occurring events. The events within the emergency category that were the most stressful were: "You witness an inmate physically assaulting staff" and "You see an inmate threatening staff."

The most stressful events within the administrative issues category were: "Administrators minimize problems within the institution," "You find that what counts at work is who you know, not what you know" and "You do not have the opportunity to discuss matters before the administration takes actions that impact you."

The most stressful event within the work in corrections category was: "There are staff shortages when and where you work" (also one of the most frequently occurring events). Within the policy and procedures category, the most stressful events were: "You see inconsistencies regarding staff discipline," "You witness errors resulting from rotations or from people working in places that they shouldn't" and "You see people get promoted because of who they know, not what they know."

The frequency and stressfulness ratings were multiplied for each event to determine which categories were the most important sources of stress. These calculations suggested that work in corrections was the most important source of stress. Within this category, the specific events that seem to be the most important sources of stress included: "There are staff shortages when and where you work," "Staff are outnumbered within specific areas, such as the dining hall or the visiting room," "You are aware that inmates have weapons even though you don't know for sure who or where," "You have to deal with management problems stemming from overcrowding" and "You do not know what to expect or what might happen during your shift."

## Job Assignments

In terms of differences among job assignments, it was found that uniformed staff reported higher stress levels associated with all seven categories. The only difference based on rank occurred in the emergencies category. Lieutenants and unit managers reported higher stress levels for this category than did first-level ranks (officers, corporals and unit caseworkers).

Females reported higher levels of stress than their male counterparts in all categories except emergencies, the category in which the two groups were relatively the same. Caucasian staff reported higher stress related to administrative matters and emergencies than did non-Caucasian subjects. The remaining categories were rather similar.

In terms of how this stress affects staff, it was found that uniformed staff tended to report more symptoms of strain, such as physical problems, emotional exhaustion and feelings of less personal accomplishment, while females reported increased symptoms of strain, such as physical problems, less personal accomplishment and tendency to depersonalize the people with whom they work. When measures of strain for correctional employees were compared to other occupations, such as social service workers, medical staff, teachers and mental health employees, it was found that correctional employee scores were significantly higher.

It is conceivable that job assignments of the non-uniformed staff in the study allowed more flexibility and creativity than those of uniformed staff, who often are confined to their work areas and limited in the ways they can perform their job duties.

## Possible Solutions

In summary, the research suggests that the day-to-day work environment and organizational problems that arise in the corrections field can be seen as the most important sources of stress. The unfortunate impact of these events could be diminished if administrators would improve their relationships with employees. One way to do this is to increase the opportunities for employees to provide input into the development of the policies and procedures that impact daily institutional functions. This could alleviate the perceived lack of control correctional staff often report.[13] It also could decrease the amount of cynicism staff have toward administrators.[14] The improved relationship between administrators and their subordinates likely would increase the professionalism and efficiency of everyone involved.

Perhaps some of the stress officers report could be decreased by allowing more flexibility or variety within their job responsibilities. Officers, corporals and unit caseworkers were significantly less likely than lieutenants and unit managers to rate emergencies as a source of stress. Perhaps the higher-ranking employees view emergencies as more stressful because their role is to prevent such incidents and to ensure that any incidents that occur are handled appropriately. This accountability can be within the department (i.e., administrative investigation), extra-departmental (i.e., civil lawsuits) or both.

Another possibility is that the higher-ranked personnel perceive less control over such events because often they are on the periphery of emergency situations. Administrators must address the implications of this finding. Administrators should investigate emergency responses with the goal of improving future responses rather than of placing blame; in this way, they may be able to lessen the degree of stress associated with emergencies that higher-ranking personnel experience. It also may be helpful for supervisors to work with subordinates to develop emergency response strategies. This not only could increase the amount of control supervisors perceive, but also increase the amount of support subordinates perceive in such situations.

In terms of stressfulness of the job for females, it could be hypothesized that because of the limited number of female role models, the lack of acceptance and lack of support, females experience more job-related stress in this field. This is a trend that hopefully is changing. Because of the limited numbers, conclusions regarding Caucasian and non-Caucasian staff were not drawn.

## Impact of Stress

How does this stress impact staff? As noted, correctional employees were found to have higher scores of emotional exhaustion and depersonalization of clients than other occupational groups. This should be somewhat alarming to administrators. This, coupled with the fact that various groups of correctional employees in the current study experienced similar amounts of strain (i.e., everyone was experiencing strain regardless of job assignment, rank, gender or minority status), should be even more alarming. These findings could be an indication of the elevated degree of strain that correctional employees experience. Clearly, it is important to provide training to all employees on appropriate ways of dealing with stress. The likelihood of decreased productivity related to the experience of strain should make this an issue that requires immediate attention.

## Conclusion

The implications for the findings in this study are varied. Administrators should be able to use the current results to guide attempts to address the problems associated with the stressors in correctional work. For example, it may be helpful to provide training to staff on the stressors commonly associated with working in corrections, on the symptoms of strain resulting from that stress and on the coping strategies useful in dealing with those symptoms of strain. There also appears to be a need to train administrators on issues likely to affect staff in their facilities and how administrators can address these issues most effectively. This training could help administrators improve their relationships and communication with staff, especially uniformed and lower-ranking staff.

If administrators contend that the primary role of all employees is security, they must enforce that position. For example, the Federal Bureau of Prisons requires that everyone capable of responding to an emergency do so, therefore, secretaries, psychologists, associate wardens, unit managers and officers are expected to respond to requests for assistance. This system also requires administrative personnel to stand in the dining hall during meals so inmates and line staff have easier, less-threatening access to them. It also tends to show inmates and staff that the administrators are not "above" that aspect of correctional work.

Of course, administrators must be cautious about how they approach such a task so it is not perceived as just another opportunity to scrutinize staff performance. For this to be taken seriously, administrators must carry out this responsibility consistently. If their appearances occur haphazardly, staff are more likely to become suspicious of their motives. It also can be beneficial for administrators occasionally to tour their institutions so they may improve their relationships with staff. But if those tours only serve as an opportunity for them to draw attention to problem areas, they quickly can become another source of stress. It would be more productive for administrators to use these opportunities to provide direct verbal support and encouragement to employees. This is something that is sorely lacking in correctional environments; inmates do not frequently compliment staff on the good job they are doing.

Correctional employment obviously is stressful and can negatively impact both staff and administrators. Staff must use healthy coping strategies such as exercise, hobbies, family activities and supportive friendships. Other strategies such as smoking, drugs or alcohol use, and overeating tend to intensify the effects of stress and strain rather than reduce them. Administrators must be aware of the impact on staff and provide support and training to deal with those situations. Some systems do this better than others.

The Nebraska Department of Correctional Services uses emergency preparedness concepts, including critical incident stress management, victim advocacy for staff and staff support services. This is a step in the right direction, but more can be done to ensure the health and wellbeing of corrections' most valuable assets—staff.

## Reference

Brodsky, C.M. 1982. Work stress in correctional institutions. *Journal of Prison and Jail Health,* 2(2):74–102.

## Endnotes

1 Cherniss, C. 1980b. *Staff burnout. Job stress in the human services.* Beverly Hills: Sage Publications.

2 Cherniss, C. 1980b. *Staff burnout. Job stress in the human services.* Beverly Hills: Sage Publications.

3 Drory, A. and B. Shamir. 1988. Effects of organizational and life variables on job satisfaction and burnout. *Group and Organizational Studies,* 13(4):441–455.

4 Dignam, J.T. and S.B. West. 1988. Social support in the workplace: Test of six theoretical models. *American Journal of Community Psychology,* 16(5):701–724.

5 Maslach, C. 1979. The burnout syndrome and patient care. In *Stress and survival: The emotional realities of life-threatening illness,* ed. C. Garfield, 111–120. St. Louis: Mosby.

6 Maslach, C. and A. Pines. 1977. The burnout syndrome in the day care setting. *Child Care Quarterly,* 6:100–113.

7 Cheek, F.E. and M.D. Miller. 1983. The experience of stress for correction officers: A double-bind theory of correctional stress. *Journal of Criminal Justice,* 11:105–120.

Dignam, IT., M. Barrera Jr. and S.B. West. 1986. Occupational stress, social support and burnout among correctional officers. *American Journal of Community Psychology,* 14(2):177–193.

Dignam, J.T. and S.B. West. 1988. Social support in the workplace: Test of six theoretical models. *American Journal of Community Psychology,* 160:701–724.

Gerstein, L.H., C.G. Topp and G. Correll. 1987. The role of the environment and person when predicting burnout among correctional personnel. *Criminal Justice and Behavior,* 14(3):352–369.

Patterson, B. 1992. Job experience and perceived job stress among police, correctional, probation/parole officers. *Criminal Justice and Behavior,* 19(3):260–285.

8 Dignam, J.T., M. Barrera Jr. and S.B. West. 1986. Occupational stress, social support and burnout among correctional officers. *American Journal of Community Psychology,* 14(2):177–193.

Drory, A. and B. Shamir. 1988. Effects of organizational and life variables on job satisfaction and burnout. *Group and Organizational Studies,* 13(4): 441–455. Gerstein, L.H., C.G. Topp, and G. Correll. 1987. The role of the environment and person when predicting burnout among correctional personnel. *Criminal Justice and Behavior,* 14(3):352–369.

Hall, J.K. and P.E. Spector. 1991. Relationships of work stress measures for employees with the same job. *Work and Stress,* 5(1):29–35.

9 Gerstein, L.H., C.G. Topp and G. Correll. 1987. The role of the environment and person when predicting burnout among correctional personnel. *Criminal Justice and Behavior,* 14(3):352–369.

Hepburn, J.R. 1984. The erosion of authority and the perceived legitimacy of inmate social protest: A study of prison guards. *Journal of Criminal Justice,* 12:579–590.

Hepburn, J.R. 1987. The prison control structure and its effects on work attitudes: The perceptions and attitudes of prison guards. *Journal of Criminal Justice,* 15:49–64.

10 Hepburn, J.R. 1987. The prison control structure and its effects on work attitudes: The perceptions and attitudes of prison guards. *Journal of Criminal Justice,* 15:49–64.

11 Beaver, S.L. 1992. Stressors, coping strategies and indicators of strain among male and female correctional personnel. Unpublished master's thesis, University of Nebraska-Lincoln.

Crouch, B.M. 1984. Pandora's box: Women guards in men's prisons. *Journal of Criminal Justice,* 13:535–548.

Etheridge, R., C. Hale and M. Hambrick. 1984. Female employees in all-male correctional facilities. Federal Probation, 25(4):551–566.

Fry, LI and D. Glaser. 1987. Gender differences in work adjustment of prison employees. *Journal of Offender Counseling, Services and Rehabilitation,* 14(l):121–132.

Horne, P. 1985. Female correction officers: A status report. *Federal Probation,* 49(3):46–54.

Jurik, N.C. 1985. An officer and a lady: Organizational barriers to women working as correctional officers in men's prisons. *Social Problems,* 32(4):375–388.

Walters, S. 1992. Attitudinal and demographic differences between male and female corrections officers. *Journal of Offender Rehabilitation,* 18(1-2):173–189.

Zimmer, L. 1987. How women reshape the prison guard role. *Gender and Society,* 1(4):415–431.

12 Etheridge, R., C. Hale and M. Hambrick. 1984. Female employees in all male correctional facilities. *Federal Probation,* 25(4):551–566.

Fry L.J. and D. Glaser. 1987. Gender differences in work adjustment of prison employees. *Journal of Offender Counseling, Services and Rehabilitation,* 14(l):121–132.

Jurik, N.C. 1985. An officer and a lady: Organizational barriers to women working as correctional officers in men's prisons. *Social Problems,* 32(4):375–388.

13 Hepburn, J.R. 1984. The erosion of authority and the perceived legitimacy of inmate social protest: A study of prison guards. *Journal of Criminal Justice,* 12:579–590.

Hepburn, JR. 1987. The prison control structure and its effects on work attitudes: The perceptions and attitudes of prison guards. *Journal of Criminal Justice,* 15:49–64.

14 Ulmer, IT. 1992. Occupational socialization and cynicism toward prison administration. *Social Science Journal,* 29(4):423–443.

**Review Questions**

1.  Discuss the factors responsible for stress of a corrections officer.

2.  Discuss the strategies for preventing stress for corrections officers.

# Police Fatigue: An Accident Waiting to Happen
*Dennis Lindsey, M.Ed.*

After working almost 35 hours straight on a case that involved high-stress surveillance, the controlled delivery of nearly 2 tons of marijuana, and the arrest of 5 suspects, a detective on a narcotics task force was driving over 350 miles back home. The judge in the case advised the prosecuting attorney that if the detective was not in court that day by 2 p.m., the case would be dismissed without prejudice. As the detective approached the midway point on his route home, his vehicle, according to witnesses, swerved left, traveled through the median strip, crossed the oncoming traffic lanes, flipped several times, and ultimately came to rest on the opposite side of the interstate. The detective was severely injured and out of work for over a year.

Accounts of tragedies associated with law enforcement fatigue are not new. In fact, such stories become more commonplace each year. Convincing federal, state, and local law enforcement organizations of the seriousness of fatigue as an occupational health, commercial, public safety, and legal issue ultimately will require law enforcement managers to have a paradigm shift to address this concern. Agencies must acknowledge this problem to improve working conditions for their personnel and to protect them from the scientifically documented consequences that fatigue can cause. For example, researchers assessed neurobehavioral functions after 17 hours of wakefulness and reported performance impairment on a range of tasks.[1] Impairments after 20 hours of wakefulness equaled that of an individual with a blood-alcohol concentration of 0.10, twice the presumptive level of intoxication in most states.[2] Further, the ability to maintain speed and road position on a driving simulator is significantly reduced when the awake period is prolonged by 3 hours.[3] The magnitudes of the decrements were similar to those found at and above the legal limits of alcohol consumption (0.05).[4] All of these studies indicated that moderate levels of sleepiness can substantially impair the ability to drive safely even before an individual actually falls asleep.

Exhaustion due to shift work, voluntary and mandatory overtime assignments, seemingly endless hours waiting to testify in court, physical and emotional demands of dealing with the public, and management expectations of doing more with less, combined with family responsibilities, puts the modern law enforcement professional at serious emotional and physical risk. Law enforcement fatigue and sleep deprivation also are becoming serious political and legal liabilities for police managers. What department can sustain multimillion dollar lawsuits or afford to lose a veteran officer for years?

The cumulative work hours for many professionals, such as pilots, locomotive engineers, ship captains, public transportation and commercial truck drivers, firefighters, and emergency room doctors, are standardized and regulated through federal or state regulatory commissions (e.g., U.S. Department of Transportation or Federal Aviation Administration). Unfortunately, no such regulations exist for the majority of federal, state, and local law enforcement employees. "Police work is the one profession in which we would want all practitioners to have adequate and healthful sleep to perform their duties at peak levels. Not only is fatigue associated with individual misery, but it also can lead to counter-productive behavior.

It is well-known that impulsiveness, aggression, irritability, and angry outbursts are associated with sleep deprivation. It is totally reprehensible that the cops we expect to protect us, come to our aid, and respond to our needs when victimized should be allowed to have the worst fatigue and sleep conditions of any profession in our society."[5]

Throughout the last century, the standard work week was 9 a.m. to 5 p.m., Monday through Friday, designed to not intrude on workers' premium social time, such as evenings and weekends. As such, the 8-hour workday evolved from the widely held belief that the 24-hour day should be split evenly between work, recreation/relaxation, and sleep. While many people take the 8-hour day for granted as a part of normal life, such working conditions are a relatively recent industrial development.

Traditionally, law enforcement personnel work long hours for four main reasons. First, they seek monetary gain-the more they work, the more money they make. Traditionally, wages for law enforcement personnel have been low; therefore, the dependence on overtime, night-shift premiums, and moonlighting (working other jobs) has been necessary. Second, they encounter organizational or occupational expectations (we have to do more with less). "Many companies (law enforcement agencies) foster workaholism and actively seek out and reward workaholics."[6] Third, employees want personal satisfaction. The majority of law enforcement professionals could make substantially more money doing something else, but the job is fun, stimulating, exciting, challenging, unpredictable, and dangerous. It attracts risk-aggressive individuals who have chosen not to passively sit behind a desk. Finally, they belong to an exclusive fraternity. Law enforcement gives a person a sense of self-identity, belonging, and self-worth.

Not surprisingly, as long hours, shift work, and irregular hours of work increase, the hours, quality, and quantity of sleep decrease, causing a sleep debt. Conversely, fatigue levels rise, leading to detrimental effects on both health and on-the-job performance.

## Fatigue

What is fatigue? How does it relate to sleep? Although there is no universally accepted definition of fatigue, several exist. Fatigue is a "tiredness concerning the inability of disinclination to continue an activity, generally because the activity has been going on too long"[7] or "a feeling of weariness, tiredness, or lack of energy."[8]

People often use drowsiness and fatigue interchangeably, but they are not the same. Drowsiness is a feeling of the need to sleep or the state in which the body is ready to fall asleep. Fatigue is a lack of energy and motivation. Apathy, a feeling of indifference or not caring about what happens, and drowsiness can be symptoms of fatigue. It should be noted that fatigue can be a normal, healthy, and important response to physical exertion, emotional stress, boredom, or lack of sleep. However, it also can signify a more serious psychological or physical disorder. Because fatigue is such a common complaint, sometimes a potentially serious cause may be overlooked.

In the last 25 years, the job of enforcing the law has become increasingly complex from a cognitive perspective. Further, policing the community is creating tasks that require much higher levels of attentiveness than in the past. Long work hours are widely accepted as a major contributing factor to fatigue.[9] As hours of work increase, sleep is reduced with a concomitant elevation in fatigue and reduced levels of alertness.[10]

## Sleep

Humans typically have four to six sleep cycles that each last 70 to 90 minutes. At the end of each cycle, they are nearly awake. In light sleep, body movement decreases and spontaneous awakening may occur. People spend most of the night in intermediate sleep, which helps refresh the body. Deep sleep, the most restorative stage, lasts 30 to 40 minutes in the first few cycles and less in later ones. In this stage, people are the most difficult to arouse. Dreaming occurs in REM (rapid eye movement) and heart rate increases. This stage lasts about 10 minutes in the first cycle and 20 to 30 minutes in later ones. During a full night's sleep, these sleep cycles are repeated four to six times, moving from one stage of sleep to another.[11]

Several functions occur during sleep. These include—
- consolidation and optimization of memories;
- conservation of energy;
- promotion of physiological processes that rejuvenate the body and mind (some studies suggest that sleep restores neurons and increases the production of brain proteins and certain hormones);

- the process of unlearning that prevents the brain from becoming overloaded with knowledge; and
- avoidance of danger (pre-historic people adapted the pattern of sleeping in caves at night because it protected humans from species physiologically suited to function well in the dark, such as saber-toothed tigers).

Lack of sleep is considered one of the primary causes of fatigue. Humans need to sleep—it is not a matter of choice but essential and inevitable. The longer a person remains awake, the greater the need to sleep and the more difficult to resist falling asleep. Sleep will inevitably overpower the strongest intentions and efforts to stay awake.[12]

Little is known about the physiological role of sleep and ways in which it restores the brain to its full function, but the effects of fatigue on the brain can be measured. Studies have shown that after 24 hours of sustained wakefulness, the brain's metabolic activity can decrease by up to 65 percent in total and by up to 11 percent in specific areas of the brain, particularly those that play a role in judgment, attention, and visual functions. One study highlights nine dimensions of workplace performance susceptible to the effects of fatigue, including the inability to—

1. comprehend complex situations, such as processing substantial amounts of data within a short time frame, without distractions (the lack of focused attention associated with sleep deprivation is likely to reduce efficiency of such processing);
2. manage events and improve strategies;
3. perform risk assessment and accurately predict consequences;
4. think latterly and be innovative;
5. take personal interest in the outcome;
6. control mood and behavior;
7. monitor personal performance;
8. recollect timing of events; and
9. communicate effectively.[13]

People know when they feel tired-their eyes become a little glassy, they tend to have less eye movement, and yawning is more pronounced. As they try to fight through periods of fatigue, the human body, in an effort to rest, goes into microsleeps where a person literally falls asleep anywhere from 2 to 10 seconds at a time. It is difficult to predict when a person, once fatigued, might slip into a microsleep. Additionally, research has found that as little as 2 hours of sleep loss on one occasion can result in degraded reaction time, cognitive functioning, memory, mood, and alertness.

**Accident Risk**

Research suggests that fatigue-related errors are common well before the point at which an individual no longer can stay awake. Inattention may get much of the blame, but fatigue often is the culprit. Thus, fatigue studies likely are a conservative estimate of the overall incidence of reported fatigue-related accidents. "Human fatigue is now recognized around the world as being the main cause of accidents in the transportation industry."[14]

In addition to studying the direct link between accidents and fatigue, experts also have thoroughly researched the cognitive impairment thought to mediate the relationship. Major findings show that mood, attitude, and cognitive performance (judgment and competence) deteriorate with sleep deprivation.[15] Moreover, research shows that fatigue is four times more likely to cause workplace impairment than alcohol and other drugs.[16] Ironically, alcohol and drug abuse normally are addressed immediately by management. However, the lack of sleep, probably the most common condition adversely affecting personnel performance, often is ignored.

Fatigue in and of itself is not the key problem. Rather, the risks associated with fatigue impairment include poor judgment, accidents, and injuries. As such, fatigue is a context-dependent safety hazard, an important distinction because it can carry a significant risk in some situations and little or none in others. In some cases, fatigue-induced impairment and accidents may be inconsequential, creating only minor delays in completing a task, or may be detected by checks and balances (e.g., search warrants and fact patterns for probable cause court hearings are reviewed, checked, and proofread for accuracy before submission to judicial systems). In other situations, however, the risks of equipment damage, personal injury, and public safety can be far greater.

## Reduced Social Time

The primary effect for law enforcement professionals working long hours is reduced social interactions and isolation from traditional community and social support systems, resulting in the "us against them" point of view. Furthermore, studies have shown that long work hours negatively impact an individual's family relations.[17]

## Health Consequences

Fatigue is a symptom common to many diseases directly related to irregularity of daily life. Higher consumption of alcohol, caffeine, and tobacco; reduced physical exercise; stress; depression; social isolation; unbalanced diet and nutrition; and irregularity of daily meals all are hallmarks of law enforcement personnel around the world and can lead to an unhealthy increase in weight gain.[18] In fact, literature has indirectly linked long and irregular work hours with negative health issues to include disruptions of the body's biological rhythms, which may—

* change eating and sleeping habits;[19]
* raise blood pressure;[20]
* affect psychological well-being;[21]
* cause negative effects for pregnant women and fertility rates;[22] and
* result in gastrointestinal disorders,[23] stress-related disability claims, decreased productivity, and increased absenteeism.[24]

## Recommendations

Law enforcement agencies should make a concerted effort to provide a strong and coherent research base for the development of sound policies. Equating fatigue-related impairment to blood-alcohol equivalent gives policy makers, employees, and community leaders a clear index of the extent of impairment associated with fatigue. Agencies should develop preventative strategies to implement within the diverse range of political, economic, and social environments in which the law enforcement community functions and ensure cooperation with federal, state, and local court systems.

Departments should establish strict policies and implement effective enforcement regarding employee moonlighting. Administrators should review the policies, procedures, and practices that affect shift scheduling, overtime, rotation, the number of work hours allowed, and the way the organization deals with overly tired employees. Administrators should review recruit, supervisor in-service, and roll-call training, as well as executive retreats, to determine if personnel receive adequate information about the importance of good sleep habits, the hazards associated with fatigue and shift work, and strategies for managing them. Are personnel taught to view fatigue as a safety issue? Agencies should consider either implementing and enforcing regulations regarding a strict time-based work/rest policy, placing responsibility on the organization, or an education-based policy that focuses responsibility on the individual.

Finally, agencies should consider several different work/rest rules. The most common policy is the 16/8 formula. For every 16 hours of work, departments must provide 8 hours of rest time. Work/rest policies are most appropriate for agencies that have sufficient manpower to work in shifts. If resources are limited, managers may have to choose between using volunteers/reserves, implementing mutual aid agreements, or declaring an emergency and breaking the work/rest policy; therefore, any policy must include flexibility. Also, officers should not consider vacations just as missed days of work. They should turn off their cell phones and advise courts of scheduled leave. They always should take the time off that their departments provide and use it, remembering that no one is irreplaceable.

## Conclusion

Modern law enforcement practices have developed well-entrenched unwritten rules that treat sleep in utmost disregard and disdain. Agencies often encourage and reward workaholics. A recent news report covering a large party proudly declared: "Four hours into his second 12-hour shift, [the officer] has been busy answering questions, giving directions, listening to drunken declarations of love, and drunken jokes amid the endless roar of the crowd."

When a person is deprived of sleep, actual changes occur in the brain that cannot be overcome with willpower, caffeine, or nicotine. The decline in vigilance, judgment, and safety in relation to the increase in hours on the job cannot be trivialized. Community perceptions of fatigue-related risk have changed and now are viewed as absolutely unacceptable, as well as preventable. As a consequence, law enforcement professionals face a greater reactive pressure both politically and legally to rethink and implement proactive strategies to reduce fatigue-related incidents.

Fatigue is a serious, challenging problem that requires informed, forward-thinking managers to take action sooner, rather than later. Police leaders and sleep research experts need to work in concert to assess each individual agency to minimize the threat that fatigue poses to the community and the individual law enforcement professional. Fatigue is not just an industrial issue to negotiate between employers, unions, and employees but an occupational health, commercial, and public safety concern.

Local, state, and federal law enforcement organizations that fail to sensibly manage fatigue today certainly will face a broad range of damaging and enduring legal, ethical, physiological, and personal consequences in the future.

## Endnotes

1   N. Lamond and D. Dawson, "Quantifying the Performance Impairment Associated with Fatigue," *Journal of Sleep Research* 8 (1999): 255–262.

2   Ibid.

3   J. Arendt, G. Wilde, P. Munt, and A. McLean, "How Do Prolonged Wakefulness and Alcohol Compare in the Decrements They Produce on a Simulated Driving Task?" *Accident Analysis and Prevention* 33, no. 3 (2001): 337–344.

4   Similar levels of decrement in driving performance have been reported; see N. Powell, K. Schnecchtman, R. Riley, K. Li, R. Troell, and C. Guilleminault, "The Road to Danger: The Comparative Risks of Driving When Sleepy," *Laryngoscope* 111, no. 5 (2001): 887–893.

5   William C. Dement, M.D., Ph.D., in Brian Vila, *Tired Cops: The Importance of Managing Police Fatigue* (Washington, DC: Police Executive Research Forum, 2000): xiv.

6   Lawson Savery, "Long Hours at Work: Are They Dangerous and Do People Consent to Them?" (Curtin University, Australia).

7   European Transport Safety Council.

8   U.S. National Library of Medicine and the National Institutes of Health.

9   The author bases this conclusion on his extensive research on this topic.

10  J.C. Carey and J.I. Fishburne, "A Method to Limit Working Hours and Reduce Sleep Deprivation in an Obstetrics and Gynecology Residency Program," *Obstetrics and Gynecology* 74, no. 4 (1989): 668–672.

11  Information in this paragraph is derived from "Sleep: Your Body's Means of Rejuvenation"; retrieved on November 28, 2006, from http://health.yahoo.com/topic/sleep/overview/article/mayoclinic/F422495-751C-4684-AOA50B88AB19B576.

12  Royal Society for the Prevention of Accidents, "Driver Fatigue and Road Accidents: A Literature Review and Position Paper," February 2001; retrieved on December 5, 2006, from http://www.raspa.com/roadsafety/info/fatigue.pdf.

13 Y. Harrison and J.A. Home, "The Impact of Sleep Deprivation on Decision Making: A Review," *Journal of Experimental Psychology Applied* 6 (April 2000): 236–249.

14 http://www.aph.gov.au/house/committee/cita/manfatigue/mfcontents.htm

15 A. Nocera and D.S. Khursandi, "Doctors' Working Hours: Can the Medical Profession Afford to Let the Courts Decide What Is Reasonable?" *Medical Journal of Australia* 168 (1998): 616–618.

16 T. Akerstedt, "Consensus Statement: Fatigue and Accidents in Transportation Operations," *Journal of Sleep Research* 9 (2000): 395.

17 D.L. Bosworth and P.J. Dawkins, "Private and Social Costs and Benefits of Shift and Nightwork," in *Night and Shiftwork Biological and Social Aspects: Advances in the Biosciences* 30, eds. A. Reinberg, N. Vieux, and P. Andlauer (Paris, France: Pergamon Press, 1980), 207–213.

18 M. Shields, "Long Working Hours and Health," *Health Rep* 11, no. 2 (1999): 33–48.

19 G. Costa, "The Impact of Shift and Night Work on Health," Applied Ergonomics 27, (1996): 9–16.

20 T. Uehata, "Long Work Hours and Occupational Stress-Related Cardiovascular Attacks Among Middle-Aged Workers in Japan," *J. Hum Ergol* 20, no. 2(1991): 147–153.

21 S. Babbar and D. Aspelin, "The Overtime Rebellion: Symptom of a Bigger Problem? (Implications of Forced Overtime)," *The Academy of Management Executive* 12, (1998): 68–77.

22 C.W. Henderson, "Study Links Long Hours, Job Stress to Miscarriages," *Women's Health Weekly,* June 9–16, 1997, pp. 9–10.

23 G. Costa, "Shift Work and Health," *Med Lav* 90, no. 6 (1997): 739–751.

24 C. Mulcany, "Workplace Stress Reaches Epidemic Proportion," *National Underwriter* 95, no. 4 (1991): 20–21.

## Review Questions

1. State 5 reasons to support the importance of sleep.

2. As an administrator in law enforcement agency, what policies will you implement to prevent fatigue for the officers?

# A Guide to Effective Stress Management
*J. F. Volpe*

Stress is defined as "a physical, chemical or emotional factor that causes bodily or mental tension resulting from factors that tend to alter an existing equilibrium."

From the moment we are born to the second before we die, our bodies and minds react to surrounding stimulus and change in some way to adapt. Stress takes us out of our "comfort zone" and forces us to change and adapt.

While stress is a factor in every job, law enforcement officers must handle an above-average level of stress. Those who assume a leadership role take on an even greater burden. Leaders often choose to be the problem-solver, buck-stops-here individual, and they get pushed out of their "comfort zone" unpredictably and, many times, over an extended period of time.

Although the term "stress" usually has a negative connotation, not all stress is bad. In fact, without some stress, we would not be challenged as leaders to develop intellectually, emotionally or physically. But stress that is not managed can have a serious negative impact on a person's physical and psychological well-being.

To a psychologist, stress is "anxiety produced when events and responsibilities exceed an individual's coping abilities." Conversely, stress to the physiologist is "the response of the body to any demand placed upon it to adapt."

To Dr. Hans Seyle, who began studying stress in the 1930s, stress is simply a "single, nonspecific reaction of the body to a demand made upon it."

It is important to understand the psychological and physiological aspects of stress to manage it successfully and, in turn, create a positive impact on our physical and psychological well-being. Further, proper stress management plays a critical role in a law enforcement leader's ability to make sound, principle-based decisions.

Causes of stress are known as "stressors." A large variety of physical and emotional stimuli cause stress. From major life events, such as a divorce or the purchase of a new home, to minor things, such as being stuck in traffic, stressors affect each of us in different ways. A person's genetic make-up, diet and coping strategies are just a few controlling factors. Also, the amount of time we subject ourselves to certain stressors is a critical consideration in stress management. With this in mind, psychologists classify stress as either Acute or Chronic.

Acute stress is temporary stress that creates peak performance. Strategically directing officers to an armed robbery-in-progress and high-risk emergency driving are examples of acute leadership-induced stress.

Acute stress can be good for leaders in small doses. It keeps us alert, challenged and assured all of our systems are responding. It can actually improve our leadership performance as it takes us out of our "comfort zone" and forces us to adapt to the new stimulus. Physically, blood rushes to the brain, breathing increases, blood pressure goes up and our senses become finely tuned to the surrounding environment.

The body releases large amounts of Adrenaline and Cortisone, the body's primary "stress fighting" hormones, and we are poised to "fight or flee."

Psychologically, we focus on specific problems better and think more clearly because the brain gets more blood and oxygen. The detrimental effects of stress are of no great concern if the stressors are temporary, as they are in the acute stress mode.

Chronic stress, on the other hand, can have a critical impact on the ability to make competent, principle-based decisions. In this mode, our bodies are in a "continuous state of siege." A serious lawsuit, a

Reprinted from *Law & Order Magazine,* October 2000, pp. 183–188 with permission of *Law & Order Magazine.*

lengthy internal disciplinary investigation, or supervising a problem officer over a long period of time may cause a chronic stress reaction in a leader.

One problem with chronic stress is that we tend to adapt to it. While battling chronic stress, a strong leader will compensate, both physically and mentally, for such a long time their mind and body may actually become comfortable. If not managed properly, chronic stress will have a detrimental physical and psychological effect on a leader. While individual leaders may handle the same types of "stressors" differently, some physical and psychological reactions are consistent among individuals.

Physiologically, as the heart and brain receive more blood, the vital organs receive less blood. Blood sugar levels rise, as well as levels of cholesterol and fat. The longer a person is forced to handle these physical changes without management, the more our physical well-being suffers.

How damaging can this be physically? Studies show stress that is not managed properly can lead to serious physical problems, such as myocardial ischemia (reduced blood flow to the heart), high blood pressure, premature arterial aging, immune system deficiencies, and vitamin and bone density depletion. Psychologically, stress causes problems with the brain's Biogenic Amine/ Endorphin system, which is responsible for the production and transportation of Serotonin, Noradrenaline and Dopamine. As this chemical transportation system fails, several physical and emotional things happen.

First, a lack of Serotonin, which converts to Melatonin, causes the body clock to fail. The resulting insomnia leaves us feeling tired with a lack of motivation. Second, the absence of Noradrenaline leads to our body's inability to set energy levels properly, creating a sluggish, lethargic feeling. Finally, when Dopamine levels decline, the brain's "pleasure center" becomes inoperative and we become more sensitive to physical and emotional pain.

As the weight of stress continues without proper management, we may experience the following symptoms:

- Sleeplessness
- Nausea or upset stomach
- Fatigue or lethargic feeling
- Frequent headaches
- Teeth grinding
- Susceptibility to illness
- Lack of concentration
- Lack of clarity
- Anxiousness
- Impatience
- Irritability
- No sense of humor

While all of the above symptoms cause concern, the most important symptom that may occur is the inability to make decisions based on sound leadership principles, such as Integrity, Courage, Discipline and Loyalty. It is here that leadership-induced stress leaves many casualties. If we lose the ability to make principle-based decisions, we will fail as leaders long before the physical effects of stress take their toll.

We must, therefore, be challenged as leaders to recognize the physical and psychological symptoms of stress and employ effective strategies for stress management before our leadership ability is detrimentally affected.

### Ten Steps to Effective Stress Management

Researchers generally agree the first step in stress management is to identify stressors and eliminate them. Unfortunately, assuming a leadership role in law enforcement usually means adding stressors to our lives, not eliminating them. Even though leaders must deal with more stressors, we can employ both physiological and psychological strategies to effectively manage the resulting stress.

**Step 1:** *Mental Preparation.* While we may not be able to eliminate some of the common leadership stressors, such as taking command of an incident or handling the discipline of a problem officer, we can prepare for some known stressors. We can mentally create stressful incidents and determine, with the luxury of time, research and peer group counsel, some effective ways to properly handle them. This technique, called visualization, boosts self-confidence and eliminates certain stressors, such as uncertainty and confusion.

We can take this step further by creating mock scenarios and role-playing stressful incidents to become more familiar with our duties and responsibilities, should the actual incident arise. Many of the stressors associated with an incident can be diminished if we rehearse our performance in a nonthreatening learning environment.

**Step 2:** *Mind Over What Matters.* Meditation is a psychological counterattack to stress. With meditation we replace the stressors attacking our minds with peace and tranquility. This does not mean we have to join a Buddhist Monastery and chant away the hours. Meditation techniques, such as clearing the mind and mentally placing ourselves in a tranquil, pleasurable place, lower blood pressure, decrease anxiety and renew energy levels. Simple things, such as gazing into an aquarium, listening to music or tranquil sounds, or imagining a past pleasurable experience are examples of effective meditation techniques.

**Step 3:** *Share the Load.* Discussing our stressors with others (usually peers) is an effective way to ease a stressful burden. In such a discussion we usually discover we are not alone with our "world-ending catastrophe." This realization goes a long way in easing stress and its effects. Additionally, sharing a problem with a peer can lead to helpful advice on how to handle the problem, which, in turn, could eliminate the stressors completely.

**Step 4:** *Work (it) Out.* From a physical perspective, most researchers agree physical exercise is probably the best stress reduction strategy available. Physical exercise, even in a mild form such as walking, can increase the brain's release of Beta-endorphins. Collectively, Endorphins are morphine-like molecules responsible for regulating our body's sensitivity to pain and promoting a feeling of "well-being." Physical exercise also metabolizes stress hormones in our blood, which helps us relax and stay calm. If that is not enough, consistent physical exercise keeps body fat down, muscular strength and tone up and serious health problems, such as heart disease or high blood pressure, in check.

**Step 5:** *Don't Play Too Hard.* Leisure activities, while sounding nonstressful, may be quite the contrary. In fact, intense competitive leisure activities may cause more stress than they relieve. A truly relaxing activity will rejuvenate minds and bodies, not stress them further. Hobbies, such as gardening, painting or photography, are beneficial stress reduction activities because they allow relaxation without intense competition or concentration.

**Step 6:** *Don't Forget to Breathe.* The simple act of breathing, when done with thought and technique, can be a significant stress reducer. By concentrating on diaphragm breathing (lower lungs) instead of chest breathing (upper lungs), we get oxygen to the tissues more efficiently. This causes less stress on the heart because it does not have to beat as fast.

Next, by concentrating on slowly releasing the exhaled air, we can truly relax all the muscles, including the diaphragm, that contract when we inhale. Finally, a slow, concentrated release of air from the diaphragm causes the diaphragm to press on the Vagus Nerve, which stimulates a relaxation response in our bodies. The benefit of this breathing technique is it can be done anytime, anywhere with almost immediate results in stress relief. Leaders should take periodic "breathing breaks," especially when emerged in a lengthy, stressful incident.

**Step 7:** *Eat to Win.* Diet plays a major role in stress management. First, by keeping blood sugar levels from fluctuating too much we can avoid mood swings and feeling tired. Complex carbo-hydrates (tightly interlinked sugars which break down slowly), as opposed to simple sugars, should be the primary source of sugar. These sugars break down over long periods of time to keep sugar, and energy levels, more constant.

Next, eat fruits and vegetables, specifically fresh fruits and vegetables. Many fresh fruits and vegetables contain the amino acid L-Tryptophan, a substance that is very difficult, as well as illegal, to get in synthetic form. In its natural state, L-Tryptophan is critical for muscle building and assists in the production of Serotonin. Fresh fruits and vegetables are high in protein and complex carbohydrates, low in fat, and great for small, fast meals when time is short.

Vitamins can improve overall health by preventing the oxidation process in our bodies. The same oxygen that keeps cells functioning properly can oxidize tissues. Lipofuscins (oxygen waste products or "radicals") can build up in the heart and brain, causing genetic damage in the tissue. Certain vitamins, such as vitamin C and E, are powerful antioxidants that link to the "radicals" and allow the body to flush them out. Consequently, vitamins C and E taken together help keep the cardiovascular system clear and the arteries elastic and relaxed.

Eating balanced meals in terms of Proteins, Carbohydrates and Fats is important, but eating frequent meals throughout the day is just as critical to maintain proper nutrition and health. While it may seem contradictory to keeping body fat low and lean muscle mass high, eating more frequent, smaller meals keeps metabolism burning at a more constant rate, allowing the food eaten to be utilized more efficiently with fewer calories stored as fat.

**Step 8:** *Say No to Drugs.* A big mistake in managing stress is depending on medication and/or drugs, including alcohol, tobacco, caffeine, sugar and over-the-counter drugs, to feel better. A leader who uses these items to feel better may simply be "masking" stress-related problems instead of managing them. Limiting the use of these "pick-me-ups," while employing effective stress management techniques, will result in a more even, consistent feeling of well-being.

This does not mean we should disregard brain chemical re-balancers. While using effective stress management techniques work for most, some people, due to genetics or other physical problems, need prescription medication to help rebalance their brain Serotonin, Dopamine or Noradrenaline while they effectively manage stress. For example, someone with genetic low-stress tolerance may use a Selective Serotonin Reuptake Inhibitor (SSRI) or a tricyclic for long periods of time without becoming addicted or developing a tolerance to them. The above-noted prescription medications are prescribed after meeting with a physician, carefully reviewing laboratory results and medical history and other stress management strategies prove ineffective.

**Step 9:** *Sleep it Off.* A well known sleep study found men who slept seven to eight hours a night and women who slept six to seven hours a night had significantly lower mortality rates than those who slept less. Our bodies have natural internal "clocks" that control our sleep patterns. When it gets dark, our bodies begin to secrete melatonin, a hormone that increases drowsiness. As the sun starts to rise, the adrenal gland begins to secrete cortisol, a stimulant that helps us wake up.

Stress places a tremendous strain on both our physiological and psychological systems. Sleep is the natural way to shut our bodies down to allow our systems to recover. Unfortunately, as mentioned, stress can also decrease the production of serotonin, which causes insomnia. If we have difficulty sleeping, we will not get the stress recovery our bodies need. This vicious circle will continue unless we take proactive steps to ensure we get the proper amount of restful sleep.

Surprisingly, ensuring a restful sleep and managing stress have a lot in common. Physical exercise after waking up improves the quality of sleep. Eating foods that contain Melatonin or Serotonin before going to sleep can make a significant difference in sleep quality. Drugs should be avoided, but may be temporarily beneficial with a doctor's advice and supervision.

It is not a myth that we can "catch up" on sleep. Sleeping more when we have the opportunity can be very beneficial as restorative sleep. Leaders often find themselves with "too much to do and too little time to do it." We must be mindful, however, to stop and rest, with the knowledge we will be more productive leaders in the long run.

**Step 10:** *It Ain't as Bad as You Think.* While every decision made as a leader may have some impact, not every decision has critical impact. If we worry about the possible catastrophic outcomes of every item handled, we place ourselves in a constant state of stress (remember chronic stress?).

Certainly we must give certain high-risk items careful consideration and be mindful of the possible safety and/or civil liability outcomes. With this in mind, we should spend a significant amount of time training for these high-risk incidents to develop proficiency in making critical decisions.

On the other hand, we must be careful to avoid "beating ourselves up" over every minor mistake or wrong decision. Mistakes are going to happen and we will make some poor decisions. A strong leader acknowledges a poor decision, rectifies the matter (if possible), and learns from the experience. General Colin Powell claims his first rule to live by is, "It ain't as bad as you think. It will look better in the morning." It usually isn't and it usually does.

## Stress Management Assistance

Most stress can be handled by employing sound management strategies. At certain times, however, stress may overload our systems to where normal strategies are ineffective; especially following a critical incident. Fortunately, when we experience this type of overload a professional group that specializes in assisting over-stressed law enforcement personnel can help. One example is the Northern Illinois Critical Incident Stress Debriefing Team. This is a select group of psychologists, firefighters, paramedics, emergency room nurses, EMS members, police officers, chaplains and social workers who have received specialized training in Critical Incident Stress Debriefing procedures. This team offers its services for no fee.

In Florida, the Central Florida Police Stress Unit, Inc., assists officers with stress related concerns. They offer training in stress management and a 24-hour hotline for officers who need immediate assistance.

Many communities offer similar types of units for emergency service personnel at no charge. Additionally, most hospitals and medical centers have doctors on staff to assist with stress-related problems.

While a law enforcement officer has a significant level of stress, leaders take on all this stress, and more. Leaders must be able to make competent, principle-based decisions in short periods of time, discipline subordinates fairly, and be effective trainers. Further, they must be able to effectively manage the stress brought on by assuming a leadership role—or suffer from the physical and psychological stress-induced problems.

Stress can cause many undesirable qualities within a leader, such as anxiousness, irritability, low confidence, fatigue, insomnia and depression. Above all, stress critically affects our ability to make decisions based on sound leadership principles, such as Integrity, Courage, Discipline and Loyalty. With this in mind, we must develop effective stress management strategies to effectively manage our individual stressors and not succumb to the detrimental effects of stress.

We should be able to effectively manage stress if we employ psychological and physical strategies, such as meditation, visualization, physical exercise, proper diet and sleep, to their fullest reasonable extent. If, however, our inability to manage stress is genetic, we should seek a physician's assistance to explore other stress management strategies, including medication.

Once we understand leadership-induced stress and the significant problems it poses, we can make the strategic adjustments in our lifestyles to effectively manage stress and perform our jobs as competent, principle-based law enforcement leaders.


## Review Questions

1. Discuss the process of stress reaction in the body.

2. What is the definition of stress?

3. Explain the ten steps to effective stress management.

# PART FIVE
# Nutrition Issues

## Basic Nutrition Information
*Davidson C. Umeh*

Nutrition is the study of food and the effects it has on the body. Adequate intake of essential food nutrients is essential for good health. Evidence shows that uniform services personnel do not eat the right foods at the right time due to shift duty and unpredictable emergency assignments. Poor eating habits by uniform services personnel have played a significant role in the incidence of cardiovascular problems, obesity, and diabetes among people in the profession. The personnel in uniform services can improve their eating habits through better nutrition knowledge and a change in eating behavior. There are six major nutrients that are required in the daily diet to maintain good health. These nutrients include: carbohydrates, fats, protein, vitamins, minerals, and water.

### Carbohydrates
Carbohydrates are made up of different combinations of sugar units. The main function of carbohydrates is to provide energy. In the absence of carbohydrates, the body utilizes fats as its source of energy. Protein is oxidized to release energy when carbohydrates and fats are not available. Carbohydrates serve as an oxidant to enhance the burning of fat in the body.

Carbohydrates can be classified into monosaccharides—one unit of sugar, disaccharides—two units of sugar, and polysaccharides—three or more units of sugar. Monosaccharides are the simplest form of carbohydrates (glucose). It is in the form of glucose that carbohydrates are absorbed into the blood. The glucose is transported by the blood to the cells where it is oxidized to produce energy for the body. Disaccharides (sucrose – fructose + glucose ) are broken down into single units during digestion before absorption into the blood. Polysaccharides have many units of sugar and are known as complex carbohydrates. Complex carbohydrates (starches) are the best source of carbohydrates in the diet.

Starches contain fibers that play important roles in the process of digestion. Fibers (1) reabsorb water from the lining of the intestine; (2) enhance the passage of waste products through the intestine thereby reducing the incidence of colon cancer; and (3) absorb fatty substances from the intestine system to reduce the cholesterol level, which may cause cardiovascular problems. It is best to obtain carbohydrates in the diet from starchy foods. The daily recommended amount of carbohydrate in the diet is 60%. Carbohydrates may be obtained from pasta, rice, vegetables, celery, whole wheat bread, fruits, and carrots.

### Fats
Fats are essential nutrients in the body even though there is an erroneous concept that fat is bad. It is important to state that too much fat is what creates health problems in the body. Fat has the most concentrated source of calories in food. However, it takes twice the amount of oxygen required to oxidize carbohydrates for the same energy production from burning fat. Fats provide the following functions in the body: (1) transporting fat soluble vitamins (A, D, E, K); (2), regulating the temperature of the body through its insulation effects; and (3) providing shock absorption for vital organs.

Fats are classified into saturated and unsaturated. Saturated fats are solid at room temperature. They are obtained mainly from animal sources. They have a higher level of cholesterol which can increase the blood cholesterol level and predispose the body to cardiovascular diseases. Saturated fat can be obtained from butter, meat, eggs, lard, coconut oil, and palm oil.

Unsaturated fats are made up of monounsaturated and polyunsaturated fats. They are obtained mainly from plant sources. They are liquid at room temperature and contain less cholesterol. It is advisable to select most of the required fat in the diet from unsaturated fat sources. The sources include sunflower oil, canola oil, corn oil, and safflower oil. The daily recommended amount of fat in the diet is 30%.

Cholesterol is a naturally occurring substance in the body. The body manufactures cholesterol to perform some physiological functions in the body. There are two types of cholesterol in the body. High Density Lipoproteins (HDL) and Low Density Lipoproteins (LDL). An indication of the cholesterol level shows how much fat is in the blood. The normal cholesterol level is 200 mg. HDL plays a role in the elimination of cholesterol from the blood to the liver. Participation in exercise helps to increase the level of HDL (good cholesterol). The LDL is increased by dietary fat particularly saturated fat. An accumulation of LDL (bad cholesterol) is not good for one's health. The excess fat is deposited in the blood vessels thereby creating susceptibility to cardiovascular diseases.

## Proteins

They are formed by different combinations of amino acids. Proteins are a part of every living cell. There are 20 naturally occurring amino acids, of which the body can synthesize 11 and the remaining 9 must be obtained through dietary sources.

Proteins are essential for the following functions: (1) They build and repair cells; (2) they constitute the enzymes and hormone structure; (3) they help in the formation of hemoglobin which transports oxygen; (4) they serve as a source of energy.

Protein can be obtained from milk, meat, eggs, legumes, and grains. The recommended daily requirement in the diet is 12%.

## Vitamins

Vitamins are needed in very small amounts by the body. However, they play a major role in the physiological process in the body. They act as catalysts to enhance the activities of various enzymes in the body in the following processes: energy production, growth and repair of tissues and adequate nerve and muscle functions.

Vitamins are classified as water soluble and fat soluble. Water soluble vitamins can dissolve in water, for example: vitamin B-complex and vitamin C. Fat soluble vitamins dissolve in fat, for example: vitamins A, D, E, and K.

Vitamins are obtained from a variety of food sources: milk, vegetables, meat, beans, and carrots. Adequate amounts of vitamins can be derived by eating a balanced diet. It is a misconception to assume that one requires a vitamin supplement unless the person has a special health problem that demands it.

## Minerals

Minerals are inorganic materials needed in small amounts by the body. They help in the formation of the structural parts of the body and play a role in the regulation of body processes. Minerals are obtained from a variety of food sources, which include fruits, vegetables, grains, meat, and milk. A balanced daily diet will provide a sufficient amount of minerals.

## Water

Water is the most important nutrient. The body weight is about 75% water. Water is essential in the transportation of nutrients and removal of waste materials in the body. Water plays a significant role in all biochemical reactions in the body. Living things cannot survive for a long time without water. It is recommended that 6 to 8 glasses of water be taken daily.

## Review Question

1. Discuss with relevant examples the nutrients that constitute a balanced diet.

# Stay Alert & Comfortable on the Job
*Tim Fletcher*

It's 2 a.m. You're in the stake-out van. It's quiet, and the subject isn't moving. *Nothing* is moving at 2 a.m. OK—time for a snack. Your well-trained hand reaches out for the bag of chips and the can of soda, and with practiced economy of motion, the bag is decapitated and the soft-drink tab popped. In seconds, the snack starts converting into—what?

## Mind-and-Body Numbing Fat

Worse, minutes after consumption, the drowsies hit. Now you're *really* tired. What happened? It's simple: you told your body to go to sleep! The time of day, your choice of food—your body gets the message loud and clear. Seconds after your chin hits your chest, your subject strolls out and down the street, bright and alert.

Our bodies operate on a natural cycle called our "circadian rhythm" (CR). It plays a major role in regulating bodily activity. With knowledge of our CR in conjunction with proper use of food, we can limit the "down" effects of our CR. Throw in some simple "stay-awake" exercise tips, and you have the formula for maximizing your surveillance potential.

For this article, surveillance can be categorized as physical, static, or monitoring. "Physical surveillance" is tailing: you actually follow someone on foot or by vehicle. "Static" is the stereotypical stakeout: sitting in a room or vehicle, unmoving, covert, waiting for something to happen. It's mostly boring as hell, but it can get real interesting if something goes down. The third style, "monitoring" is the most common: sitting in front of a row of flickering monitors, perhaps making the odd door shakedown tour in a deserted building.

There are food and drink-related problems associated with all three. Eventually, you will have to use a washroom. You may feel tempted to fall asleep. You may run out of energy and the will power to make the last set of rounds. Herewith are strategies, in a simplified form, to help combat these very real problems.

Static and monitoring surveillance present the biggest problems, especially on a night shift. Just sitting and waiting gets old real fast: you want to do *something*. Eating may be all you can do, so you pour some java from the thermos and grab chips from the munchie bag. *Wrong!*

Here's what happens. Your body has two natural "down" times—about 2 a.m. and 2 p.m. The 2 a.m. dip especially is necessary for your body to divert energy for repairs. Your blood concentrates in the core, and your pulse slows, which cools you down. This dip is in the middle of the night shift—but that's just about meal time. Fatty foods and those with lots of carbohydrates get our body producing melatonin, a sleep-inducing chemical, within minutes of consumption. So, these foods give you a sleeping pill just when your body already wants to nap and is cooling itself down. You get a triple whammy: you're fighting natural and food-induced snoozies *and* your ability to concentrate lessens (ever try studying in a cold room?).

What you want to do is take a slug of water—tap water or bottled water—and pull out some protein: a meat sandwich (hold the mayo, use mustard), fish, skinless broiled chicken, or hard-boiled eggs. These are the best when you're in a CR dip.

These high protein foods heat the body, and help us keep alert. Yes, bread is a carbo, but a lot less than a bag of chips! But note: make sure it's not *fried* chicken, *fatty* meat, or *coated* fish. All the grease or carbohydrates can offset the protein and send you into that "carbo-dump" after all.

Snacking is OK in moderation, if you can handle the calories, but try carrot sticks, an apple, bananas, something of that sort. These do contain carbohydrates, but far fewer than chips, doughnuts, or even muffins. Cauliflower is also good, but it's "gassy" (OK if you're working alone).

**Reprinted from** *Canadian Security Magazine*, **April/May 1996, pp. 19–20 with permission of author.**

Water makes the best drink for surveillance. Forget so-called power drinks—you probably aren't sweating enough for electrolyte replacement, and the sugar which most contain in one form or another will cause that dreaded "carbo-dump." Even fruit juice from concentrate, or "fruit drinks" don't do the trick. If you want flavor, then "natural" fruit juices aren't bad, but water is the ideal.

As with anything, moderation is best. When you're covert, a full bladder or bowel is uncomfortable at best. At worst, when you finally give in to the urge—hopefully someplace where you can—Murphy's Law says the subject will vanish moments after you do, or you'll be "burned" when you move. Even in a van equipped with a camper potty, you may lose the subject if you're alone, or be caught literally with your pants down in a confrontation.

Starting well before you head out, eat only enough to stave off that hungry feeling, and drink lightly. If your location is very hot, and you're sweating, only drink enough to replace that fluid loss. You won't be on stakeout forever, and you can tank-up after.

Coffee is another surveillance no-no. Caffeine will provide a wide-awake feeling, but it's short-lived and then produces a crash. Having another cup will peak you again, but it will be of shorter duration, and the crash will be deeper. It gets shorter and deeper with each cup. Coffee is also a diuretic—you'll need to urinate more frequently, and it may also get your bowels moving. In addition, one teaspoon of sugar in your coffee is as much as the sugar in four apples.

If your situation allows it, try some exercises at your low points. Even a few pushups will push the blood back to the extremities and raise body temperature and thus fight off drowsiness. Try "air-sitting": put your back to a wall, or the inside of your surveillance van, and sit as if you had a chair under you, letting your legs do the support work. Do some sit-ups or curl-ups. Bring a pair of "grips" with you.

Don't do stretches. Stretching is a passive exercise; that is, there is no real physical exertion. It does help your muscles to relax, but with relaxation … *snoooore*! As an aside, if you haven't been physically active, your body may not be ready for sleep even if the brain is, so stretching, by relaxing your muscles, aids in rest *after* surveillance.

Physical surveillance may need more energy, and in this case, it's OK to eat more. But again, keep away from fatty foods. Your body is like a gas tank. If your muscles have been heavily used (as in running a marathon), and their store of energy (gas tank) is way down, you may get away with fatty foods.

Remember though, a pound of body fat represents about 3500 calories. One bag of chips can contain 2500 calories. When your car's gas tank is full, you can keep buying gas, but you will have to store it in the garage. When your body's gas tank is full, the excess is stored as fat, either under your skin or in your arteries. If it comes in as fat already, the process is accelerated.

Shift work makes this picture even more complicated, but that's for another article. It is safe to say, however, that the better shape you are in, the more you balance your food intake, and the more you pay attention to your circadian rhythm when scheduling off-duty sleep and activity periods, the more effective you will be at surveillance.

Keep in mind that the suggestions in this article are geared to specific surveillance conditions and not general nutrition. This is *not* a weight-loss program! When not trying to stay awake all night or for extended periods, you may wish to eat more carbohydrate foods. As always, check with your doctor for specifics as they relate to you, especially if you have heart disease, are obese, or are really out of shape. The Canada Food Guide (obtainable from libraries, your doctor, your local health unit) will also be valuable.

**Review Questions**

1.  Describe the ideal nutrition habit to enhance effectiveness in static and monitoring surveillance.

2.  Discuss 3 diet plans that will induce an officer to sleep during static surveillance by 2:00 a.m.

# Eating on the Run
*Mike Bahrke*

*"The eating habits of police are poor, at least on the job. You might be called out several times during your meal, or you don't have time to stop so you go through a drive-thru. You can eat only so many hamburgers and cheeseburgers before it starts affecting your diet. And how many diners are open at midnight? In my area there are four: two doughnut shops and two restaurants—both greasy spoons."*

—State police officer

Sound familiar? With so little time to eat, law-enforcement officers have difficulty finding satisfying, nutritious meals and the time to eat them. Because poor nutrition affects strength, endurance and body weight, performance and health can be adversely impacted.

High-fat and high-calorie diets, linked to America's two biggest killers—heart disease and cancer— affect all Americans, including police officers. Obesity carries with it additional risks of heart attack, stroke, high blood pressure, diabetes, lung disease, gallbladder disease and certain types of cancer. Cardiovascular disease is a major problem among police officers, with the risk of having a heart attack doubling with each decade of law enforcement service. Research finding show that cops frequently have unacceptably high levels of cholesterol and blood pressure and low-than-average aerobic fitness and lean body mass.

Fortunately, police officers can make healthy choices even with their irregular schedules. Changing bad habits and choosing to eat better are the keys. Balance, moderation and variety are important ingredients to being nutrition wise. Cops who want to improve their dietary habits should follow the same eating regimen that bodybuilders do: lots of wholesome grains and other starches and avoidance of high-fat and sugary foods. Whole-grain crackers are great low-fat munchies for a high-carbohydrate snack. Low-fat muffins and bagels, along with nonfat yogurt and orange juice, make a well-balanced meal-on-the-run that's usually available from a convenience store or cafeteria as well as from home.

Officers who eat and run often don't eat enough fruits and vegetables. Include a banana or orange juice with your breakfast. Dried fruits are another convenient and portable way to include more fruit in your daily diet. Snack on tomatoes, carrots and green peppers, which offer more nutrients than paler vegetables such as lettuce, celery and mushrooms. Tomato and vegetable juices are another way to increase your vegetable intake.

Lean meats, fish, poultry and beans are good sources of protein that assure proper muscle development; hamburgers and steaks are loaded with fat. A rule of thumb: Include 4 to 6 ounces of protein-rich food at each meal. Nonfat milk and other calcium-rich dairy products should be an important part of an officer's diet throughout his or her lifetime. Dairy products help maintain strong bones, reduce the risk of osteoporosis and protect against high blood pressure and muscle cramps.

Most fast-food restaurants have at least a few low-fat menu items such as a grilled-chicken sandwich, a side salad and maybe even a frozen yogurt cone. Carry a few healthy snacks in the patrol car too, so you fill up on muscle-building nutrients instead of sugary, high-fat foods. You'll have more energy and be far healthier.

**Review Question**

1. Describe a nutritious diet plan for uniform services personnel on duty.

**Reprinted with permission from *Muscle and Fitness Magazine*, April 1995, Vol. 57, No. 4, p. 77.**

# Good Nutrition Benefits All Officers

*Carol Chapola*

Proper nutrition contributes to an appropriate body weight and optimal health, both of which enhance fitness levels and job performance. Physically fit officers of every rank are more likely to adapt to the physical and mental challenges of the profession than officers suffering from poor health and inadequate conditioning.

Perhaps the most observable outcome of eating a well-balanced diet is a normal body weight, which has a positive impact on physical appearance. The way an officer looks influences how citizens perceive him. Many departments understand this and recognize the significance uniforms have when it comes to presenting a professional image.

The shape and fitness level of the officer wearing the uniform are equally important. In an appearance-conscious society, negative biases abound against those who carry too much body fat. This especially holds true for officers because the public expects them to be lean and fit. Law enforcement officers want their supervisors to look like effective leaders. Well-dressed officers of all levels who are at a suitable body weight come across as highly competent and professional, and are good role models for the department and community.

An appropriate weight is not so much a number on a scale, but a body composition that maximizes health and minimizes the risk of certain diseases and disorders. In other words, a strong bone structure, optimal lean muscle and a desirable level of body fat should be considered with weight. Individuals vary considerably in size and shape. However, by eating right and staying physically active, most officers can attain a proper body composition and avoid many of the problems associated with being overweight.

Excess body weight increases the risk for joint problems, hypertension, diabetes, gallstones, heart disease and some cancers. It may also interfere with job performance by hindering agility and speed, thus slowing officers down during physical altercations, and when running and clearing obstacles in foot pursuits. Cardio-respiratory systems are often affected as well, leading to fatigue and breathlessness. Being overweight also contributes to poor flexibility, which increases the chance for injury and lower back problems.

Technically, overweight refers to weighing more than recommended ranges found in standard height-weight tables. These charts are good sources for determining a desirable weight, but they do not estimate body fat percentage, which is ultimately what matters. Among several methods used for evaluating body fat are skin-fold measurements, underwater weighing and bioelectrical impedance—an electronic device that generates a harmless current through the body to measure percent body fat.

These techniques are fairly accurate, but depend on the skill of the person administering them. Since height-weight tables are convenient and easy to use, they are regularly employed as a guideline to evaluate whether weight loss (fat loss) is necessary. In general, overweight refers to carrying extra body fat, and obesity pertains to an excessive accumulation of fat.

Avoiding weight problems is possible by balancing caloric intake with energy output. Genetics play a role in body composition, but even those prone toward obesity can avoid excessive body fat through good dietary habits and exercise. Physical activity is an important factor for controlling weight: it burns energy, raises the metabolic rate and builds muscle tissue.

Staying physically active has many other advantages, including muscular strength and endurance, cardiovascular health and a lowered risk of various disorders, such as diabetes and heart disease. Nevertheless, even with an exercise program in place, unwanted fat will accumulate if continually more calories are consumed than the body needs.

Calories are units of energy contained in food. The body converts this energy into fuel that is used for normal functioning (growth, maintenance, and repair) and physical movement. Individual activity levels, age, health, body size and other factors determine how many calories the body requires. Calories consumed but not needed are stored as energy reserves, mostly in the form of body fat.

In past years, there has been much emphasis on limiting the intake of dietary fat to control weight. The reason is that fat contains nine calories per gram, compared to four for carbohydrate and protein. In addition, dietary fat is stored in the body more efficiently than the latter two nutrients. This has led many people to believe that as long as their diet is low in fat, they can eat as much as they want.

However, even carbohydrates and proteins, when eaten in excess, will supply unnecessary calories to the diet and lead to weight gain. Fat-free snack foods are not an exception. Most of these items contain added ingredients that are used to replace fat and give the food a better taste. Fat-free snacks frequently have just as many calories as their higher-fat counterparts.

With abundant food choices available it is easy to overeat, and it takes discipline and self-control to avoid consuming extra calories. When weight loss is necessary, efforts should focus on losing body fat slowly through a gradual reduction in calories and increase in activity levels. Severe food restriction and fad diets are not healthy, and any results are usually temporary.

Long-term strategies that work include gradually cutting back on serving sizes (especially in restaurants), limiting the intake of junk food and dietary fat, and reading nutrition labels to understand the nutrient content of selected items. An overall well-balanced diet that incorporates a variety of healthful foods, such as vegetables, whole grains, lean meats, low-fat dairy products and fruit, helps ensure that the right amount of nutrients are being consumed and, along with exercise, facilitates in maintaining muscle mass and bone density.

A nutritious diet not only assists in weight loss, it also promotes health and lowers the risk of many disorders, including high blood cholesterol, hypertension, osteoporosis and various cancers like prostate, breast and colorectal. Heredity is a strong predictor of whether or not a disease will develop, but environmental factors, especially diet, greatly reduce or increase the likelihood.

Many of the leading causes of mortality in America are related to nutritional habits. Heart disease is the number one cause of death, and research has shown that diet has a significant impact on either its prevention or development. It is known that a high intake of saturated fat—a type of fat found in butter, whole milk products and fatty meats—elevates blood cholesterol levels, which may lead to narrowed arteries and eventually a heart attack or stroke. On the other hand, a diet low in saturated fat and cholesterol, with adequate intakes of fiber, helps lower blood cholesterol and reduce the risk of heart disease.

Another connection exists between certain dietary factors and cancer, the second leading cause of death in America. Health recommendations stress the importance of eating plenty of fruits, vegetables and other plant-based foods (whole grains, nuts, beans) to help protect against malignancies. These foods contain hundreds of natural substances that have many beneficial effects in the body, ranging from neutralizing agents that cause cancer to blocking tumor growth.

Good health is important for all officers, not only because of high stress levels, but also because of the physical and mental challenges of police work. For instance, having normal blood pressure and desirable cholesterol levels aids in cardiovascular health, and helps the body better adapt to physically demanding situations. It lessens the chance of having a heart attack as well. Not having to worry about health problems helps officers to focus on the situation at hand. And the ability to think clearly and concentrate effectively is enhanced when energy levels are high and fatigue is absent, both signs of good health.

Several studies have indicated that law enforcement officers, as a group, are prone to certain health problems and have above-average risks for heart disease and increased mortality rates for a few cancers. It is believed that a stressful work environment and unhealthy lifestyle practices, including poor nutrition, lead to inadequate health among some officers.

Officers are somewhat of a disadvantage when it comes to eating right because job factors, such as overtime, shift work and rotating schedules, usually affect dietary patterns. This may lead to skipping meals, excessive snacking and poor food choices. In addition, regularly eating in restaurants makes it harder to control caloric intake because portion sizes are often too large and high in fat. Nevertheless, it is certainly possible for officers to practice sound nutritional habits and work around problem areas.

Taking the responsibility to eat healthfully is up to each officer, but the department can provide an environment that focuses on helping officers do so, starting at the top with management as role models. Lean, fit supervisors give a nonverbal message that they take care of themselves and set a good example for those they manage.

A basic understanding of proper nutrition and how to practice it is necessary for officers, and should be taught in the academy. Much of academy training centers on physical conditioning, yet the importance of diet in achieving maximum fitness levels are frequently overlooked. Nutrition classes that focus on weight-management, heart disease, stress and immunity, and how job factors affect dietary patterns, address the specific needs of officers and should be taught by a qualified nutritionist.

Once in the department, reasonable incentives can be offered for maintaining an appropriate weight and other nutrition-related outcomes, such as desirable blood pressure and cholesterol levels. Attending nutrition classes or seminars through a local college or hospital can be encouraged as well. Departments that have the financial resources available should consider contracting a dietitian to provide nutrition-counseling services to officers who need assistance, or hiring a staff nutritionist if an employee wellness program has been implemented.

Additional means include making sure snack bars, if provided, offer a variety of nutritious foods like fresh vegetables, salads, whole grain breads, lean deli meats, fruit, and low-fat milk and cheese. Break rooms should be supplied with a refrigerator, microwave, table and utensils, so officers have a place to prepare and eat food they bring from home. Health and nutrition information can also be posted on bulletin boards or included in employee or city newsletters.

Budgetary constraints, of course, often determine what is or is not implemented in a department. But costs are usually offset by long-term savings in health care, better job performance, less absenteeism, and officers with good attitudes because they believe management values them as employees, and takes an interest in their health and well-being.

Undoubtedly, proper nutrition plays a vital role in optimal physiological functioning, and its importance should not be overlooked among law enforcement officers or their leaders. The benefits of eating healthfully extend far beyond an appropriate body weight and professional appearance; everything from job performance to health is impacted.

## Review Questions

1. Develop a position paper on why proper nutrition is essential for law enforcement personnel.

2. What strategies can be used by the department to encourage officers to develop proper nutrition habits?

# The Nitty-Gritty of Proper Nutrition
*Kathleen Vonk*

In the last article we discussed how many calories you personally require each day. Now that you know how much you should eat, how do you know what you should eat to optimize health and nutritional benefits while maximizing weight loss at the same time?

In 1997, the Food and Nutrition Board of the National Academy of Sciences created Dietary Reference Intake (DRI) recommendations with respect to nutritional intake. DRIs have been established for just about every nutrient, vitamin and mineral, and they have been tailored to each life stage (age), gender, and even for pregnant or lactating women. They are extremely comprehensive and can be viewed by visiting the Web site (www.usda.gov).

## Carbohydrates

Carbohydrates have been given a bad rap in the past, however, they are the most important food group for emergency service professionals and athletes alike. The brain, muscles and heart utilize and require adequate carbohydrates to function properly. A constant supply of blood sugar, or carbohydrates in their simplest form, allow you to fight longer, deliver more powerful strikes, and allow you to think and respond more rapidly or perhaps even more appropriately during the fight-or-flight response.

Examples of carbohydrates include fruits, vegetables, pasta, bread, rice and potatoes. They contain 4 calories per gram, and should comprise the majority of calories consumed each day.

The DRI for carbohydrates is 45–65% of total calories per day. To maximize weight loss, stay near the lower end of the recommended intake, but don't go below the minimum DRI.

## Protein

The muscles in the body are made of protein strands, and it is important to ingest the essential amino acids that the body cannot produce itself. Adequate protein intake also allows the body to repair and build muscle fiber, fingernails, hair and blood cells. Proteins are not a significant source of energy during exercise unless it is a prolonged event such as running a marathon or competing in a triathlon.

Examples of food that contain mostly protein include meat, milk and dairy products, tofu, soy beans, egg whites, some nuts, whey, beans and lentils. The DRI for protein is 10–35% and depends on age and activity level. To maximize weight loss and to stay within a safe and healthy range of protein intake, stay near the upper end of the DRI, but don't go over.

## Low Carb/High Protein Diets

Very low carbohydrate/high protein and fat diets have resulted in fainting spells that are not exactly conducive to officer safety. These diets have also been shown to cause high cholesterol, kidney disease, kidney stones, and even kidney failure, osteoporosis, ketosis (unhealthy metabolic state), and even cancer through the avoidance of carbohydrates, which contain cancer-fighting vitamins, minerals, fiber, and antioxidants.

## Fat

Although fat seems to be the culprit to weight gain, it is actually essential for normal functioning of the body. It is important to the nervous system and aids in the transport of fat-soluble vitamins. It acts as insulation from external elements and cushioning for the internal organs. Excessive body fat is unhealthy and can lead to many conditions such as diabetes, cardiovascular disease, and metabolic syndrome (a cluster of unhealthy conditions that can lead to coronary heart disease and diabetes).

**Reprinted from *Law and Order Magazine,* Feb. 2009, pp. 14–16 with permission of *Law and Order Magazine.***

There are "good fats" and "bad fats," and it is beneficial to be familiar with each. Good fats are usually liquid at room temperature, come from plant and fish sources, and are considered "good" because they have some health benefits such as lowering cholesterol. Bad fats are usually solid at room temperature, usually come from animal products and high fat dairy products, and are considered "bad" because they have some negative health consequences if consumed in excess. An example would be the fat seen around a cut of beef, which can clog arteries and lead to cardiovascular disease, heart attack, and stroke.

Trans fats fall into the "bad fat" category and are altered by manufacturers to increase stability and shelf life of food products. They are considered "bad" because they negatively affect the cholesterol level in the blood and increase the risk for coronary heart disease. They are so bad for you that some states and cities across America have banned their use in restaurants. Trans fats have been used mostly by manufacturers and restaurants to deep fry foods because the liquid grease can be reused every day, and it lasts a long time without having to replace it.

The DRI for fat is 20–35%. Fat is fat, and excess consumed fat is stored as fat in the body. Although both good and bad fats contain the same energy content, the diet should consist mostly of good fats such as olive, canola, and fish oil (healthy Omega 3s), and bad fats should be restricted for health reasons.

### Example

We will use Officer Chubby from the last article as an example to figure daily intake for carbohydrates, protein, and fat. Stay within the DRI guidelines but maximize weight loss potential by using 50/25/25 for the ratios. His daily calories figured to be 2,400. Fifty percent carbohydrates = 1,200 calories, or 300 grams/day (1,200 divided by 4 calories per gram). Twenty-five percent protein = 600 calories, or 150 grams /day (600 divided by 4 calories per gram). Twenty-five percent fat = 600 calories, or 67 grams / day (600 divided by 9 calories per gram).

Now that we've worked through the math, there are really only three things you will need to remember, and the rest will fall into place: Total calories = 2,400. Protein = 150 grams/day. Fat = 67 grams/day.

Knowing your personal numbers is essential, but you'll also have to keep track during the day making sure to stay within your guidelines. This is where most of us fall short and consume too many calories each day. Just 100 calories too many each day equates to a 10-pound weight gain in one year. This illustrates just how easy it is to gain weight and how tough it can be to take off! Weight loss should be slow to be permanent, so make the decision to be in this for the long haul and turn it into a lifestyle rather than a temporary diet.

### Water

Water is probably the most important nutrient because it is required for just about everything in the body. Once the water consumed in food is taken into account, the DRI for water is 100 ounces/day for men and 73 ounces/day for women. This is easier to track when setting a simple goal of drinking 4 to 5, 20ounce bottles of water each day. If plain water is hard on your palate, drink flavored water, making sure to count the calories if applicable.

### Other DRIs

Fiber is important not only for weight loss but for good health as well. The DRI for fiber is 25 grams/day for women and 38 grams/day for men. Adequate fiber aids in cancer prevention because it cannot be digested by the body, so it moves through the system and prevents anything from sitting in the intestines for an extended period of time and becoming toxic to the body.

The DRI for salt is 3,800 mg/day or less, with an upper limit of 5,800 mg/day. Too much salt in the diet can increase blood pressure, which is hard on the heart and cardiovascular system.

The DRI for cholesterol is 300 mg/day, however lowering blood cholesterol is more consequential by limiting saturated fat intake rather than consumed cholesterol.

There is even a DRI for physical activity, which is 60 minutes per day. Even the lowest recommendation is 30 minutes per day and comes from the newly revamped MyPyramid, which replaces the old Food Guide Pyramid. This can be viewed at www.mypyramid.gov.

Physical activity is just that—it should be physical. Try to get your heart rate up to at least 120 beats per minute and maintain that level of exertion for the duration. More information on exercise and heart rate will come in the next article. It will help you increase not only fat-burning metabolism but police-specific performance.

**Review Question**

1. Describe in detail the nutrients found in food that are essential for maintaining good health.

# Law Enforcement and Nutrition

*Kathleen Vonk*

Why does it seem so hard to eat right and stay fit? Why is it such a task to count calories and to "just say no" to that second helping or to that chocolate dessert? It seems hard because it really is hard. It does take effort. But let's face it ... you know you feel better when you eat healthy and work out. And as an added benefit, you perform your job better. In this profession, that's a huge benefit because any incident can turn into a life-and-death struggle.

From a simple trouble with subject to a domestic turned deadly, your life may depend on whether you can outlast the suspect in a violent struggle. Although training plays a part, fitness does as well. And, yes, proper nutrition does equate to better physical and mental performance. If it didn't, college and professional athletes wouldn't care about what they ate, what their protein to carbohydrate to fat ratios were, or what legal supplements they took.

Since cardiovascular disease is the number one killer of law enforcement officers, making healthy nutrition choices and staying physically fit will add years and quality of life with your family, well beyond retirement and into your second career if you so choose.

Most police officers do care about their health, fitness levels, and weight. Most, however, have no idea how much they actually eat in a day, and weight gain in the form of body fat slowly shows up over the years. From saturated and trans fats to soy products to omega-3 fatty acids to fruits and vegetables, it can all be pretty confusing.

Is it really that difficult though? How hard can it be to understand the good, the bad, and the ugly when it comes to making good nutritional choices throughout the day? Do you choose the apple or the bag of chips? Let's try to simplify the process and take it step by step.

## Calories

First, let's figure out how many calories you actually require each day. Then we'll figure out the protein, carbohydrate, and fat ratios. You'll only have to do this once, so work through it, and you'll have your numbers until your age or weight significantly changes.

BMR stands for basal metabolic rate, i.e., your "metabolism." This equates to the amount of calories you burn at rest in a 24-hour period and can be figured using the Harris-Benedict equation. Men: 66 + (6.23 x weight in pounds) + (12.7 x height in inches) – (6.8 x age in years). Women: 655 + (4.35 x weight in pounds) + (4.7 x height in inches) – (4. x age in years).

Once you have determined your minimum calories for the day, you can figure your maximum calories by multiplying your BMR by your activity factor. This will depend on your goals and physical activity level each day. For weight loss, multiply your BMR by 1.1 ; if your goal is to maintain your current weight and you are sedentary, multiply by 1.2; if you are lightly active (light exercise 1–3 days/week), multiply by 1.375; if you are moderately active (moderate exercise 3–5 days/week), multiply by 1.5; if you are very active (hard exercise 5–6 days/week), multiply by 1.725; and if you partake in a special forces-type training program or exercise very hard two times each day every day, multiply your BMR by 1.9.

Take Officer Joe Chubby, for example. He is a 30-year-old male, 5' 11" tall and weighs 230 pounds. Plug him into the Harris-Benedict equation for males. 66 + (6.23 x 230) + (12.7 x 71) – (6.8 x 30) = 2,196 calories per day. Round this off to 2,200 calories/day. His goal is weight loss, so multiply 2,200 by 1.1 to get 2,420 calories/day. In most cases, calories consumed in a day should never go below 1,200, because this will depress your metabolism and cause a troublesome starvation cycle, making it more difficult to take and keep unwanted weight off.

**Simple Tips**

If the Harris-Benedict Equation seems too complicated, simply start counting your calories and writing the information down every day. This will at least help you to accurately read labels and pay attention to portion sizes. Then, with weight loss as a goal, subtract 500 calories from your average over those two weeks and try to stay at or below your new number for the weeks to come. When you become comfortable with this new routine, venture out and delve into the carbohydrate, fat, and protein ratios.

Too much, too soon can easily cause frustration and misery, so take it slow and be patient. The weight gain is tallied over the course of several years, so don't expect it to come off and stay off in a few weeks. There are also free BMR calculators online; all you have to do is plug in your personal stats and the program will figure your daily calories for you.

Packing a lunch and having preplanned food in the patrol car can help avoid times of extreme hunger when fast food restaurants make nutritious choices difficult. It's hard to avoid that drive through when you've just cleared a three-hour traffic point on an empty stomach. Having food available in your lunch box and eating a few hundred calories every few hours or so also ensures that you have a consistent blood sugar level.

This not only helps avoid times of extreme hunger but also equates to instant energy to your brain and muscles if needed. It also guarantees that you are getting proper nutrition because you have packed it yourself and made sure that you stuck to your calorie, protein and fat requirements.

Variety and moderation are keys. Choose colorful, natural foods (and lots of them) because fruits and veggies are full of nutrients and low in calories. Foods high in man-made or manipulated processed foods such as potato chips and cookies are high in chemicals, fat, and calories, so avoid them as much as possible.

Both fat and carbohydrates are burned during aerobic exercise, but the longer the session, the higher percentage of the energy provided comes from fat. When the session starts, carbohydrates are the primary source of energy with fat being a secondary contributor, but as the session goes on, more fat and fewer carbohydrates are utilized. By the time the 60-minute mark is reached, the primary source of fuel comes from fat.

Although fat is used during aerobic exercise, it cannot be used as fuel to the body in very intense physical activity such as in an all-out sprint or a fight with a suspect. In these cases, carbohydrates are the primary source for energy and muscle metabolism. This is another reason why carbohydrates should comprise the majority of calories consumed each day, especially for an officer who works the street and runs the daily risk of physical encounters.

Combining exercise with appropriate nutrition is the recommended method to losing weight and bettering health, rather than one or the other. Remember to have fuel in your system before your workout to reap the benefits of exercise, such as a simple carbohydrate sports drink. It is equally important to replenish your system within an hour of your fitness session, with two to three hundred calories including both carbohydrates and protein.

Chocolate milk (skim or low fat) is an excellent post-exercise drink, and if you're looking for a snack near bedtime, go for a serving of low fat cottage cheese to ward off the initiation of the starvation state that begins several hours after sleep begins. Lastly, remember that you have to eat to lose weight! Skipping meals can depress metabolism, destroy energy levels, and lower insulin sensitivity, which is detrimental to glucose storage (fuel for your brain and muscles). Figure your numbers. Plan your meals. Eat up and lose weight! Adopt the attitude, "Just Do It!"

**Review Question**

1. Describe the plan for a healthy diet and maintaining good health for a law enforcement officer.

# PART SIX
# Physical Fitness Issues

## Fitness for Duty Evaluations: A Sample Policy
*Michael Hyams*

Most agencies will order or request a psychological fitness for duty evaluation when an employee exhibits behavior that makes us question whether he or she is still fit to carry out their public safety duties. However, very few of us have comprehensive policies that protect both the agency and employee in these situations. While most California police agencies have established practices for confidential counseling after critical incidents such as officer-involved shootings, many of us do not have consistent practices for ordering an evaluation that may lead to the end of a career for the involved employee.

Because we can compel these evaluations to insure the public safety and guarantee a "stable, reliable and productive workforce" (*Yin v. State of California, 95 F.3d 864*), it is incumbent upon us that we do so in a fair and consistent manner, and not overstep the limits of our authority. It would be counterproductive to order the evaluation and then face a lawsuit for invasion of privacy or wrongful termination. (See e.g., *Pettus v. Cole, 49 Cal. App.4th 402.*)

The following sample policy is derived from several existing policies throughout the state and incorporates current legal decisions regarding the extent and scope of the evaluations. It is in place in at least two Southern California police departments and has been reviewed and approved by at least one active police labor representation law firm.

Depending upon your labor-management relations and associated contracts, the establishment of a fitness for duty policy may require a "meet and confer" process. (See e.g., *Holiday v. City of Modesto, 229 Cal. App. 3d 528*). You should consult your legal advisor prior to implementation.

This policy is intended to be an operational policy. It is not intended to be advisory regarding what psychological tests should be administered or the criteria you should use in selecting your evaluator, although it does suggest minimum qualifications. You should consult your existing providers of psychological services regarding their recommendations, licensing, scope of practice, avoidance of dual relationships and other issues important to the practice of psychology, especially in this highly specialized area of fitness for duty evaluations.

Finally, it is important to stress that a fitness for duty evaluation should not substitute for discipline or confidential counseling. Nor should it be conducted just to protect the decision maker. Ordering a fitness for duty evaluation is a serious matter that can have a long lasting effect on both the employee and organization, as well as the public they both serve.

### Fitness for Duty Evaluations: Purpose
The purpose of this policy is to establish consistent procedures for ordering and implementing psychological fitness for duty evaluations of sworn personnel and other personnel involved in public safety functions. Such evaluations are necessary for the safety and welfare of the community and department personnel, and to insure compliance with California law.

California Government code Section 1031 (f) mandates that all peace officers in California "[b]e found to be free from any physical, emotional or mental condition which might adversely affect the exercise of the powers of a peace officer."

**Reprinted with permission from the *Journal of California Law Enforcement*, Vol. 32, No. 1, 1998, pp. 10–13.**

It is not the intention of this policy to interfere with a supervisor's ability to recommend or suggest personal counseling to a subordinate, nor is this policy intended to alter or replace confidential counseling provided by the department as a result of critical incidents. Rather, this policy is intended to provide a mechanism for the assessment of an employee's mental and emotional ability to perform essential functions of their position when the employee's conduct, behavior and circumstances indicate to a reasonable person that continued service by the employee may be a threat to public safety, the safety of other employees, the safety of the particular employee, or, may interfere with the city's ability to deliver effective police services.

## Procedures

**Criteria.** To assist in determining the continuing emotional and mental fitness of (department) officers to carry out their essential duties as armed peace officers, and other employees whose duties affect the public safety, all supervisory employees should be alert to any indication that an employee may not be emotionally or mentally fit. Such indications may include but are not limited to the following factors. *The mere presence of any one factor or combination of factors may not be sufficient to order the evaluation.* However, such presence should not be ignored and may lead to the ordering of an evaluation. While there is a great variety and range of acceptable behavior among employees, dramatic or sudden changes in any particular employee's customary behavior may increase concern.

- One or more personnel complaints, whether originated internally or externally, particularly complaints of the use of unnecessary or excessive force, inappropriate verbal conduct, or any conduct indicating an inability to exercise self-control and self-discipline. **Reporting:** Any supervisor observing circumstances indicating that the emotional or mental fitness of an employee may be in question should meet with the employee, if to do so will not aggravate the situation. If the meeting does not relieve the supervisor's concerns, or no meeting is conducted, the involved supervisor shall contact his or her division commander and prepare a written report of the circumstances if so directed. The division commander or designee shall advise the chief of police of the circumstances.

- An employee is not required to disclose a disability to a supervisor, however, a supervisor may inquire regarding the conduct, behavior or circumstances that give rise to his or her concerns. Where appropriate, a supervisor and employee may also discuss reasonable accommodations that may enable the employee to perform the essential functions of his or her position.

**Relief from Duty.** In aggravated circumstances, such as when an employee's conduct immediately or directly threatens safety, a supervisor may immediately relieve the employee of duty pending further evaluation. In other cases, employees may be relieved from duty or reassigned as necessary for public safety or the efficient operation of the department, pending completion of an evaluation. Any readily accessible or department provided weapons or other department property may be seized by the supervisor and where appropriate, the employee ordered not to exercise peace officer or other official powers. Nothing in this policy is intended to prevent or limit a supervisor from taking any emergency action reasonably necessary to protect life or property.

**Order for the Evaluation.** The chief or his designee may determine, in the exercise of his or her discretion and with or without additional investigation, that a fitness for duty evaluation is or is not warranted. If an examination is warranted, it should be scheduled for the earliest opportunity.

The employee should receive a written order for the evaluation. Such order should include a brief description of the reasons for the evaluation. It should also specify the date, time and place of the evaluation; the name of the psychologist conducting the evaluation; a directive to cooperate with the psychologist's and/or staff requests and completely and honestly answer any questions posed by the psychologist and or staff; and notice that the evaluation is being conducted for use by the department. The notice shall also state that the evaluation is confidential between the employee and the evaluator to the extent required by the Confidentiality of Medical Information Act (Civil Code Section 56 et seq.), which allows the evaluator to release limited information to the department as specified below.

**Requirements for the Evaluator.** The evaluator will be designated by the department and must meet the requirements of 1031 (f) of the Government code, which requires the mental and emotional condition of officers "shall be evaluated by a licensed physician and surgeon or a licensed psychologist with a doctoral degree in psychology and at least five years of postgraduate experience in the diagnosis and treatment of mental disorders." The evaluator shall be instructed by the department to only release that information as allowed under this policy or as otherwise required by law.

**Limited Scope of Report.** The department has a right to information that is necessary to achieve a legitimate purpose. The evaluation is ordered by and conducted for the department. It is not for the purpose of treatment but to determine fitness for duty. The limited verbal and/or written results of the evaluation will be provided to the department as a confidential personnel record. The report and information received by the department shall be limited to: An employee may waive in writing any or all restrictions on the information reported to the employer.

**Disposition of Report.** The department shall establish appropriate procedures to protect the information from unauthorized use or disclosure. The report will be placed in a sealed envelope and retained in the employee's separate secure medical file in the _____. The report may only be used or disclosed in a legitimate and appropriate proceeding to the extent authorized or compelled by law or agreement.

**Refusal to Cooperate.** Refusal to comply with the order or any of its parts, or with reasonable requests by the evaluator shall be deemed insubordination, and shall be grounds for disciplinary action, up to and including termination. Statements made to the evaluator shall be considered compelled and may not be used in a criminal or civil proceeding against the employee.

**Disposition.** Depending upon the results of the evaluation and the recommendation of the evaluator, the department may:

- return the employee to full duty;
- place, mental or physical condition, or treatment, the report may contain information, which is relevant to that action;
- place the employee on temporary light or modified duty; from any duties pending treatment and re-evaluation; allow full or modified duty on receipt of treatment; resume disciplinary proceedings as appropriate; where possible, it is always the department's intent to rehabilitate an employee and achieve a return to full-duty status.

**SAMPLE ORDER LETTER**
Fitness for Duty Evaluation

CITY OF [                    ] POLICE DEPARTMENT
[date]
TO: [Name of Employee]
FROM: Chief [         ]
SUBJECT: Notice of Psychological Fitness for Duty Evaluation

This memorandum will serve as a written order directing you to submit to a psychological Fitness for Duty Evaluation.

The reason (s) for the evaluation are:

[Summarize the behavior, circumstances, etc., and refer to any of the appropriate factors that are listed under the Procedures section of this General Order]

The evaluation is scheduled for [day, date, and time] and will be held in the office of Dr. [NAME]. The address is [ ].

You are directed to cooperate with the psychologist's and/or staff requests and honestly answer any questions posed by them. The evaluation is being conducted for use by the department, however, the evaluation is confidential between the employee and the evaluator to the extent required by the Confidentiality of Medical Information Act (Civil code Section 56 et. Seq), which allows the evaluator to release limited information to the department. You may authorize the evaluator to release additional information to the department.

Refusal to comply with this order or any of its parts, or with the reasonable requests of the evaluator, shall be deemed insubordination and shall be grounds for disciplinary action, up to and including termination. Statements made to the evaluator shall be considered compelled and may not be used in a criminal or civil proceeding against the employee.

(signed)
CHIEF OF POLICE (OR DESIGNATE)

**Review Questions**

1. Describe the steps in conducting an objective fitness for duty evaluation.

2. Identify the factors that necessitate a directive for a fitness for duty evaluation.

# Health and Fitness Programs

*Glenn R. Jones*

Imagine a police department that does absolutely no firearms training. Its officers would not have to demonstrate proficiency with weapons, and the department would have no standards for assessing officer performance in the use of firearms.

Such a situation is, of course, unthinkable. The ability to use firearms proficiently is an indisputable necessity in modern law enforcement. And yet, even on today's violent streets, the majority of officers never fire a weapon in the line of duty.

Physical abilities, by contrast, are called upon regularly in police work. Endurance, strength, and physical conditioning are often critical factors in determining the outcome of an encounter between officers and law breakers. Despite this, serious efforts to address the health and fitness of police officers are generally dismissed as well-intentioned but somewhat impractical. Some departments simply do not regard fitness as a critical issue.

However, there is a growing understanding that the benefits of health/fitness programs for law enforcement agencies are far more tangible and broad-based than weak excuses would indicate. Not only can a well-developed fitness program help to reduce injuries, boost morale, and foster a more effective crime fighting force, but it can also be a cost-effective component to a department's overall health care policy. The benefits of an effective and fairly administered health/fitness program for law enforcement agencies should no longer be ignored.

## Current Standards

Because of the sheer number of departments and the lack of a universally accepted standard for health/fitness policies, it is difficult to determine the prevalence of serious health promotion programs in American law enforcement agencies. Studies attempting to gauge the status of fitness programs tend to yield confusing results due to classification inconsistencies. For example, does a policy of pre-employment physicals classify a department as having a health promotion program? A 1988 survey of the largest police department in each State revealed that at least 22 of the responding agencies had relatively in-depth health promotion programs.[1] Still, the results of this survey were somewhat relative, since no parameters were defined for an "in-depth" program.

## Implementing a Program

Once a department's administration decides to develop a health/fitness program, several steps should be taken to ensure its success. First and perhaps most important, the proposal must be "sold" to two groups: (1) The city council and budget appropriators, and (2) the people who will be directly affected—the officers, and if applicable, civilian personnel.

## Budget Considerations

Often, the first tactic in promoting health/fitness programs is to quote the abundance of data showing reduced health care costs and absenteeism and improved productivity and morale.[2] Although these specific goals are very compelling reasons for initiating a program, they are difficult to measure objectively. And while some effort to measure these goals should be made, departments should not rely on attaining them to *justify* a health/fitness program.

Instead, it is more reasonable for departments to justify a fitness program by arguing that a compelling interest exists in law enforcement to have officers who are healthy and fit. If this effort saves a department money in health care costs, then all the better. However, departments should not determine

Reprinted with permission from *FBI Law Enforcement Bulletin,* July 1992, pp. 6–11, Courtesy of the *FBI Law Enforcement Bulletin.*

the success or failure of health/fitness programs by whether a cost savings results. The ultimate result should be an improved department, with employees who are healthier, personally more secure, and better able to provide effective policing services.

## Personnel Considerations

It is unwise to underestimate the negative power of a disgruntled group of officers. For this reason, a significant effort should be made to ensure that a health program gains the approval of the personnel directly affected. Much of this effort will involve eliminating the "they're out to get us" attitude. Department leaders should emphasize that the intentions are not only to produce more capable police officers but also to help individuals become healthier and more physically fit.

## The Program

Health/fitness programs should ideally consist of four components: Health promotion, medical screening, exercise, and fitness assessment. Each element is important and should be considered in the framework of the overall program.

## Health Promotion

Too often, departments become focused on fitness assessment and fail to provide education to assist officers in developing healthier lifestyles. But forcing an overweight, hypertensive, chain-smoker with a cholesterol level of 350 to run a mile and do a round of sit-ups once a year will do little to improve that individual's health. Such an officer requires assistance to change negative fitness habits and to adopt a more health-oriented lifestyle.

For this reason, exercise counseling should be included in any departmental fitness program. Ideally, departments should make available any community resources that will assist personnel in increasing health awareness. Usually, such community assistance is available at minimal or no cost to departments.

## Medical Screening

A thorough medical screening policy is also essential to a comprehensive fitness effort. A well-implemented screening program will not only identify potential health risks but it will also reduce the legal liability on departments in the event an individual encounters serious health-related problems during exercise or in the line of duty.

In addition to being an excellent disease prevention tool, medical screening should be performed in order to determine if it is safe for an individual to participate in an exercise program and to perform the duties normally associated with law enforcement. Again, this is for the protection of both the individual and the department.

However, it is not necessary or advisable to perform a complete medical screening of all officers every year. The screening process, in fact, will probably be the most expensive component of the health promotion program and should not be overused. Therefore, good guidelines for departments to follow are:

— *For personnel 35 years of age and below*—a yearly blood pressure check and completion of a medical history questionnaire (assuming all officers underwent a thorough pre-employment screening that revealed no medical problems). A more complete screening would then be performed only if apparent risks were detected.

— *For personnel 36–49*—a thorough medical screening every 2 to 3 years, including blood work, urinalysis, mammogram for females, and stress test with EKG monitoring. Eye exams may also be considered. On off years, personnel should be screened only if a medical change has taken place or if an individual begins to complain of a specific symptom, such as chest pains.

*— For personnel 50 and above*—a complete medical screening at least every other year. During evaluations, doctors should be required to sign an opinion regarding the safety of the individual to participate in exercise and to perform job duties.

## Exercise

Any department with a serious commitment toward health and fitness promotion should assist officers by making exercise resources readily available to them. Departments that cannot realistically provide on-site facilities may consider assisting officers with the purchase of memberships to local health clubs. However, on-site facilities offer more convenience and usually prove more cost effective in the long term.

Choosing a facility is only one of the important decisions that departments have to make concerning an exercise program. Another important issue is whether to allow (or to the other extreme, require) officers to work out while on duty. There is no conclusive evidence that on-duty exercise programs are cost effective in terms of significantly reduced health care expenditures. However, as mentioned, cost should not be the primary concern for police departments instituting a fitness program.

Departments should adopt a plan that best fits the needs of the personnel affected. This may mean providing on-duty workout time but not demanding that all employees take part. Some employees may prefer to work out on their own time and should not be forced to change their routine, as long as they pass standard departmental assessment tests. However, departments contemplating mandatory physical fitness standards should seriously consider allowing on-duty workout time before the consequences of the program take effect.

## Fitness Assessment

Fitness assessment is often the first component considered by administrators when designing health programs. Unfortunately, it is also the element that will cause the most dissatisfaction if not instituted fairly and after much analysis by program managers. Several important issues must be addressed when formulating the assessment program.

### Who to test

Departments often attempt to ease the assessment component of the program onto officers by initially calling for voluntary participation. Typically, an incentive, such as a percent pay increase, is offered to promote participation. However, this approach usually results in a program for people who are already in shape. While this group should be commended for their efforts, they are not the population who need the most help. Therefore, it is preferable to implement the program by making everyone (including supervisors) participate, but not to penalize officers for poor performance during a reasonable initiation period.

Although officers, particularly older ones, may argue that any comprehensive fitness standard has to be "grandfathered" in, this argument is inaccurate from a legal perspective. If the proposed standard is otherwise lawful and application of the standard to senior officers is reasonable and implemented in a reasonable manner, giving adequate time for adjustment to the standard, the department should be on safe legal ground.[3]

### Types of tests

Assessment protocols can be categorized as either job-related or health-related. There are important physiological, practical, and legal implications between the two that departments must consider before any type of assessment program is initiated.[4]

The vast philosophical differences between job- and health-related tests must be considered carefully before departments choose an assessment protocol. As with most other major decisions departments must make, fitness testing programs should not be considered in a vacuum but should be discussed within the framework of what will best fulfill the needs of the department and of the community.

### Job-related tests

Job-related tests typically involve an obstacle course format. The activities included are intended to represent physical actions typically encountered by police officers (such as scaling fences, climbing stairs, or dragging victims.) A job-related testing format must consist of a single standard for all participants being tested. To adjust the standard in an effort to compensate for performance differences related to gender or age tends to negate the entire purpose of job-specific testing.

Because single standards may result in more test failures by females and older officers, many agencies have been discouraged from adopting job-related tests. This situation compels departments to prove that test items are, in fact, job-related and necessary. Obtaining this proof involves an extensive validation process that can be expensive and complicated, as well as time consuming.[5]

However, standards that either impact unequally based on race, color, religion, sex, or national origin, or on account of disability and which are used as a component of employment decisions, such as hiring and promotion, must be shown to be necessary for and directly related to successful performance in the position in question.[6] Therefore, agencies that plan to use fitness test scores for any employment decision should consider contracting with a qualified consultant to validate the test.

### Health-related tests

Health-related assessment protocols test an individual's overall health and fitness, without emphasizing job-related tasks. The health-related fitness components test body composition, muscular strength, flexibility, muscular endurance, and cardiovascular endurance. Tests can be designed to assess these components. Protocols and standards can be attained from other departments or can be developed within the department.

Health-related tests are more useful than job-related tests for providing feedback to officers regarding potential fitness improvements and for assisting them in setting individual goals. However, results of health-related tests not directly related to job performance should not be used for making employment decisions, such as hiring, promotion, assignment, or dismissal.[7]

### Use of The Results

Perhaps, the most potentially controversial aspect of health/fitness programs is the manner in which departments use the test scores. There is a very wide range of possibilities, but they generally fit into two broad themes.

## Wellness Programs

As the name implies, wellness programs focus on the benefits to the employee and the organization of health and fitness. Such programs use measurement of fitness to assist employees in assessing their own fitness and health. These programs provide information on training and fitness and encourage employees to actively pursue health and fitness through knowledge and activity. Since no employment actions are based on assessment results, wellness programs are less likely to experience legal challenge.

## Mandatory Standards

Mandatory standards are those which are used as a basis in evaluating officers for employment actions, such as pay raises, promotions, assignment, and termination. Because such standards have significant consequences, they are the most likely to face legal challenge. Consequently, mandatory fitness standards should be imposed only after considerable practical and legal scrutiny.[8]

## Measuring The Results

In measuring the effectiveness of health promotion programs, departments should consider two issues: (1) Is the program improving health and fitness among officers? and (2) is the program saving money in health care costs? Procedures for tracking progress should be built into the program from the beginning and related directly to the program's stated objectives. Improving health and fitness is, by far, the most important objective and can be measured through tracking fitness scores, cholesterol levels, blood pressure levels, dietary trends, smoking habits, and levels of obesity. Program options can then be redirected to those areas requiring the most attention.

If possible, a database should also be established to track health care-related information, such as absenteeism, injuries, and the number of insurance and workman's compensation claims filed. While relating these factors to health promotion efforts may be difficult, any tangible positive effects that can be documented could be of tremendous value to justify a health promotion program. Again, however, efforts to improve health and fitness within departments are of value even if monetary savings cannot be demonstrated.

## Conclusion

Police administrators are realizing the importance of improving the health and fitness levels of their officers. Health/fitness programs demonstrate a concern for officers not only as crime fighters but also as valuable employees and individuals whose fitness and well-being should be proactively cared for to some degree by their departments. Well-developed health promotion programs can also lead to reduced overall health care costs. Most importantly, however, they can increase the effectiveness and security of officers and enhance morale within law enforcement agencies.

## Endnotes

1   R. Boyce, "Physical Fitness/Health Promotion Questionnaire," 1989, conducted at University of North Carolina at Charlotte, Department of Health and Physical Education, Charlotte, North Carolina (unpublished).
2   R. J. Shepard, "Current Perspectives on the Economics of Fitness and Sports with Particular Reference to Worksite Programs," *Sports Medicine*, 7, 1989, 286–309.
3   See Kelly v. Johnson, 425 U. S. 238 (1976).
4   J. Hogan and A. M. Quigley, Physical Standards for Employments and the Courts," *American Psychologist*, November 1986, 1193–1217.
5   See *Harless v. Duck*, 619 F.2d 611 (6th Cir. 1980); *Evans v. City of Evanston*, 881 F.2d 382 (7th Cir. 1989); *Zamlen v. City of Cleveland*, 906 F.2d 209 (6th Cir. 1990).
6   Ibid
7   See International Union, UAW v. Johnson Controls, 111 S.Ct. 1196 (1991).
8   For a detailed discussion of potential disparate impact problems in establishment of health and fitness standards for law enforcement officers, see Schofield, "Establishing Health and Fitness Standards: Legal Considerations," *FBI Law Enforcement Bulletin*, June 1989, pp. 25–31.

## Review Question

1.  Discuss the steps for implementing a health/fitness program for a uniform service department.

# Functional Fitness, Part 1
*Kathleen Vonk*

You have probably heard the hot new term floating around the fitness profession, but what exactly is "functional fitness"? It's exactly that—functional. It is that which serves a purpose and makes sense. Functional training will help develop the necessary strength, power, and balance for performance on unstable surfaces in the unpredictable environments in which officers operate.

Rarely does a forcible arrest take place on an ideal, flat, soft surface, and often we must negotiate these altercations in and around obstacles and on less-than-ideal surfaces: snow, ice, grass, dirt, gravel, off camber, and so on. For public safety officers, functional training can be described as training that will assist in performing physical skills on the street, more explosively, more efficiently, with as much force as possible, and with reduced risk of injury.

Functional training will give us the best possible odds of sustaining the fight at high intensities, complete with all the unplanned events and surprises that a real fight on the street can include. That is unlike choreographed DT drills in the mat room and unlike a predictable bout on a treadmill or a controlled weight-lifting session.

An added benefit to intense functional training is that the calorie bum can be off the charts if so chosen, and even though appropriate rest periods are incorporated into each routine, the heart rate stays elevated during recovery, thus improving and maintaining the cardiovascular system also.

The key to developing and maintaining explosiveness is to train explosively: train slowly, be slow; train quickly, be quick; train explosively, be explosive. Yes, training slowly has its place in physical fitness, such as in high weight / low rep resistance training for brute strength or body building. Slow, steady cardio has its benefits as well, such as fat burning and cardiopulmonary rehab.

However, "power," which incorporates an element of speed, is a finely tuned balance between resistance (weight) and speed. The fastest sprinters are not the biggest, most muscular athletes, and neither are the very thin and light distance athletes with little muscle mass. Optimal power falls somewhere in between.

Velocity is the rate of change of position. Absent trunk rotation, punching someone straight out in front of you would be an example of linear velocity. Since our limbs are fixed to our bodies at specific points of origin, most of our strikes are done with rotation about those fixed points or axes, i.e., the point at which the arm attaches to the torso at the shoulder, or where the thigh attaches to the pelvis at the hip.

Power relative to delivering strikes with the greatest amount of rotational power develops with maximal rotational or angular velocity. Whether throwing a ball, swinging a bat, golf club, fist, baton, or foot, that rotational power starts from the ground and works its way up the body and out to the extremity that is rotating. The body itself relative to the ground and acts as the very first axis about which we rotate to swing the bat or throw the punch.

Imagine if you tried to punch somebody and kept your torso rigid with no rotation—you would have very little power by the time the fist met the nose, and you would surely suffer the consequences of an inadequate strike. Training the body to improve rotational torque is an enormous benefit to applicable job tasks on the street, and it requires rotational movement in a fitness routine.

A solid fitness base should be built before incorporating interval training, plyometrics, and functional training into any routine. If you're just starting out, work your way up to a solid cardiovascular base: work up to running 30 minutes per session, 3 to 6 times per week or more. For weight loss and management, this should eventually increase to an hour each day, 5 to 6 days a week.

Other forms of cardiovascular training are acceptable as long as your heart rate is elevated and sustained at 80% of your max (max heart rate is figured by subtracting your age from 220).

**Reprinted from *Law and Order Magazine*, March 2009, pp. 17–19, with permission of *Law and Order Magazine*.**

Build a solid strength base with resistance training. Start out with a full-body workout using your personal 15 rep max, then progress to 10 rep max lifting. You can continue to progress to higher weight and lower reps to build muscle mass and raw strength, but wait until you've built this base before incorporating intervals and plyometrics into your functional training routine.

Start to incorporate intervals into your cardio workouts. For example, warm up for 5 minutes, do 20 minutes of intervals, then cool down for the last 5. For your intervals, go hard for 30 seconds then easy for 90, repeat 10 times for a total of 20 minutes, then cool down for 5 minutes. You can increase speed, elevation, or difficulty level for your intervals.

If you're working on a stair stepper, don't hang onto the rails because this defeats the purpose of climbing steps. By not holding onto the rails, you will have to support your entire body weight, which will result in a higher calorie burn and a higher cardiovascular ROI.

Once a cardiovascular and strength base has been built, you're ready to integrate functional training into your workouts. Start out by using just your body weight, then gradually progress to light dumbbells and increase as you feel necessary. The body was meant to rotate. Start to incorporate core rotation into your training for added power development and injury prevention.

Much emphasis is placed on perfect form in weight lifting with good reason. However, if you have no lower back issues, move the way you would out in the field. When you reach into the trunk to retrieve a box of flares or an evidence kit, you most likely round your back and reach down in front of you while doing so. Hence, train the way you move in life and you may avoid injury while performing such tasks.

For example, while doing fast stationary lunges with light dumbbells in your hands, reach down as if you're tying your shoe lace while rounding your back- just like you do in everyday life, and just like you're bending over reaching into the trunk. This is much different than keeping perfect form with appropriate spinal alignment as required when squatting with heavy weight.

**Review Questions**

1. What is the definition of functional fitness?

2. Design a week's cardiovascular training program for police officers.

# Functional Fitness, Part 2

*Kathleen Vonk*

One of many potential functional workouts is the 3D Dumbbell Matrix by Gary Gray. There are many variations to this workout, but the routines basically incorporate the performance of several consecutive movements with no rest in between—performing them as fast as possible while maintaining sound form. All exercises are performed standing up, as the entire core will be engaged for stability and support. Tightening the abdominal and core muscles will also help to perform more reps and push more weight.

Here is one sample workout: 10 alternating military press (5 each arm), 10 alternating "Y" presses (like the song YMCA), 10 alternating reaches straight out to your sides (like a "T"), 10 alternating straight punches, 10 alternating cross reaches (right hand crosses in front of the body toward the left hand with torso rotation and vice versa), 10 alternating upper cuts, 10 alternating cross upper cuts with torso rotation, 10 alternating bicep curls, 10 alternating stationary lunges (step out in front), 10 alternating lateral lunges (to the sides while keeping the toes pointing forward), 10 alternating transverse lunges (torso rotation at a 45 degree angle behind you, keeping the front foot stationary and toes pointing forward), and then repeat the last three lunge exercises but add a military press or bicep curl on each return.

Plyometric training is specific work for the enhancement of explosive power. Vertical jumps, squat jumps, tuck jumps, single and double leg hops, long jumps, push-ups with clapping in between reps, trunk rotation with a medicine ball in hand, and many forms of passing and throwing a medicine ball are all examples of plyometric exercises. Keep the work interval short and the rest interval longer for adequate recovery, but upper body plyos can be alternated with lower body plyos to save time and maximize workout efficiency.

For example, start by doing 10 stationary squat jumps with no extra weight. Drop and do 10 military pushups with an airborne phase in between each rep. Continue with 10 tuck jumps, then hold a dumbbell or medicine ball out in front of you and quickly spell out your name in the air (standing). Move to skipping in place getting as high as you can with your knees, then do 10 vertical wood chops out in front of your body with the ball or weight.

If you can't do standard full-body push-ups in the plank position, start from your knees and let your upper body fall toward the ground. Catch yourself with your hands and explosively push your body back up to the kneeling position. Work your way up to full-body push-ups, then work toward incorporating an airborne phase into the push-up.

Another great upper-body plyometric workout is medicine ball tennis. With a partner and a tennis court, use a medicine ball of your choice (weight varies). Use only one half of the entire tennis court, with each person responsible for the smaller doubles area on each side. The goal is the same as in tennis, with only one bounce of the medicine ball allowed.

You must utilize side trunk rotation rather than throwing the ball over the net, but try to throw it so hard that your competitor misses or cannot handle the medicine ball after the bounce. Again, keep the intervals short and allow for adequate rest. Other options include granny shots, chest pass, overhead throws, torso twist throws, sit-up throws, and slamming the medicine ball on the ground in front of you.

If you don't have room and/or a partner for these types of plyometric drills, you can easily use a concrete wall for similar drills. You can also swing dumbbells in a torso twist, wood chop, or write your name or the alphabet in the air in front of you while you stand with the medicine ball in your outstretched arms. The key is to move the ball, dumbbell, or weight plate as quickly as you can. Plyos require adequate recovery in between sessions, so schedule at least two days of rest before you engage in your next plyometric session.

Even though cleans, jerks, snatches, and variations of all three seem to be reserved for more advanced athletes, there is a lot to be said for such exercises in the public safety profession. Optimal sports performance is usually based on the ability to develop power. This is also true in our occupation when our lives may depend on our explosive functional abilities.

Therefore, it would be advantageous to explore and incorporate these exercises into the fitness routines of police, corrections, court, fire, EMS, and security occupations. Consult the National Strength and Conditioning Association (www.nsca-lift.org) for proper technique and protocol before performing these exercises. Keep in mind that they can be done with lighter weights and dumbbells as well.

Pull-ups with hands facing away from the body are also an overlooked requirement when addressing police fitness, as you may or most likely already have had to pull yourself up and into a window or over a fence. If body weight pull-ups are not possible or too difficult, take advantage of some of the available training aids such as a 1%-inch elastic band that will assist in the pull up and eventually get you to the point of performing them with no assistance. An officer should be able to do at least one pull up with the added weight of full duty gear for obvious reasons!

Today's kids (future criminals), as well as current criminals are all watching the ultimate fighting shows and practicing on each other. Some develop a "no fear, no consequence" mindset with little restraint and/or remorse. One day you may have to fight these very products of our society, if you haven't already.

The tools we carry on our duty belts are not 100% reliable, and you may not even have time to access them. Kickboxing cardio classes and actual sparring drills with appropriate protective gear, coupled with resistance, cardiovascular, and functional training, are outstanding options and even necessities to help deal with such adversaries.

If you enjoy any competitive sport, you will find significant improvements in your performance after incorporating functional training and plyometrics into your workouts. If you never have, try some type of individual or team sport you have had an interest in, without worries of whether you're good at it or not.

Anything that involves reactionary movements, hand-eye-foot coordination, or elements of speed, agility, and quickness will benefit your performance in public safety. As an added benefit, it will most likely result in feelings of accomplishment, well-being, and social fulfillment.

**Review Question**

1. Develop a week's fitness program for a law enforcement officer.

# Physical Fitness Training for Police Officers
*Scott Oldham*

Most officers come out of the academy in the best physical shape of their lives. Shortly thereafter the strains of shift life and rigors of police work begin to take their toll. Unfortunately, the reverse is true for offenders who go to prison: many enter the system suffering from the effects of a chemical addiction or a life as a couch potato. Through a program of mandated sleep through confinement, three meals a day and all the weights they care to lift, they come out musclebound, hardened criminals.

As officers age they undergo the normal trappings of life, including family responsibilities, incidental injuries and the continual deprivation of sleep that many assume is part of the cost of doing business. Cops do not lead normal lives; no shift is the usual nine to five. It does not matter what division or job responsibility an officer has been assigned, they are all outside what a "normal" person experiences. As a result of this job related peculiarity, many things that officers enjoyed in their early professional life such as team sports, weightlifting and other fitness-related activities, are the first to be sacrificed for time spent doing other things.

Many officers take their physical condition for granted until it is much too late. Every year more officers die from heart attacks or diseases related to the degradation of the body than all those who die from violent attacks and traffic accidents combined. Even more officers are forced to retire early because of similar conditions.

Physical conditioning was once a fact of life with many in the police service. Most recruits came to the job as large men, most straight out of the military where physical conditioning was inculcated into them from basic training. Today many different types of individuals are seeking careers in law enforcement and the profession is without a doubt much better as a result. However, many officers have not had the training to maintain their bodies the way they should have had.

Many freshly hired recruits, while in good shape upon entering the field-training program, do not have the knowledge, time or desire necessary to maintain that physical fitness. As a result, they begin to let it lapse. The officers who stay in good shape are the ones who have learned to continue conditioning and training the body throughout their career.

There are three areas of concern for those wanting to achieve or maintain physical conditioning and health: physical strength, cardiovascular conditioning and nutrition.

## Physical Strength

When planning a physical fitness program determine in advance what a specific job requires. It does an officer no good to train for something he will not do. For example, most of the law enforcement community does not need incredible upper body strength, but SWAT officers do. Most of law enforcement doesn't run or walk miles a day, but foot patrol officers do. Officers should train for a specific job function or for those they are aspiring to achieve.

No matter what professional assignment an officer is in before he sets about any physical fitness routine several questions need to be answered. What physical characteristics are they trying to enhance or preserve? What does the specific job require? What physical traits are needed to achieve those goals?

Most officers come from the patrol division and want to enhance the fitness characteristics needed for that assignment. What specific function does the patrol officer need in order to perform his or her job safely? Without a doubt there is a need for cardiovascular fitness. Ever see, or better yet hear, the vastly overweight and out of shape cop chasing someone down the street? Often these officers sound as though they will have a heart attack prior to retaining the suspect into custody. There is also a need for physical strength conditioning as well. Officers do not need to be able to crush steel in their bare hands or run a four-minute mile to be a cop, but they do need to be able to pick themselves up and get out of their own way otherwise they can put not only themselves but also their partners at risk.

For strength, particularly upper body strength, there are several exercises but the simplest and most basic remains the best: the push-up. A push-up is a learned exercise that can rapidly build strength in many areas of the upper body. Many officers think of themselves in good condition but when asked to perform 20 push-ups find themselves winded and nearing exhaustion.

Start slowly when beginning a pushup routine. Get a calendar and mark goals on it. Begin on a Monday with five push-ups twice daily. Once in the morning, once at night. Add one push-up to both sets each weekday. Take the weekends off and repeat the same amount of push-ups done on Friday the following Monday. Do the same for sit-ups or crunches (whichever is more comfortable). With these two exercises, which are very basic building block exercises, dramatic increases in physical strength and stamina will be realized in a very short period of time. Once officers have achieved a level of fitness they are comfortable with they can move on to other, more challenging strength exercises.

Remember that strength and stamina are different. Someone may be incredibly strong, like the weight lifters who bench-press 350 lbs. However, if they can only be that strong once without being completely spent for the rest of the day, then it isn't useable strength. If officers cannot be counted upon to have strength coupled with stamina they really aren't doing themselves or other officers much good.

### Cardiovascular Fitness

"Cardiovascular disease is without a doubt a killer and one that can be especially so in the high stress environment that a police officer occupies," says Tom Tartar, MD, an emergency room trauma physician in Bloomington, IN. In fact, cardiovascular disease is such a killer that in the United States over 600 people die each day from its effects.

While strength is good, cardiovascular fitness is crucial. If the heart can't pump blood to the body in sufficient quantities to oxygenate the muscles, officers will not be able to exercise all of that strength they just spent time building. Walking is one of the easiest and most beneficial of all cardiovascular exercises. Recent studies have found little difference between walking and running. Walking is a much lower impact aerobic event than running and places less strain on knees and other joints that may be susceptible to career ending damage.

Again, just as with push-ups and sit-ups, start small and build. Do not try to walk a marathon the first day out. Go slowly at first then build. Use the walk as a relaxation tool as much as a tool to build cardiovascular endurance. Use exercise to reduce stress. Once comfort is built with walking several miles progress can be made to other activities.

For those who have become comfortable with a walking routine and want to progress to other cardiovascular exercises the questions are raised, what kind of exercises and what kind of fitness goals to pursue? Again, just as with physical strength training, examine the specific job and then determine how to train.

For periods. The best example of the needed physical fitness is the average foot pursuit. A short, hard sprint followed by a hopefully short and victorious wrestling match. The average police foot pursuit lasts less than 100 yards, but 100 yards can be a long way to go if an officer hasn't conditioned himself to run that far that fast.

Training by running miles and miles does in fact build stamina, but is it the same kind of stamina needed in this situation? This is the difference between anaerobic and aerobic exercise. Aerobic exercises are those that take longer and require that the individual take deeper, longer breaths, like long distance running. Anaerobic exercises are those such as sprints and other activities that require short intense bursts of energy. Aerobic exercise will build anaerobic endurance but if one never trains for those short all out gut busting runs they still won't be as prepared for them as they should.

**Nutrition**

One of the best things that an officer can do is to maintain his heart through exercise and good nutrition. Balanced nutrition is not a jelly filled and a glazed along with three cups of coffee. Nutrition is the key to many things, including the building of strength and stamina. Nutrition has to be balanced for it to be effective. The schools teach the four basic food groups for good reason: they are building blocks that create a nutritional foundation. Without a strong foundation a building will eventually degrade and collapse—a body will do the same.

Nutrition is one of the biggest stumbling blocks for police officers as a whole. Most on duty meals are spent dining on high fat, high calorie fast food. Most officers take nutrition even more for granted than they do other fitness components.

One of the major ingredients to any nutrition program is tailoring it to what an officer is trying to achieve: if he is trying to lose weight that will entail one diet routine; if he is trying to gain weight, another. Consult with qualified nutritional advisors, often the same people who can help to establish a good workout program to achieve overall fitness goals.

Many departments long ago realized that physically fit officers are just simply good business. With officers being more physically fit there is less down time from injuries and less overall sick time meaning improved officer safety, public safety and a healthier overtime budget from not having to fill in for sick or injured officers.

Recent studies indicate officers who are in good physical condition are involved in far fewer uses of force than other, less fit officers. Some departments that have seen the benefits physically fit officers bring to the job have begun allowing their officers time on duty to maintain or improve upon that fitness. Many of those that do not provide this time have none the less tried to assist the officers in their fitness goals by providing weight training facilities, cardiovascular training machines and other fitness related equipment.

Physical training is a pain. There is really no other way to phrase it. If there were a magic pill that one could take to maintain or achieve fitness while laying on the couch it would be a best seller. Short of this magical pill, however, there is no method to achieving fitness other than by working at it.

Marksmanship is something that most officers take seriously because they know their life and the lives of others will depend upon it. Physical fitness is something that should be taken equally as serious. How many gunfights are officers involved in? How many combative subjects do they have to subdue? Train for both because they both will make sure that officers come home after the shift is over.

Remember somewhere out there right now an opponent is building the ability to be victorious. The opponent may be a hardened felon or it may be heart disease. Both can be just as lethal if given the edge and the opportunity.

**Review Questions**

1. Explain why officers ignore physical fitness programs after graduation from the academy.

2. What are the benefits of participation in physical fitness for a police officer?

3. Design a fitness program for a police officer.

# PART SEVEN
# Suicide Issues

## Preventing Police Suicide
*Thomas E. Baker and Jane P. Baker*

Does being a police officer increase the risk of suicide? During 1994, a record 11 New York City police officers committed suicide; only two officers were killed by criminals that year. Two homicides and 11 suicides—at that rate, police officers are killing themselves faster than they are being killed by criminals.[1]

The research on police suicide is limited. Most of the studies on police deaths have addressed police killings and assaults committed by criminals. The available studies on police suicide generally focus on the number of suicides, the methods employed, the impact of having service weapons readily available, and the occupational factors that seem to contribute to the high suicide rate among officers.[2]

One research study found that the suicide rate among police officers was three times higher than that of the general population.[3] In addition, an unpublished research report recently found that the police suicide rate now has doubled.[4]

Answers concerning police suicide have been elusive, and many issues remain unclear. But researchers may have been asking the wrong questions. Rather than dwelling on the rates and the means of suicide, perhaps analysts should ask what kind of support systems within police departments could have intervened before those officers took their own lives.

### Overcoming Obstacles to Intervention

Typically, when police officers experience serious, long-term emotional problems that can lead to suicide, two reactions occur that hinder the helping process. First, everyone—from the affected officers to friends and co-workers to the department's hierarchy—initially denies that a problem exists. Second, even when a problem eventually is acknowledged, the affected officers often resist seeking help for fear of losing their jobs, being demoted, or having their personal problems exposed for public ridicule. These common systemic reactions must be overcome before any successful intervention can take place.

Many officers feel that referral to a mental health professional would mean the loss of their jobs. Police supervisors have a similar value system and, because of this belief, they often fail to take the appropriate action. As a group, police officers and supervisors often have protected those officers experiencing depression and denied the existence of any problems. However, such an obvious cover-up does a disservice to affected officers by denying them the help they need.

As noted, troubled officers usually resist seeking help. Officers fear that if help is sought, employment and economic security will be threatened. This myth can be dispelled through departmental policy and the approach supervisors use when dealing with potential suicide.

Education on depression and suicide should be implemented for all personnel. Officers who receive assistance might even develop into better officers. They should be informed that seeking help does not mean the end of a career, but the start of improving a new career. Asking for help signals strength, not weakness, and that must form the foundation of any prevention program.

A suicide prevention program can work only if members of the department feel free to take advantage of it. Police administrators and supervisors must play a nonpunitive role. They must communicate to officers four clear messages: (1) Seeking help will not result in job termination or punitive action; (2) all information will be respected and kept confidential; (3) other ways exist for dealing with a situation, no matter how hopeless it seems at the time; and (4) someone is available to

**Reprinted with permission from** *FBI Law Enforcement Bulletin,* **October 1996, pp. 24–27. Courtesy of the** *FBI Law Enforcement Bulletin.*

help them deal with their problems. Police training and departmental policy, as well as the everyday examples set by police leaders, must communicate these four messages consistently.

## Recognizing the Warning Sign

Identifying at-risk officers is the first step toward helping them. Is there any common pattern to be found in police suicidal behavior? In truth, any member of the department could become depressed and commit suicide under certain circumstances. However, a long trail of evidence typically leads to the final act. Many suicidal people have mixed feelings about dying and actually hope to be rescued. About 75 percent give some kind of notice of their intentions.[5] If recognized and taken seriously, these early warning signs make prevention and intervention possible.

Typically, multiple problems plague suicidal police officers, so supervisors should look for a cluster of warning signs. These might include a recent loss, sadness, frustration, disappointment, grief, alienation, depression, loneliness, physical pain, mental anguish, and mental illness.

The strongest behavioral warning is a suicide attempt. Generally, the more recent the attempt, the higher the risk factor for the officer. Police training officers need to incorporate education about suicide warning signs as a regular part of the department's mental health program.

When officers fail to perform at the optimal level for an extended period of time, the problem could be related to a major depressive episode. Clinicians agree that depression often plays a major role in suicide.[6] While anyone can have an occasional gloomy day, people dealing with depression suffer from a deeper, long-term malaise.

Depression is a mood disorder that can be characterized as a person's overall "climate" rather than a temporary "weather condition." Significant depressive episodes last for at least two weeks. During this time, a person might experience changes in appetite or weight: altered sleep patterns and reduced psychomotor activity; reduced energy levels; feelings of worthlessness or guilt; difficulty thinking, concentrating, and making decisions; and recurrent thoughts of death or suicide. Finally, this person might plan or attempt to commit suicide.[7] Behaviors such as exhibiting persistent anger, responding to events with angry outbursts, or blaming others over minor events should be considered indicators of possible distress.

## Assessing the Problem

Supervisors or managers should schedule interviews with officers who appear depressed, sad, hopeless, discouraged or "down in the dumps." During this interview, the supervisor should check the officer's body language, look for sad facial expressions, and be alert to a flat mood. The officer might complain of feeling down, not having any feelings at all, or being anxious. Complaints about bodily aches and pains might be reported to cover the officer's true feelings.

The twin feelings of hopelessness and helplessness indicate a high risk of suicide. Officers who think and speak in these terms feel that their lives are devoid of hope, or they see themselves as unable to meaningfully alter their situations. When they reach this point, they often take action. The finality of suicide might be seen as a technique to restore feelings of former strength, courage, and mastery over the environment.[8] Supervisors should listen carefully for expressions of these feelings.

Suicidal officers might have negative influences in their personal lives as well. Supervisors should look for histories that might include suicidal behavior, mental illness, chronic depression, multiple divorces, and alcoholism. Losses in an officer's life, drug abuse patterns, and stress overload also contribute to the problem. Older officers might experience physical problems or face impending retirement and feel that they will become socially isolated.[9] Such physical and social losses can generate the destructive feelings of hopelessness and helplessness.

## Taking Action

Most people have mixed emotions about committing suicide, and suicidal feelings tend to be episodic, often coming and going in cycles. Troubled officers want to be rescued, but do not want to ask for assistance or know what specific help to request. This state of confusion actually works to a supervisor's advantage because suicidal officers want a strong authority figure to direct their emotional traffic and make sense of the confusion. Therefore, supervisors should quickly assure suicidal officers that support and assistance is available.

The situational leadership style that applies here is one of directing and telling. Officers in a suicidal state of mind are open to suggestion and are likely to respond to directions. Supervisors must use their positions of authority to tell officers what action they expect. Further, supervisors should demand that officers respond to their directions.

It is important for supervisors to ask specifically whether officers are having thoughts of hurting themselves. Many find it difficult to ask such a basic question, but it must be done. Officers who indicate that they are having suicidal thoughts must not be left alone. All threats must be taken seriously. Other people might not have heard their pleas for help.

Supervisors should plan their intervention so that it leads to a professional referral. The specific methods of intervention must be thought out as carefully as possible in order to avoid violence directed inward or outward at other employees. Without careful planning, officers confronted by supervisors could react unpredictably. Because their thought processes are garbled, they could strike out at co-workers, supervisors, or family members, resulting in a homicide followed by a suicide. Even if that does not occur, a real danger of suicide exists at the point of intervention.

Supervisors should refer officers to a certified mental health professional, even setting appointments and making arrangements for the officers to be there. The department's responsibility does not end there, however. Supervisors should monitor the situation to ensure that officers are evaluated and receive continued support and counseling.

## Conclusion

The research clearly indicates that being a police officer increases the risk of suicide. Appropriate intervention can occur during a specific time frame, but within the police culture, denial often delays assistance.

Police officers throughout the ranks must stop pretending that the problem of police suicide does not exist or that it will go away. Someone must break the silence of denial and take action. With further research, innovative prevention programs, and proactive training, officers' lives can be saved.

## Endnotes

1 W. Bratton, "We Don't Want to Lose You." *Spring* 3100 57 (1994), 12–13.

2 See, for example, J. M. Violanti, J. E. Vena, and J. R. Marshall, "Disease Risk and Mortality Among Police Officers: New Evidence and Contributing Factors," *Journal of Police Science and Administration* 14 (1986), 17–23; and K. O. Hill and M. Clawson, "The Health Hazards of Street Level Bureaucracy: Mortality Among the Police," *Journal of Police Science* 16 (1988), 243–248.

3 Ibid., Hill and Clawson.

4 J. M. Violanti, "The Mystery Within: Understanding Police Suicide," *FBI Law Enforcement Bulletin* 2 (1995), 19–23.

5 E. A. Grollman, *Suicide: Prevention, Intervention and Post Intervention* (Boston: Beacon Press, 1988).

6 American Psychiatric Association, DSM IV *Diagnostic and Statistical Manual on Mental Disorders*, 4th ed. (Washington, DC: Government Printing Office, 1994).

7 Ibid.

8 P. Bonafacio, *The Psychological Effects of Police Work* (New York: Plenum Press, 1991).

9 J. Schwartz and C. Schwartz, *The Personal Problems of the Police Officer: A Plea for Action.* (Washington, DC: Government Printing Office, 1991), 130–141.

**Review Questions**

1. Identify 2 obstacles that hinder the helping process in preventing suicide.

2. Identify 4 points a police administrator should communicate to encourage suicide prevention education.

3. What are the warning signs for identifying at-risk-officers for suicide?

# The Mystery Within: Understanding Police Suicide

*John M. Violanti*

Although considerable obstacles hinder the study of police suicide, mounting evidence suggests that self-inflicted deaths within the law enforcement profession are continuing a dramatic upward trend that began in the 1980s. According to one study, between the years 1950 to 1979, a sample of 2,662 officers averaged one suicide every 2.5 years. From 1980 to 1990, the rate increased to one suicide every 1.25 years. These sobering finding indicate that police suicides now may be occurring at twice the rate they did in the past.[1]

Such statistics make it increasingly important for law enforcement agencies to deal with a problem that refuses to disappear, no matter how successfully it is ignored. Only by gaining a better understanding of the factors that lead to police suicide can administrators develop an effective response to this tragic cause of death among law enforcement officers. Resolving the underlying problems that hinder the research of police suicide may be the first step to gaining a better understanding of it.

## Problems of Research

Considerable difficulty exists in studying police suicide. Researchers often find that information on officer suicide either is not collected or departments are reluctant to allow access to such data.[2] In addition, police suicides may be misclassified routinely as either accidents or undetermined deaths. Because police officers traditionally subscribe to a myth of indestructibility, they view suicide as particularly disgraceful to the victim officer and to the profession.[3]

The police represent a highly cohesive subculture whose members tend to "take care of their own."[4] The desire to shield victim officers, their families, and their departments from the stigma of suicide may lead investigators to overlook certain evidence intentionally during the classification process. One study of the Chicago Police Department estimated that as many as 67 percent of police suicides in that city had been misclassified as accidental or natural deaths.[5]

Failure to correct for such biases could lead to false conclusions regarding the causes and frequency of police suicides. Therefore, accurate research must go beyond official rates: the preliminary results of an ongoing study of police suicides over a 40-year period indicate that nearly 30 percent of police suicides may have been misclassified.[6]

Other problems exist in the study of police suicide. Because most research focuses on large cities, very little is known about suicides in small or rural departments. Therefore, while epidemiological data reliably indicate that police officers are at a higher risk for suicide than the general population, such results may not be generalized appropriately to the entire country. However, the research that has been conducted produced various explanations as to why police officers take their own lives.

## Why Officers Commit Suicide

Studies have revealed several factors related to police suicide. Suicides have been found to be more common among older officers and are related to alcoholism, physical illness, or impending retirement.[7] Other clues have been cited to help explain the high rate of self-inflicted death among police officers: The regular availability of firearms; continuous duty exposure to death and injury; social strain resulting from shift work; inconsistencies within the criminal justice system; and the perception among police officers that they labor under a negative public image. In addition, research confirms a higher propensity for suicide among males, who dominate the police profession.[8]

A study of the Detroit Police Department found that the vast majority of Detroit police officers who took their lives were white young men, high school educated, and married. Alcohol abuse was fairly

**Reprinted with permission from *FBI Law Enforcement Bulletin*, February 1995, pp. 19–23. Courtesy of *FBI Law Enforcement Bulletin*.**

common among the sample (42 percent), as was a formal diagnosis of psychosis (33 percent). However, marital difficulties appeared to be the most prevalent problem among the Detroit sample.[9]

Examination of 27 cases of police suicide in Quebec found that one-half of the officers had a history of psychiatric and/or medical problems, and many had severe alcohol problems. Most officers in the sample experienced difficulties at work, and in *every case*, a notable drop in work performance had been observed in the 6 months prior to the suicide.[10]

## Stress

The high stress of police work generally is cited as a primary contributing factor. The constant barrage of stressor inherent with danger, and for police managers, the pressures of administration, can overwhelm even the strongest person. When officers lose the ability to cope in normal ways, they may turn to an ultimate solution to relieve the pressures of stress.[11]

## Frustration and Helplessness

Among the occupational factors surrounding police suicide, frustration often is cited as particularly important. Almost unfailingly, officers enter policing with high ideals and a noble desire to help others. Over time, this sense of idealism may transform into hardcore cynicism.

The roots of frustration emanate from the central irony of American policing: Society charges police officers with the task of regulating a public that does not want to be regulated. For individual officers, the resulting frustration is exacerbated by a largely unsympathetic press, a lack of community support, and a criminal justice system that values equity over expediency. A sense of societal isolation often ensues, compelling officers to group together in a defensive stance. When an officer feels that the frustration no longer is tolerable or that no coping alternative is available, suicide may become an attractive option.[12]

It also is possible that feelings of helplessness are brought about by the nature of the job.[13] A sense of helplessness is a disturbing realization for anyone, but especially for police officers who are conditioned to view themselves as superheroes capable of anything. Suicide is one way of dealing with helplessness and emotional pain. The finality of the ultimate solution may be an attempt to restore feelings of strength, courage, and mastery over the environment.[14]

## Access to Firearms

Another factor that distinguishes police officers from the general population also has been implicated in the high number of police suicides. That is, most law enforcement officers carry or have access to firearms. An ongoing study of police suicides in the United States reveals that 95 percent involved the use of the officer's service weapon.[15]

Another study compared suicides in New York City and London. While the police suicide rate in New York City was twice that of the general population, the police suicide rate in London, where officers do not carry firearms was similar to that of the city's civilian population.[16]

The police firearm holds special significance for officers. It is a very potent symbol of the power of life and death. Society entrusts law enforcement officers with the authority to use their weapons to take the life of another person in certain situations. In police suicides, officers, in effect, are claiming the right to take their own lives. After all, the weapon has been issued as a means to stop misery and to protect others from harm. Despondent officers may view suicide in such a way.

## Alcohol Abuse

Alcohol abuse also has been implicated as a significant contributing factor in police suicides. One study documented alcohol abuse in 60 percent of the suicides in the Chicago Police Department.[17] Administrators should be aware that alcoholism may lead to other work problems, such as high absenteeism, traffic accidents, or intoxication on duty. Given the established correlation between alcoholism and suicide, these symptoms should not be ignored. They should be considered indications of a larger problem.

### Fear of Separation From the Police Subculture

As officers near the end of their law enforcement careers, another potential threat appears—separation. To individual officers, retirement may mean separation from the camaraderie and protection of police peers. During their years of service, officers may have clustered with other officers due to a general isolation from society and its prejudices toward the police. Upon retirement, these officers must enter the very society that they perceive as alien and hostile.

While the benefits of retirement may be viewed positively by the majority of officers, separation from the police subculture can be a frightful and devastating prospect for others. Fear, coupled with increasing age (a definite suicide risk factor), loss of friends, loss of status as a police officer, and a loss of self definition, leaves some retiring officers vulnerable to suicide. A recent study found a 10-fold risk of suicide among police retirees.[18]

### Other Factors

Other factors have been suggested in an attempt to explain why officers take their own lives. One theory holds that officers commit suicide because of their continuous exposure to human misery and their constant giving of themselves.[19] Another study cites police bureaucracy, with its paramilitary structure, overbearing regulations, and negativism, as a primary catalyst in police suicides.[20]

It also has been suggested that "loner" officers who feel isolated from and uninvolved with the police subculture are more likely to commit suicide.[21] Another theory views police suicides as a response to confusing messages from society: Police are given great discretionary powers, but that power is routinely truncated by the courts, the press, and from time to time, administrators. Under these conditions, many officers experience a significant sense of conflict and confusion.[22]

Policing involves a continual barrage of boredom interspersed with acts of violence, deceit, and human misery. Many officers are exposed to a subculture of violence in which they encounter death almost daily. The average citizen generally does not witness in a lifetime the amount of death and violence a police officer experiences in one month. As a result of this exposure, Post Traumatic Stress Syndrome may lead to a breakdown of normal coping processes. Because the effects of stress are believed to be cumulative, officers exposed to many stressors may reach a breaking point leading to suicide. A study of the Royal Canadian Mounted Police found that 15 percent of the Mounties who committed suicide recently had been exposed to a traumatic work incident.[23]

Current research does not explain definitively what effects such exposure has on the psyche of police officers. It is possible that exposure to death and human suffering produces a numbing effect; that is, death becomes easier to accept as a possible solution to seemingly impossible problems.

Psychological trauma is associated closely with this exposure to death and violence. Many officers involved in police shootings suffer serious aftereffects as a result of these critical incidents. Similar to veterans of war, officers involved in such incidents experience post traumatic symptoms, such as nightmares, flashbacks, and a fear of returning to duty. Suicide can be the ultimate response to this sometimes unendurable pain.

### Asking For Help

Traditionally, no matter what their problems, police officers refrain from asking for help. There are various reasons for this reluctance. Officers do not wish to appear weak or vulnerable in front of their peers. Individuals who perceive themselves as problem solvers often have great difficulty admitting that they have problems of their own. As a result, some officers who feel that they can no longer tolerate psychological pain choose to solve the problem themselves through suicide rather than by asking others for help.

Fortunately, officers' reluctance to seek out help is being abated by successful counseling programs established in many departments. For individual officers, these programs have helped remove the stigma of admitting that they have problems. Currently the domain of large and progressive departments, intervention programs should be implemented in every U.S. law enforcement agency. Because all police officers face similar challenges and pressures—regardless of the size of the agency in which they serve—every officer should have access to comparable counseling resources.

## Effects on Survivors

### *Families*

As is true with any suicide, it is the survivors who must cope with the aftermath of a police suicide. In addition to the emotional anguish and feelings of guilt that generally haunt family members following a suicide, other difficulties often face police suicide survivors. Because suicide is perceived as "dishonorable," families may not be afforded the full honors of a police military-style funeral. To make matters worse, police departments often abandon surviving family members after 1 or 2 weeks of condolences.

Law enforcement agencies must go beyond departmental boundaries to assist the families of *all* deceased officers, including those who take their own lives. By simply maintaining contact and offering assistance with practical matters, such as finances and pension rights, agencies can help family members move through the grieving process.

### *Departments*

In addition to the immediate family, another group experiences the wrath of suicide: Police peers. A grief wave often strikes departments after an officer commits suicide. In some cases, supervisors note a lasting negative effect on the morale and work quality of surviving officers. For this reason, agencies should arrange for psychological debriefings after the self-inflicted death of any officer.

## Preventing Police Suicide

The destructive effects on survivors underscore the need to prevent suicide among police personnel. Not only can an effective intervention effort save officers' lives, but it also can safeguard agencies from the devastating effects of suicide.

Agencies must move beyond the morbidity of the subject to develop effective suicide countermeasures. Perhaps the best way to prevent police suicide is to train officers to cope better with professional and personal problems. This provides them with the means to recognize and avoid the psychological and behavioral wrong turns that eventually can lead to suicide. In addition, training supervisors to recognize the warning signs of suicide can afford agencies an opportunity to intervene before it is too late.

## Conclusion

Suicide leaves survivors shaken and in search of answers that may never be found. Police suicide can devastate the morale of entire agencies and leave individual officers with intense feelings of guilt, remorse, and disillusionment.

By its very nature, suicide is an act of desperation, carried out when less drastic avenues of relief seem unavailable or inadequate. Police agencies should ensure that these other avenues are available.

Because most studies suggests that law enforcement officers are at a heightened risk for taking their own lives, police agencies also should be at the forefront of developing and implementing suicide intervention programs. As is true with addressing any problem, the first and most important step is to recognize that the problem exists. With regard to police suicide, this fact can no long be ignored.

## Endnotes

1   J. M. Violanti and J. E. Vena, "Epidemiology of Police Suicide" (research in progress, NIMH Grant MH47091-02).

2   J. H. Burge, "Suicide and Occupation: A Review," *Journal of Vocational Behavior*, 21,206–222, 1982.

3   J. Skolnick, *Police in America* (Boston: Educational Associates, 1975), 21.

4   J. M. Violanti, "Police Suicide on the Rise," *New York Trooper*, January 1984, 18–19.

5   M. Wagner and R. Brzeczek, "Alcohol and Suicide: A Fatal Connection," *FBI Law Enforcement Bulletin*, March 1983, 7–15.

6   Supra note 1.

7   J. Schwartz and C. Schwartz, "Th Personal Problems of the Police Officer: A Plea for Action," in *Job Stress and the Police Officer*, W. Kroes and J. Hurrell eds. (Washington, DC: US Government Printing Office, 1976). 130–141.

8   S. Labovitz and R. Hagehorn, "An Analysis of Suicide Rate Among Occupational Categories, *Sociological Inquiry*, 41, 1971, 67–72; also Z. Nelson and W.E. Smith, "The Law Enforcement Profession: An Incidence of High Suicide," *Omega*, 1, 1970, 293–299.

9   B. I. Danto, "Police Suicide" *Police Stress*, 1, 1978, 32–35.

10  G. Aussant, "Police Suicide," *Rural Canadian Mounted Police Gazette*, 46, 1984, 14–21.

11  F. L. McCafferty, E. McCafferty, and M. A. McCafferty, "Stress and Suicide in Police Officers: A Paradigm of Occupational Stress," *Southern Medical Journal*, 85, 1992, 233–243.

12  Supra note 4.

13  M. Heiman, "Suicide Among Police," *American Journal Of Psychiatry*, 134, 1977, 1286–1290.

14  P. Bonafacio, *The Psychological Effects of Police Work*, (New York: Plenum Press, 1991); also S. Allen, "Suicide and Indirect-Destructive Behavior Among Police," in *Psychological Services for Law Enforcement*, J. Reese and H. Goldstein, eds. (Washington, DC: US Government Printing Office, 1986).

15  Supra note 1.

16  P. Friedman, "Suicide Among Police: A Study of 93 Suicides Among New York City Policemen 1934-40." in *Essays of Self Destruction*, E. S. Shneidman, ed. (New York: Science House, 1968).

17  Supra note 5.

18  C. W. Gaska, "The Rate of Suicide, Potential for Suicide, and Recommendations for Prevention Among Retired Police Officers" (Doctoral Dissertation: Wayne State University, 1980).

19  M. Heiman, "The Police Suicide," *Journal of Police Science and Administration*, 3, 1975, 267–273.

20  C. Nix, "Police Suicide: Answers are Sought," *The New York Times*, Sept 15, 1986, B2–4.

21  J. Slater and R. Depue, "The Contribution of Environmental and Social Support to Serious Suicide Attempts in Primary Depressive Order," *Journal of Abnormal Psychology*, 90, 1981, 275–285.

22  Supra note 4.

23  R. Loo, "Suicide Among Police in a Federal Force," *Suicide and Life-Threatening Behavior*, 16, 1986, 379–388.

## Review Question

1. Discuss the factors responsible for police suicide.

# Practical Strategies for Preventing Officer Suicide
*Laurence Miller*

Law enforcement is a dangerous profession, but not always for the reasons people think. The suicide rate for police officers is two to three times the rate of the general population; furthermore, three times as many officers kill themselves, about 300 annually, as are killed by criminals in the line of duty. This makes officer suicide the single most lethal factor in police work.

Suicidal crises rarely occur in isolation, but are most commonly seen in officers with prior histories of depression, or in those who have recently faced an overwhelming crush of debilitating stressors, leading to feelings of hopelessness and helplessness. A typical pattern consists of a slow, smoldering build-up of tension and demoralization, which reaches a "breaking point," and then rapidly nosedives into a suicidal crisis.

Importantly, suicidal crises tend to be short, which means that timely intervention can literally make a life-or-death difference. With appropriate treatment, about 70% of depressed, potentially suicidal persons improve considerably within a few weeks. This hardly means that depressed moods and suicidal thoughts won't ever occur again, but a history of successful psychological treatment provides a support resource that the individual can rely on if and when the next crisis begins to brew.

The police culture reinforces a professional ethos that resonates with the personal philosophy many officers already bring to the job from their own family and cultural upbringing. This includes a black-or-white, good-or-bad, all-or-nothing perspective on the world and the people in it. Shades of gray are often regarded as the bleeding colors of washed-out conviction and resolve, and this encompasses the officer's self-perception of his own status as a law enforcement professional and as a human being.

Two primary qualities that almost all officers endorse are self-reliance and perfectionism. Officers come to believe that they should be able to handle most situations with a minimum of help, and that a long record of success can be undone by a single mistake. At the same time, part of the gratification the police role brings lies in the respect it garners among civilians, the camaraderie felt among brother officers, and the admiration of family and friends.

Unfortunately, this orientation leaves little room for acceptance of fallibility or error. An officer's brittle shell self-esteem may shatter if barraged by professional or family stresses, especially in combination. For such an officer, shame is a far worse emotion than fear, and losing the respect of his peers or the support of his family is perceived as more critical than losing a limb or a lung to a suspect's bullet.

Worse, within this all-or-nothing value system, should the officer begin to feel overwhelmed and depressed, his inability to "suck it up" and "snap out of it" only reinforces his self-image as a loser. Completing the vicious cycle, some of this self-loathing may be projected onto others in the form of irritation or hostility, further alienating the officer from potential sources of support, which in turn, only confirms his sense of isolation and abandonment.

Add to this volatile mixture the ready access to a lethal firearm, stir in liberal amounts of alcohol, and this creates the perfect recipe for a suicidal explosion.

## Preventing Suicide

The best form of crisis intervention is crisis prevention. Much can be done by law enforcement agencies to address officer depression and suicide. First and foremost, the problem needs to come out in the open. Both command and line officers need to educate themselves as to the nature of police stress, syndromes of impairment, and ways of coping dysfunctionally and productively.

Next, officers should receive training in crisis intervention skills that they can apply to fellow officers in a similar way as they work with distressed citizens on patrol. This, in fact, is the rationale behind the Peer Counseling programs that have been set up in many departments.

**Reprinted from** *Law and Order Magazine,* **March 2006, pp. 90–93 with permission of** *Law and Order Magazine.*

Also, supervisors must be alert to signs of depression and other problems that are affecting the officers under their command. Finally, there has to be a convenient and non-stigmatized system for referring distressed officers for psychological help, and this must be framed in health-maintenance context, not as a disciplinary procedure.

### Warning Signs

Supervisors, fellow officers, family members, and friends can all be valuable resources in identifying officers in distress who may be at risk for suicide. Clues may be few or many, verbal or behavioral, direct or indirect, with any combination possible.

### Threatening Self:

Verbal self-threats can be direct, i.e., "I'd be better off eating my gun." Or they can be indirect, i.e., "Enjoy the good times while you can, they never last."

### Threatening Others:

Often, self-loathing is transmuted into hostility toward others, especially toward those believed to be responsible for the officer's plight. Verbal threats against others can be direct, i.e., "I ought to cap that boss for writing me up." Or they can be indirect, i.e., "People with that kind of attitude deserve whatever's coming to them."

### Nothing To Lose:

The officer behaves insubordinately, without regard to career repercussions and says, "I'll drink or smoke what I want, on or off duty. So what if I pee positive? What are they gonna do, fire me? Arrest me? Shoot me?" Or he recklessly puts himself in danger on the job. a kind of passive suicide.

### Weapon Surrender:

The officer may fear his own impulses, but be reluctant to admit it, i.e., "As long as I'm on desk duty this week, can I keep my gun in my locker? It's a pain to lug it around the station."

### Weapon Overkill:

This is the exact opposite pattern. The officer begins carrying more than one backup weapon, or begins to keep especially powerful weapons in his vehicle or on his person, supposedly for protection.

### Cry For Help:

"Things are getting too hairy out here. I think I may need to check into the Bug Hilton to get my act together."

### Brotherhood of The Damned:

"You know that news story about the cop in Ohio who killed his family and himself? I know how that poor bastard felt."

### Overwhelmed:

"My wife just left me, my checks are bouncing, I'm drinking again, and the Internal Affairs guys are all over me. I just can't take all this."

### No Way Out:

"If that Review Board bums me again, that's my last strike. I could go to jail for just trying to do my job? No way that's happening."

**Final Plans:**

Without necessarily saying anything, the officer may be observed making or changing a will, paying off debts, showing an increased interest in religion, giving away possessions, making excessive donations to charities, and soon.

**Intervention**

If the warning signs have been missed, the first chance to intervene with a depressed, suicidal officer may come when the crisis is already peaking. The task now is to keep the officer alive long enough to get appropriate follow-up care; this can be accomplished by applying some fundamental principles of crisis intervention.

**Define the Problem**

While some personal crises relate to a specific incident, many evolve cumulatively as the result of a number of overlapping stressors, until a "breaking point" is reached. In such cases, the officer himself may be unclear as to what exactly led to the present suicidal state. By helping the officer clarify what's plaguing him, non-lethal options and coping resources may be explored. It also shows that the intervener is listening and trying to understand.

**Ensure Safety**

Without seeming tricky or manipulative, the intervener should encourage the officer to put even a few short steps between the idea of self-destruction and the action.

**Provide Support**

Remember that the purpose of crisis intervention is not to solve all of the officer's problems in this one encounter, but to instill just enough motivation for him to emerge from the danger zone. The intervener should keep the conversation focused on resolving the present crisis, perhaps gently suggesting that the larger issues can be dealt with later-which subtly implies that there will indeed be a "later." In the meantime, just "being there" with the officer helps reduce his sense of isolation.

**Examine Alternatives**

Often, subjects in crisis are so fixated on their pain and hopelessness that their cognitive tunnel vision prevents them from seeing any way out. The intervener should gently expand the range of nonlethal options for resolving the crisis situation. Typically, this takes one of two forms: accessing practical supports and utilizing coping mechanisms.

**Practical Supports**

Are there any persons or groups that are immediately available to help the officer through the crisis until he can obtain follow-up care? The intervener must always be mindful of the risks and liabilities of relying on these support people instead of professional responders, and should be prepared to make the call to commit the officer involuntarily if he truly represents a danger to himself.

**Coping Mechanisms**

These can consist of cognitive strategies, religious faith, distracting activities, accessing positive images and memories of family, or successful handling of crises in the past that show the officer that hope is at least possible.

**Make a Plan and Obtain Commitment**

Again, this involves a combination of both practical supports and coping mechanisms, as well as both short-term and longer-term plans.

**Post-Crisis Intervention**

When the acute crisis has passed, referral to a mental health clinician is crucial for two reasons. First, the psychologist may have to perform a fitness-for-duty evaluation to determine if the officer is able to return to work; and if not, what treatment or other measures will be required. Second, specialized psychotherapeutic techniques may be applied, that involve a combination of emotional exploration, realistic confidence-building, and practical problem-solving approaches.

As in any area of crisis psychology, there is no cookbook "formula" for dealing with the problem of police officer suicide, but applying the fundamental lessons delineated here may not only save an officer's life in the short term, but even nudge his career in a more productive long-term direction.

**Review Questions**

1. Briefly explain the warning signs of suicide by uniform service personnel.

2. Describe the fundamental principles of crisis intervention to prevent officers' suicide.

# Police Suicide Is Real

*Patricia Kelly and Rich Martin*

Although not a new issue in the world of law enforcement, police suicide is a subject that law enforcement in general would rather ignore than confront for several reasons. In the general population, the most current data from the American Association of Suicidology reports that there were 31,655 suicides in the United States in 2002. The Department of Health and Human Services Centers for Disease Control and Prevention reported that 30,622 people committed suicide in 2001. Another interesting statistic from the Centers for Disease Control and Prevention was that there were 17,638 homicides in 2002 as compared to the 31,655 suicides.

The statistics for police suicides are not as easily accessible for several reasons: reporting inconsistencies, embarrassment to the law enforcement agency, protecting the officer's family, liability issues, and insurance benefits to name a few.

However, Robert Douglas of the National POLICE Suicide Foundation has studied this issue extensively. He gives numerous presentations throughout the United States each year on the subject of police suicide. These presentations focus on the number of police officers who take their own lives, the reasons behind these suicides, and intervention. He believes that officers commit suicide at a rate of 300 to 400 a year (on and off duty).

His data comes primarily from the Department of Health and Human Services Centers for Disease Control and Prevention (CDC). Since 1999 to present, the CDC has reported 60 to 130 suicides in law enforcement on average each year. So how does he make the leap to 300–400 officers a year taking their own lives? It's partially due to that fact that only 22 states require that the medical examiner list an occupation of the deceased on the death certificate. Considering that the CDC is only gathering this information from 22 states, it is conceivable that these numbers could be much higher.

The National Law Enforcement Officers' Memorial Fund Web site reports that over the last 10 years police officers have died in the line of duty at an average rate of 164 per year. If you compare the 300-400 police suicides per year, as reported by the National POLICE Suicide Foundation, or the 60 to 130 reported each year by the CDC (from 22 states) to the average number of 164 officers who died (in the line of duty) during the last 10 years, a shocking picture emerges.

Police officers are killing themselves at a rate much higher than they are dying in the line of duty. This should not be an acceptable condition of the job. Interestingly, police officers wear bulletproof vests and focus on keeping themselves from becoming a homicide victim, but die in greater numbers to suicide each year than homicide.

The sad thing about police suicides, like any suicide, is that in most cases they are preventable. In order to intervene and prevent suicides, first and foremost, education and awareness of suicidal indicators is the key. We train recruits on how to survive on the streets, but fail to train at all, or not enough, on how to survive the other potentially emotionally and physically damaging issues and situations they may encounter on the job.

Some of these might include internal politics, perceptions of or actual inequitable treatment, shift changes, ambiguous policies, internal affairs investigations, marital and/or relationship problems, traumatic incidents (also called critical incidents), etc.

The education of officers, their families, and agency personnel at all ranks and positions in identifying what types of behaviors and statements are indicative of suicidal ideation (thoughts) or suicidal intent (planning) is of grave importance. With this knowledge base, we as a police family will be able to intervene and greatly reduce the number of police suicides occurring each year.

Reprinted from *Law and Order Magazine*, March 2006, Vol. 54, pp. 93–96 with permission of *Law and Order Magazine*.

The first critical component for a successful intervention program is the administrative commitment. Without this, any attempt for implementation of such an undertaking will be doomed. This is a frightening decision with major issues.

If they decide not to undertake such a program, agency heads and supervisors need to ask themselves some painful questions like,

1. *Do we want to lose another officer instead of beginning a process of saving him?* (Proactive versus reactive)
2. *What are the consequences of not having a program in place, and/or covering up suicides?*
3. *Are we prepared to respond to another "accidental" shooting or alleged unintentional squad car accident of one of our fellow officers?*
4. *What message do we want to send to the officers, and their families, when they are seeking help?*

The commitment from the administration should be part of the educational process to reinforce to all employees the importance of how to deal, in a sensitive manner and dignified manner, with a potential suicidal intervention. People will not usually ask for help if there is a stigma attached to them. It must also guarantee that officers' benefits include insurance to cover any counseling and that the process maintains strict confidentially, unless there is an immediate threat to oneself or to others.

And lastly, this standard operating procedure should also deal with the uncomfortable topic of non-discipline. Suicidal ideation or a suicidal attempt should never, in and of itself, involve any disciplinary action. The policy should, however, include the issue of temporary versus permanent firearms/badge removal dependent on whether the problem is due to temporary short-term emotional/mental issues or severe long-term emotional/mental disorders or pathology.

Another aspect in educational awareness of suicide is a basic understanding of the primary reason for suicide: depression. We must educate others that clinical depression is in large part a biochemical illness. It is not something one can "just snap out of." This powerful emotion of being overwhelmed may also be combined with a fear of failure, anger, guilt, hopelessness, and/or revenge at something that transpired on the job or in the officer's personal life. This may equate to a feeling as if one has lost his sense of self.

Many potential suicides stem from seeking a way to remove the emotional pain that has become too much to bear. Society and police agencies often misunderstand depression by not recognizing and treating it, leading to the continuing downward spiral of valued officers.

Unfortunately, we cannot prevent all suicides. Sometimes there is no warning or indicators available. When someone decides to take his life without warning, usually while he is in sudden and extreme emotional distress, we are not afforded the opportunity to intervene.

It is important to understand that suicide is a permanent solution to a temporary problem. Many crises have a time frame when they are the most intense. As time goes on past the initial shock of the crisis, they become more manageable. Our duty to our fellow officers, their families, and ourselves is to show that there are other options to suicide and that suicide is one option you cannot change your mind about once completed.

In studies of people who attempted suicide, they primarily reported that they did not necessarily want to die but instead wanted their emotional pain to end. We, as the police community, can and must help our fellow officers before they get to the point of thinking suicide is their only option.

Several indicators (warning signs) will be observable in the person contemplating suicide. These red flags should make us aware someone may be suicidal. We should discuss these indicators with the person exhibiting them. People often think that if they ask someone if he is suicidal or has suicidal ideations this will push the person into committing a suicide. This is absolutely not the case.

If you ask someone if he is suicidal, you should ask the question directly: "Are you having thoughts of suicide?" Do not mitigate this question and ask things, e.g., "Are you thinking about hurting yourself?" or "Are you thinking about doing something stupid?" These are not helpful. If you get any answer other than, "NO," you need to take immediate action.

Anyone who is clearly indicating he will commit suicide without an immediate intervention should be taken to the nearest emergency room for a full psychological evaluation. In cases such as these, intervention outweighs everything else. The issue here for anyone attempting to help in an intervention is not to worry if this will cause someone embarrassment, loss of job, or any other concerns the suicidal person may be expressing.

Saving the person's life is the primary goal. The alternative is a potential funeral rather than an intervention. People are able to lead long and fulfilling lives even after going through a period where they were contemplating, planning, or even attempted a suicide, but first and foremost they have to survive.

If you think you or someone you know is contemplating suicide, then you must take the first step and reach out for help. Provided you feel comfortable in using your agency's Employment Assistant Program(s), e.g., Peer Support, Chaplain, Crisis Line, etc., do so immediately. However, you may also wish to contact Life Line at 1-800-273-TALK (8255) or the National Help Line Network at 1-800-SUICIDE (784-2433). You can also call your local suicide hotline, talk to your personal doctor, chaplain, or any other person who has the ability to help you intervene. It affects us all … make the call. You don't have to go through it alone.

**Review Question**

1. What are the critical components of a successful suicide intervention program?

# Police Suicide: Are You at Risk?

*Orlando Ramos*

Those of us in the profession have many reasons for choosing a career in law enforcement. We want to help others and make a difference. We care about people and often feel that it is a calling we are compelled to answer. Soon, however, we realize that it takes a special person with a heart for service to respond to the problems of society on a daily basis.

During academy training, we discovered a common theme that quickly emerged: the importance of officer survival. As impressionable new officers, we were inculcated into a quasi-military environment and taught to take control. In every situation, we must take control of the scene, the suspects, and—most of all—our emotions. The nature of police work is inherently negative. Citizens do not call us when things are good. They call us when things go bad. Over the course of an officer's career, memories of the profession often are filled with many negative thoughts and few positive ones. The bulk of service calls are geared toward taking care of others. However, who is taking care of us?

Tragically, too many times suicide becomes the way officers deal with the horrors they have witnessed in the daily performance of their duties, along with internal stressors from their departments and external problems in their personal lives.[1] Relationship problems, coupled with alcohol abuse and the accessibility of a firearm, create a recipe for disaster among troubled officers who may view suicide as the only way out. They are in so much pain that they cannot see any other option. Officers often do not seek assistance because of concerns about confidentiality, changes in duty status, perceptions of weakness, and possible issues with future promotions.[2]

## What Are Some Causes?

First, identifying solely with our professional role can increase our risk for committing suicide. If we are not careful, our career can dominate other areas of our lives. The tactics and communications skills learned on the job are effective when dealing with suspects. However, problems occur when we take these home and use them with our significant others, family members, and children.

In addition, the profession can be lonely at times. Often, we feel that only other officers can relate to what we are experiencing because they have been there before. This can lead to cynicism and a lack of trust in others. Initially, we may begin to depend exclusively on other officers and then limit these to ones in our own department. Over time, that circle can become even smaller and include only a select few of our colleagues. This dangerous cycle can easily lead to social and professional isolation.

Third, when we spend every day seeing the negatives that society has to offer, it can be difficult to find the positives. We begin to view life as one problem after another. Because we become consummate problem solvers, we try to take control by figuring out all difficult situations quickly and effectively, including those that may arise in our personal lives.

Finally, stress in the police profession is unique because it is constant. The type of stress simply varies in degree and duration.

The role of a police officer in itself is stressful because we are never off duty. Operating in an environment where we are frequently exposed to high levels of frustration and danger leads to physical, emotional, and psychological wear.

Stress in law enforcement also is kaleidoscopic in nature. It may come from many directions: our administration, the type of calls we handle, the media attention, the court system, and our personal lives. If not managed properly, stress can cause us to become prone to depression, alcoholism, anxiety disorders, and burnout that, in turn, may increase our risk for committing suicide.[2]

## What Can Be Done?

Training is critical in addressing the problem of police suicide. Law enforcement personnel and their families need to be educated about the risk factors and warning signs of police suicide. Family members should receive this information because they may be the first to see changes in an officer's mood or behavior. Such training also should include information about making the transition from workplace to home life smoother for officers.

At work, officers must remain cognizant of their individual tolerance for stress. Supervisors and peers need to respond to any deterioration in an officer's appearance, performance, or attendance, as well as an increase in citizen complaints. Agencies should encourage their officers to seek confidential assistance from personal physicians, employee assistance programs, peer support teams, and crisis intervention counselors.

## Conclusion

The law enforcement profession must convey to its members that suicide is a permanent reaction to a temporary situation. If officers were suffering from a physical condition, they would seek professional medical attention. What is the difference when an emotional one exists? Trained professionals can help prevent officers from committing suicide.

We are taught officer survival skills while on duty but seldom receive guidance on how to handle what we experience at work when we take off the uniform and go home. Training on how to make the role transition from police officer to civilian life should be required. Officer survival should not be just a day-to-day on-duty event. Instead, our goal should be to survive throughout our careers, making a commitment to living a full life well into retirement.

As law enforcement professionals, we have sworn to protect and serve our communities. We also must begin to protect and serve our fellow officers and ourselves if we are to reduce the tragic toll of officers who commit suicide. Training on the dangers of suicide and identifying resources available may help reduce the stigma of seeking professional assistance. As officers, we must begin to take an active role in helping all members of our profession understand the paramount importance of preventing police suicides.

## Endnotes

1 Orlando Ramos, *A Leadership Perspective for Understanding Police Suicide: An Analysis Based on the Suicide Altitude Questionnaire* (Dissertation.com. January 15, 2008). The author presented this research at the second annual Beyond Survival: Wellness Practices for Wounded Warriors conference hosted by the FBI Academy's Behavioral Science Unit. For additional information, see the May 2009 issue of the FBI Law Enforcement Bulletin at http://www.fhi.goy/pulilications/leh/leh.htm.

2 Access the National Police Suicide Foundation at http://www.psf.org for more information, including specialized training in police suicide prevention.

3 For additional information see Inez Tuck, "On the Edge: Integrating Spirituality into Law Enforcement," FBI Law Enforcement Bulletin, May 2009. 14–21.

## Review Questions

1. Discuss the factors that contribute to suicides for a police officer.

2. Explain the measures that should be applied to prevent officers from committing suicide.

# By Their Own Hand: Suicide Among Law Enforcement Personnel

*Audrey L. Honig and Elizabeth K. White*

Over 300 police officers committed suicide in 1998. Compare this number with the 174 line-of-duty deaths in the same year, and one can conclude that suicide surpasses accident or felonious killing as a cause of police officer death. The numbers support the widespread belief that nearly twice as many police officers die by their own hand as are killed in the line of duty.

But do police officers really have a higher that average suicide rate when compared to the general population? What, exactly, is the suicide rate among officers? And what factors contribute to police suicide? In 1998, the psychological services station of the IACP formed a committee to examine the issues of police suicide and to recommend preventive measures. Its findings offer insights into the tragedy of police suicide.

## What We Know

The rate of police suicide in the United States, while ostensibly a simple figure to calculate, is actually quite difficult to determine. Previous research and current information yield conflicting and often questionable results. In an examination of 25 different studies, some of which date from the 1930s, rates ranged from 0 per 100,000 to 203 per 100,000. The disparity, obviously, is enormous, and it continues to confound researchers.

Much of the disparity in police suicide rates can be attributed to the methodological and other serious problems in the research. Some of these problems include the following:

1. **Lack of Consistency.** The term "law enforcement personnel" is often used generically, so it does not account for differences among police officers. For example, police personnel as well, as well as the nature of police work, can vary according to jurisdiction. Although there are many basic personnel requirements for policing, there are also the specific needs of department and communities. Thus, officers in a large city may have characteristics that differ from those of officers in rural communities. Policing in California or New York is a vastly different experience from policing in Montana or Vermont.

2. **Agency Culture and Environment.** It is unclear how agency culture and environment affect police suicide rates. There appear to be differences in suicide rates among agencies, even within the same geographic area, suggesting that agency characteristics may be an important factor.

3. **Inadequate Records.** Law enforcement agencies are reluctant to share (or even record) statistics on officer suicide. As a result, most studies are prospective based solely on the recollections of respondents.

4. **Mislabeling Cause of Death.** Some researchers suggest a tendency for line staff and agencies to label a possible (or even obvious) suicide as an "accidental death." While this may be done with the best intention of protecting the officer and his or her family members, it further complicates the process of obtaining accurate data.

   *Infrequency of Suicide.* Statistical analysis is difficult because data are limited and police officer suicide is a rare occurrence. The problem is compounded when extrapolating to larger numbers.

   For example, researchers typically use ratios to describe their results. They identify the number of officers committing suicide in a few departments, and then extrapolate to 100,000.

This allows the researchers to discuss the suicide rate per 100,000 officers, but it is merely an extrapolation that should be interpreted cautiously.

*Pre-employment Psychological Screening.* The presence or absence of pre-employment screening can contaminate the research. Similarly, contamination can occur if there is little uniformity between agencies in terms of how pre-employment evaluations are conducted.

5. **Prevention and Intervention Programs.** The presence or absence of organizational interventions may affect comparisons between agencies. For example, agencies that train supervisors and line personnel to identify and approach at-risk officers may have different suicide rates. Similarly, agencies with employees' assistance programs may have different rates from agencies without such programs.

6. **Definition of Law Enforcement Personnel.** Existing studies have concluded a variety of personnel classifications (including retired personnel or custody officers) in their definition of law enforcement personnel. These studies may have also failed to adequately and accurately define their population, making meaningful comparisons difficult.

Acknowledging that there are problems with the research methodologies, the committee continued its examination of whether police have a higher suicide rate than the general population. Dr Michael Aamodt, a psychology professor at Radford University, in Virginia, reviewed all the findings to date, including the 1995 Fraternal Order of Police study involving 38,800 members in 24 states. He concluded that the suicide rate for police personnel is 18 per 100,000. When compared to the rate of 12 per 100,000 reported by the National Center of Health Statistics (1996), it appears that police suicide rates are significantly higher than the general population.

But the conclusion may not be so simple. The rates change dramatically after accounting for age, race, and gender. In the general population of white males, suicide rates are actually 21 per 100,000. This is higher than is found in both the overall population and among police officers. While police departments have diversified their workforce, the typical police officer is likely to be a white male between the ages of 21 and 65. It appears, therefore, the police may actually have a lower rate of suicide.

Other issues warrant closer examination. Owning a firearm results in a fivefold increase in suicide rates among the general population. The effect of firearm ownership among police officers, for whom firearm ownership is mandatory, is unclear. What is clear, however, is that males are much more likely to use a firearm when committing suicide. Approximately 63 percent of males use a firearm to commit suicide. In comparison, 90 percent of police personnel use a firearm when committing suicide.

Alcohol also affects suicide rates. Nine studies investigated whether suicidal officers used alcohol. The overall conclusion was that 36 percent of the suicides included alcohol use. The individual rates in the studies ranged, however, from 16 percent of 78 percent. Alcohol is frequently a factor in suicide among the general population, but there are no studies comparing the general population with police. Thus, it is unclear how alcohol rates among suicidal officers compares to alcohol rates among the suicidal public.

Another issue was the nature of the job. One study examined whether job characteristics, such as shift work or the presence of physical danger, affected suicide rates. The conclusion was that when compared to other occupations that involved shift work or danger, police officers have a significantly higher suicide rate. Other job-related concerns, such as being under investigation, being suspended, or experiencing a significant professional failure, were also indentified as precipitants for suicide. Job-related concerns appear to be more serious for an officer's mental health than personal relationship problems. Officers experiencing marital problems were five times more likely to commit suicide, while officers facing suspension were seven times more likely to commit suicide.

A final contributing factor is retirement. Retired officers were ten times more likely to commit suicide than their peers were. This has ramifications for those officers facing retirement. Officers who retired due to disability had a suicide rate of 2,616 per 100,000 compared to their age-matched peers with a rate of 34 per 100,000.

## An Immediate Need

It is unclear that there is a need for improve data gathering on a national level. Archival data is too prone to deficiencies and inaccuracies to be of use in answering the questions that are asked. By focusing future efforts on improved data gathering, police departments can better address the problem of police suicide. If the characteristics of those committing suicide are identified, prevention and early intervention programs have a greater chance for success. Similarly, the effectiveness of these programs can be incorporated into the overall data-collection process to improve success ratios.

In the interim, there is an immediate and pressing need to prevent both loss of life and secondary trauma to affected personnel. The committee recommends that police chiefs take the following common sense steps to prevent suicide attempts:

- Conduct psychological pre-employment screening of all applicants.
- Assess officers seeking high risk/high stress job assignments (e.g., undercover, special weapons, homicide) and look for personality/job match and the ability to cope with the stressors inherent in these assignments.
- Educate officers and their families about depression, suicide, stress management, and resources (e.g., employee assistance, and counseling).
- Conduct middle management education on depression and the signs and symptoms of suicide. Adopt appropriate polices and procedures should an employee be identified as potentially suicidal. This is particularly important since a majority of those who commit suicide communicate their intentions beforehand. In one study of the New York City Police Department, 29 percent of officers surveyed admitted to knowing a fellow officer who was in crisis or had contemplated suicide.
- Make resources, including chaplains, peer support, 24-hour hotlines, and mental health personnel available to officers and their families.
- Watch individuals who meet specific "at-risk" criteria. These criteria can include changes in personal and professional circumstances (e.g., divorce, under investigation) or signs and symptoms of distress (e.g., sudden drop in performance, increase in complaints, anger, and negativity).
- Debrief after high-stress incidents.
- Reexamine department policies that require sworn personnel to carry a firearm while off duty.
- Prepare officers for the emotional and social changes of retirement by providing retirement transition seminars and assistance.

While the death of any officer is sad, the death of an officer by suicide is especially tragic. Police departments expand considerable resources on officer safety, with great success, but only a small fraction of the department's budget goes toward addressing the psychological needs of their officers and families. Surely, departments should be equally concerned with the mental health of their officers.

Police suicide is costly and potentially devastating to a department. Any chief executive will confirm that suicide is tragic for anyone associated with the officer, from family, friends, co-workers, and supervisors, to even the chief. It is imperative that departments begin allocating resources to prevent officer suicide.

National P.O.L.I.C.E. Suicide Foundation Website (hhtp://www.psf.org). Based on an account of names added to the National Law Enforcement Officers' Memorial In Washington, D.C.

M.G. Aamodt and N.A. Werlick, "Police Officer Suicide: Frequency and Officer Profiles" (Paper presented at the FBI Conference on Law Enforcement and Suicide, Quantico, Virginia, 1999).

The National Center for Health Statistics report was presented at the FBI Conference on Law Enforcement and Suicide, Quantico, Virginia, September 1999. Publication is pending by the U.S. Government Printing Office.

Racial and ethic minorities comprised 21.5 percent of full-time sworn officers in 1997, compared to 19.1 percent in 1993, 17.0 percent in 1990, and 14.6 percent in 1987, according to the Bureau of Justice Statistics' *Local Police Departments 1997,* NCJ 178934, Department of Justice, Washington, D.C., October 1999.

K.B. Hill and m Kravitz, "Linking Work and Domestic Problems with Police Suicide," *Suicide and Life Threatening Behavior 24* (1994): 267–274.

C.W. Gaska, "The Rate of Suicide Potential for Suicide and Recommendations for Prevention Among Retired Police Officers" Ph.D. diss., Wayne Sate University, 1990).

A. Ivanoff, *The New York City Police Suicide Training Project* (New York: Police Foundation, 1994).

**Bibliography**

Labovits, S., and R. Hagehorn. "An Analysis of Suicide Rates among Occupational Categories." *Sociology Inquiry* 41 (1971): 67–72.

McCafferty, F.L., E. McCafferty and M. McCafferty. "Stress and Suicide in Police Officers: Paradigm of Occupational Stress." *Southern Medical Journal 85* (March 1992): 233–243.

Stack, S., and T. Kelly. "Police Suicide: An Analysis." *American Journal of Police* (1994): 73–90.

Violanti, J.M. *Police Suicide: Epidemic in Blue.* Springfield IL: Charles Thomas, 1996.

Violanti, J.M. and F. Aron. "Ranking Police Stressors." *Psychological Reports 75* (1994): 824–826.

**Review Questions**

1. Discuss the factors responsible for conflicting information on the number of officers that commit suicide.

2. Explain the various ways for preventing suicide by police officers.

# PART EIGHT
# Environmental Issues

## Drink or Die: Some Lifesaving Products and Advice for the Outdoor Officer

*Roland V. Dorman*

*With a hydropack, water is always instantly accessible. An officer can easily keep a constant flow of liquids into his or her body, which is a key factor in avoiding a heat-related illness.*

Today, whether by horse, ATV, boat, bike, motorcycle or on foot, there are few places where a police officer cannot be found. However, during the summer months many real dangers can accompany these methods of patrol.

Heat related injuries such as heat exhaustion or heat stroke can result in anything from a trip to the hospital to death. Fortunately, a new breed of products called hydration packs have emerged to insure that officers can safely enjoy their day in the sun.

I first learned of hydration packs when I went to work for the Boarder Patrol several years ago in San Diego, California. I was assigned to the Brown Field Station, which is primarily responsible for arresting illegal aliens around the Otay Mountain Range, near Tijuana, Mexico and the International Border. The mountains are approximately 4,000 feet tall, and on a summer day can reach temperatures in excess of 115 degrees.

Because of the rugged nature of the terrain, boarder patrol agents must work on foot for up to 10 hours a day, descending and climbing the mountain in search of aliens. After my third experience in as many months with severe heat exhaustion, I realized that the issue two quart military canteen I was using was grossly insufficient and I searched for something better. What I found was a hydration system, which virtually solved all of my problems.

A hydration system, or hydropack, is a generic term used to describe one of several products available from various manufacturers such as Ultimate Pack, Bianchi, or Camelbak. The packs come in many shapes, sizes, and colors, with a wide array of features to choose from. With a hydropack, water is stored in a plastic bladder carried in a backpack. A tube is connected to the bladder and draped across the shoulder for drinking. With such a system, an officer is able to carry up to 200 oz. of water in a manner that is comfortable, efficient, and convenient.

With a standard canteen an officer must stop what he or she is doing and unscrew the lid in order to drink. In most cases, an officers is only willing to stop and drink if he or she is already very thirsty, which is too late, dehydration has already begun.

With a hydropack, water is instantly accessible through a plastic tube that extends from the water bladder and drapes across the shoulder where it is easily secured to the shoulder strap. The tube is sealed with a bite valve. When you want to drink just place the valve in your mouth and gently bite down to release the water. With this system, an officer can easily keep a constant flow of liquids into his or her body, which is a key factor in avoiding a heat related illness.

Another feature of a quality hydration system is water capacity. The standard military canteen only holds two quarts of water. Depending on the intensity of the activity being performed, an officer working in the sun should drink between 5–10 oz. of water every 15 minutes to maintain proper hydration levels.

**Reprinted from *Law and Order Magazine*, August 1998, pp. 44–48 with permission of *Law and Order Magazine*.**

While this may seem high, in extreme heat and humidity a person can lose between 1–2 liters of sweat per hour. With a hydration system, a person may carry between 100–200 oz. of water.

A junior agent, new to the mountain, asked me "How much water should I carry?" My response was "How much water can you carry?" Just because you plan on spending only two hours outdoors on patrol doesn't mean you won't get involved in something and get stuck outside for five. Things happen, carry lots of water.

Hydropacks are very comfortable. Canteens are carried on a web belt around the waist or across the shoulder and water is heavy. Over a period of time that weight takes a toll on your body. If you're working on uneven or unstable terrain, a heavy canteen can also set you off balance, making you more susceptible to a stumble or fall.

With a hydropack, the water bladder is carried in a backpack. The weight is evenly distributed across the upper torso, which preserves comfort and balance.

One system, the Nimbus Ultimate Pack, offers padded shoulder straps as well as a torso belt that further distributes the weight of the pack and adds to stability. Canteens also slosh as you remove water. Hydration systems are slosh proof as there is no air within the bladder. My canteen was also notorious for snagging on tree branches and vegetation. A hydration pack hugs the contour of your back, making it almost snag free.

In addition to water, some manufacturers have designed their hydration systems to carry cargo as well. An example of this is the Camelbak H.A.W.G. In my personal pack I carry maps, chemlights, extra batteries, a field knife, a small medical kit, a disposable camera, 'SQWINCHER' FastPacks, Power Bar 'Power Gel' carbohydrate gel packs, flexi-cuffs, extra ammunition, water proof matches, and a compass.

The H.A.W.G. gives me the space to carry some very valuable equipment that in the past was left behind. Because of its support system, the H.A.W.G. is also very comfortable, even when fully loaded.

When it comes to working in the heat, a hydropack is only part of the equation. The following are some tips, hints, and advise that will help you beat the heat:

1. If possible, pre-hydrate before you begin work. Try to drink at least 10–24 oz. of water before you begin work.
2. Drink cold fluids. Cold beverages are absorbed more quickly into the body. Most hydropack manufacturers make insulated sleeves for the water bladders to keep them cold, even in the middle of the summer.
3. Water is not always enough. Your body loses valuable electrolytes and carbohydrates while you work which must be replaced. SQWINCHER FastPacks are great for doing just that. This is a re-hydration drink packed with electrolytes and carbohydrates that comes packaged in a small 6 oz foil packet containing a concentrated syrup. Tear off the top, mix water with the concentrate, and drink. Because of their small size and powerful formulation I carry several in my pack.
4. Refrain from sodas and fruit juices. Drinks with a high fructose (sugar) content can slow absorption and cause stomach cramps. Caffeine in sodas promotes urine production and fluid loss, which impairs the rehydration process. Carbonation inhibits drinking so you don't drink enough. It can also cause throat burn and stomach bloating. The best all around rehydration drink is still Gatorade.
5. Observe the color of your urine during the day to see if your fluid intake is adequate. A clear or light-colored urine can be an indicator that you are well hydrated.
6. Don't wait until you are thirsty to drink—by then it might be too late. Dehydration can occur in as little as 30 minutes. Drink constantly throughout the day.
7. Carbohydrates are the most efficient source of fuel for physical activity. However, this supply is limited in your body and once it is depleted your body will become fatigued and much more susceptible to a heat related illness. Power bars restore lost carbohydrates, however, they are in my opinion difficult to eat and taste like charcoal. An alternative is a carbohydrate gel such as the

Power Bar 'Power Gel'. It is available in a 1.5 oz single serving foil packet, comes in several flavors, and can be consumed quickly and easily.

8. Know the symptoms of a heat related illness: Dizziness and light-headedness, muscle cramps, nausea, headache, cold, clammy skin and high body temperature may indicate heat exhaustion. Hot, dry skin may indicate heat stroke. If this happens seek medical help immediately.

Patrolling outdoors, whether on foot or on a mountain bike, can be a challenging and exciting experience. However, during the summer months, there can be some very real dangers.

Heat related injuries seriously injure or kill many people each year. The bodies my agency discovers on the mountain each year are a testament to this fact. With a little planning, preparation, and common sense, these risks are easily avoidable.

## Review Questions

1. Discuss the advice you will give to new officers for the prevention of heat exhaustion/heat stroke.

2. Compare the military canteen and hydration system as to their suitability for officers assigned to duty on a hot and humid mountainous location.

# Hazardous Chemicals from Clandestine Labs Pose Threat to Law Enforcement

*Edward F. Connors, III*

One of the most dangerous emerging trends in narcotics enforcement is the rapid increase in clandestine drug laboratories in the United States. These illicit labs, which manufacture a variety of controlled substances, pose a significant threat to the safety and health of law enforcement officers involved in investigating, searching and seizing the labs. Illegal drug labs also potentially threaten the environment with chemical contamination.

Many clandestine labs contain hazardous toxic chemicals, and exposure to these chemicals can often be life-threatening. Exposure can result from inhaling vapors, getting chemicals in the eyes, absorbing chemicals through the skin, acids burning the skin, accidentally ingesting chemicals and other forms of contact. Some chemicals in these labs are also highly flammable and can explode with slight contact or heat. Ether, a common solvent used to make methamphetamine, explodes with the force of dynamite. Runoff of chemicals from clandestine labs may also contaminate water sources or soil, and toxic vapors may even permeate building structures.

In addition to the health and safety hazards of the clandestine labs, police agencies face the threat of civil liability for lack of training, improper handling and storage of chemical waste and negligent decontamination of the lab sites.

According to a recent survey by the Institute for Law and Justice (ILJ), the presence of clandestine labs is proliferating, particularly in the western and southwestern states. The 10 states contacted reported nearly 1,200 illegal lab seizures in the past 18 months. Administrator John Lawn states that the Drug Enforcement Administration (DEA) investigated 810 clandestine labs in 1988. This is a significant increase over the 184 labs investigated in 1981.

Most clandestine drug labs produce methamphetamine and amphetamine; but labs have also been seized that were manufacturing methadone, phencyclidine (PCP), fentanyl, MDMA ("ecstasy") and other controlled substance analogues.

Many medical experts expect the field of illegal synthetic drugs to increase rapidly as "entre-preneurial chemists" take advantage of improved technology in computers and communications.[1]

Some law enforcement experts in the West think that methamphetamine ("speed" or "crank" ) will replace crack cocaine as the national drug crisis for the 1990s. Methamphetamine is cheaper than cocaine and produces a longer-lasting euphoria. The number of methamphetamine-related hospital mentions reported nationwide in 1988 increased 110 percent over 1985 totals.[2] Some police officials estimate that current clandestine labs could produce 25 tons of methamphetamine a year, generating $3 billion in illegal profits.[3]

## Health and Safety Regulations

Handling hazardous substances is extensively regulated by health and safety agencies because of potential harm to employees and the public.

Law enforcement involvement with clandestine drug labs is a hazardous substance response operation that falls under the regulations of the Occupational Safety and Health Administration (OSHA) (29 CFR Part 1910 *et seq.*). OSHA regulations require the following actions by employers to protect employees dealing with hazardous substances:

1. *Communicate clear and unambiguous warnings on the hazards and dangers of chemical substances.* These warnings must be reinforced with educational programs. This applies not only to investigators in the field who come in contact with chemicals, but also to technicians and chemists in the crime lab who analyze the seized chemicals.

2. *Train all employees exposed to hazardous substances.* These employees must be thoroughly trained in recognizing and dealing with safety and health hazards present in clandestine lab sites, use of protective equipment, safe work practices and other safety measures. An initial 40 hours of safety training is required, coupled with three days of actual field experience. These employees are also required to receive eight hours of refresher training annually. This specialized training must be certified in accordance with OSHA standards.

3. *Provide proper protective equipment.* OSHA regulations require a range of safety equipment for workers exposed to dangerous substances. This equipment must meet specific standards established by the National Institute for Occupational Safety and Health for exposure levels. Examples of standard protective equipment in clandestine lab situations include coveralls (chemical-resistant suits), gloves, respirators, boots, goggles and atmosphere monitors.

4. *Examine and monitor the health of employees exposed to hazardous substances.* A continuous medical surveillance program is needed to identify as soon as possible signs and symptoms indicating possible overexposure to hazardous substances. Exposure situations should always be documented carefully and thoroughly for future medical reference. Prior to training or working with clandestine labs, employees should receive thorough medical screening to determine their fitness for the assignments.

In addition to federal OSHA regulations, many state health and labor safety agencies have authority to enforce laws governing hazardous substance operations. Last year, a small police agency in Oregon was fined nearly $3,000 for a variety of violations of the Oregon Safe Employment Act. The violations included failure to provide adequate warnings, training and protective equipment for employees exposed to hazardous substances in seizing illegal methamphetamine labs.

The U.S. Department of Transportation (DOT) regulates the packaging and transportation of hazardous substances (49 CFR Parts 170-172). Hazardous substance carriers must meet DOT's secure transportation standards before dangerous chemicals can be moved over the highways.

Operations involving hazardous substance storage, disposal and site clean-up are governed by the Environmental Protection Agency (EPA) under the Comprehensive Environmental Response, Compensation and Liability Act of 1980 as amended (42 U.S.C. 9601 *et seq.*). Costly liability may attach to a hazardous waste generators who allow hazardous substances to release into the soil, water or air.

### Investigating Clandestine Labs

Information from informants and the public, such as reports of "strange" odors from residences, probably provide law enforcement with the greatest number of tips on clandestine lab operations, but tracking precursor chemicals and lab glassware may lead to the greatest volume of illegal drug seizures.

In 1988, as part of the omnibus Anti-Drug Abuse Act of 1988, Congress passed the Chemical Diversion and Trafficking Act. Under this law, DEA has recently proposed regulations that, among other things, impose new record-keeping and reporting requirements on chemical supply companies.

These companies must keep records (name, address, phone number, form of identification presented) of regulated transactions (including sales) involving listed chemicals, tableting machines and encapsulating machines. Companies must also report to DEA any regulated transaction involving an extraordinary quantity of a listed chemical, an uncommon method of payment of delivery or any other circumstances that the regulated person believes may indicate that the chemical will be used in violation of the act.

DEA also has authority under this law to stop export shipments of listed chemicals if there is sufficient reason to believe the shipment is not destined for legitimate industrial, commercial or scientific use.

A number of states, including California, Oregon, Washington and Texas, also have state laws that require chemical companies to maintain records of the sale of certain precursor chemicals and glassware.[4] These laws enable law enforcement to track the sale of chemicals and other supplies frequently used in clandestine labs.

## Lab Raids and Seizures

Trial and error over the past five years has led a number of police agencies to develop a structured set of procedures for raiding and seizing a clandestine lab.[5] Pioneered by some key states and DEA, clandestine lab raid and seizure procedures involve the following stages:

*Pre-raid planning.* This involves meeting to review intelligence information and coordinate the tactical operation. Many raids on illegal labs involve the presence of law enforcement personnel from different agencies and jurisdictions, as well as back-up support from fire and emergency medical services. The pre-raid plan should include a combination of standard drug raid strategies (e.g., physical layout of building, presence of weapons, tactical approach, communications, perimeter security, etc.) and plans for dealing with hazardous materials (e.g., evacuation plans, first aid, etc.)

*Initial entry:* An initial entry team, similar to a SWAT unit, is used to secure the lab site, arrest suspects and remove them to an uncontaminated location. This entry team wears safety equipment that protects against hazardous chemical exposure and violence by the suspects, yet does not restrict necessary movement. The entry team must be trained to recognize lab-related dangerous situations such as a highly flammable manufacturing process or the presence of booby traps. For example, the back door of a lab recently raided in Oklahoma was guarded with a trip wire connected to a hand grenade.

*Site assessment:* Once the lab is secure, an assessment team enters the lab to assess the hazards. *This team must always include a qualified chemist.* The team also wears adequate protective equipment and, since the initial danger is unknown, often wears self-contained breathing apparatus. It is responsible for determining the presence and levels of toxic or explosive gases or vapors, determine oxygen levels and deactivating and ventilating the lab.

*Processing and dismantling the lab:* The processing team consists of experienced chemists and crime lab personnel. This team, which also wears adequate protective equipment, is used to identify, document and collect evidence of criminal activity. Some of the activities of the processing personnel include taking samples of chemicals, labeling chemical containers (placing warning signs on hazardous chemicals), photographing or videotaping the scene and original setup and lifting of latent fingerprints, if required.

As the last two stages indicate, chemists are an integral part of clandestine lab raids and seizures. Trained chemists are necessary to determine the potential hazards associated with exposure to toxic substances and document the manufacturing process used in the illegal lab.

Chemists have also been used to interview suspects outside the lab to obtain an accurate history of the manufacturing process. Sometimes a "chemist" engaged in illegal drug manufacturing is more likely to open up to another chemist.

Care must be taken in storing hazardous substance evidence recovered from a clandestine lab. The storage facility, which should be away from the regular evidence storage area, must meet EPA and OSHA standards.

One of the key positions recommended to oversee clandestine lab raids and seizures is a safety officer. This officer ensures that essential personnel wear adequate protective equipment, reports exposure situations and supervises the transportation of hazardous substances, decontamination of personnel and site clean-up. This position should compile a report of the hazardous substances found and forward it to the appropriate local or state health/environmental agency or to a regional EPA office.

It is recommended that, as part of the pre-raid planning, the raid coordinator ensure that the team has adequate back-up from the fire and emergency medical services personnel.[6] In fact, one of the better clandestine lab programs in the nation is a joint police-fire approach by the city of Portland, Oregon. While police agencies are just now training to deal with hazardous substances, fire service agencies have been training and using hazardous materials units for years.

The final aspect of an agency's clandestine lab operating procedures must deal with site clean-up and disposal of contaminated materials.

**Clean-up and Disposal**

The aspect of clandestine labs that may cause the most problems and expense for law enforcement in the future is hazardous waste clean-up and disposal. Responsibility for hazardous waste clean-up and disposal ultimately rests with the individual or organization that produced the waste, or first caused the waste to become subject to regulation. EPA has ruled that DEA is the "generator" of hazardous wastes from clandestine labs it handles, making DEA legally liable for clean-up and disposal.

In response to this problem, DEA contracts with a licensed hazardous waste disposal company to remove chemicals, equipment and glassware from the lab site.[7] The hazardous substances are carefully packed and transported to storage or disposal facilities. Non-evidentiary hazardous substances are destroyed. DEA procedures recommend treating all drug lab chemicals, glassware and equipment as if they are hazardous wastes. The contractor may also assist in decontaminating all individuals exposed to the hazardous substances in the clandestine lab and in cleaning up the site.

As an additional measure to protect the public, DEA posts a warning sign on the site notifying others that hazardous substances or waste products may still be present in the buildings or ground. The agency also notifies the legal owner of the property as to the condition of the property.

One state responding to ILJ's survey reported spending as much as $70,000 to clean up and dispose of hazardous waste at a single clandestine lab site.

In order to deal with the growing impact of the hazardous wastes produced from clandestine labs, Congress created a federal interagency task force to address the problem. Under authority of the anti-Drug Abuse Act of 1988, the task force is to formulate, test and implement a program for clean-up and disposal of hazardous wastes produced by clandestine labs. The task force consists of representatives from DEA, EPA and the Coast Guard.

This joint task force has produced proposed guidelines to help state and local law enforcement agencies better manage the clean-up and disposal of hazardous wastes from illegal drug labs.[8] In terms of site clean-up, the joint task force recommends that the local or state law enforcement agency complete its responsibility after disposing of all contaminated materials and turn the oversight of the clean-up of "residual contamination" to the "lead state agency" responsible for hazardous waste clean-up. Such a relationship must be worked out on a state-by-state basis.

**Conclusion**

The investigation and handling of clandestine drug labs poses special problems for law enforcement. The hazardous waste law is new for police. It is also an area of the law that holds a significant potential of civil liability for police employers in terms of claims by injured workers, fines by OSHA and EPA and lawsuits by the public.

While law enforcement is struggling to deal with hazardous substance issues and laws, some of the programs implemented by DEA and a few of the states may be helpful. BJA has funded four states and one city to develop model clandestine lab programs: California, Washington, New Jersey, Pennsylvania and Portland, Oregon. Several of these states have worked with DEA to develop certified safety training programs.

Proposed guidelines in lab clean-up and hazardous waste disposal are available from the DEA/EPA task force. In addition, ILJ and the National Sheriffs' Association provide overview training on investigating and handling clandestine labs.

In summary, law enforcement must better prepare to deal with clandestine drug labs. Few comprehensive guidelines for law enforcement exist.[10]

The objective of police agencies investigating and handling clandestine labs should be to ensure the safety of employees and the public by reducing or avoiding exposure to hazardous chemicals. Some recommendations gleaned from agencies successfully dealing with the problems posed by illegal drug labs are as follows:

***Develop and document policy and procedure for investigating and handling clandestine drug labs.*** Several agencies have accomplished this by creating an ongoing safety committee chaired by a hazardous materials coordinator. If possible, the approach should be multi jurisdictional, since the problem typically overlaps jurisdictions. The approach should also include coordinating with fire and emergency medical services and state agencies responsible for enforcing worker health and safety and environmental laws.

***Develop safety training and medical screening and surveillance for employees exposed to hazardous substances that meet OSHA standards.*** Police departments should work with state and federal agencies involved in enforcing worker safety regulations to develop certified training programs that meet OSHA standards for training employees exposed to hazardous substances (29 CFR 1910.120(e)). Fire department HAZMAT personnel may also help with this training. Personnel involved with hazardous substances should also be medically screened and their health continuously observed.

***Provide adequate protective equipment for employees exposed to hazardous substances.*** Proper safety equipment is critical for the health and safety of employees exposed to hazardous chemicals. Employers have an affirmative duty to warn and educate employees about the dangers of hazardous substances in the workplace.

***Contract with a licensed hazardous waste disposal company for clandestine lab site clean-up, decontamination and storage and disposal of hazardous substances.*** Hazardous waste clean-up and disposal is a highly technical field and law enforcement should rely on private industry to help in this area. Law enforcement cannot assume the burden alone of cleaning up hazardous waste caused by clandestine drug labs. State agencies responsible for environmental protection and for workers' health and safety must be involved in the problem.

## Endnotes

1   Terra Ziphoryn, "A Growing Industry and Menace: Makeshift Laboratory's Designer Drugs," *Journal of the American Medical Association*, Vol. 256, No. 22, 1986, p. 3063.

2   *Methamphetamine Abuse in the United States,* National Institute on Drug Abuse, US Department of Health and Human Services, Sept. 1988, p. 6.

3   "Rural Drug Users Spur Comeback of 'Crank,'" *Washington Post*, February 20, 1989, p. A1.

4   National Narcotics Intelligence Consumers Committee, *The Supply of Illicit Drugs to the United States*, 1988, p. 56.

5   *Clandestine Laboratory Manual of Instruction and Procedure*, State of California, Department of Justice, 1987 (update in 1988).

6   Phillip L. Currance, "EMS Crosses Hazmat Line," *Journal of Emergency Medical Services*, February 1989, p. 58.

7   Randolph D. James, "Hazards of Clandestine Laboratories," *FBI Law Enforcement Bulletin*, April 1989, p. 16.

8   Joint Federal Task Force, *Proposed Guidelines for the Clean-up of Clandestine Drug Laboratories*, May 8, 1989.

9   Ibid., p. 11

10  See Training Key #388, "Clandestine laboratories," International Association of Chiefs of Police, 1989.

## Review Questions

1.  Discuss OSHA regulations for protection of employees dealing with hazardous substances.

2.  Describe the stages involved in the raid and seizure of hazardous clandestine labs.

3.  As a supervisor in a Drug Enforcement Agency, describe the comprehensive guideline you will follow in establishing a program for dealing with hazardous clandestine labs.

# Safety Means Learning from Our Mistakes
*Murrey E. Loflin*

The loss of two firefighters in the line of duty last year compelled the author to ask again what can be done to mitigate risk and improve firefighter safety? What can we learn from our fatal incidents?

March 18, 1996, and the events of that day will be etched in my memory for the rest of my life. It was an overcast yet warm Monday morning in Virginia Beach, Va., with our usual weekly staff meeting at 0830 hours. I had another meeting afterward with the Virginia State Police to discuss implementing safety procedures for our members when operating on the interstate roadways within Virginia Beach.

After these meetings, I went back to my office to catch up on some paperwork. I was behind because I'd spent the week before at an NFPA Fire Service Occupational Safety and Health Technical Committee meeting.

At about 1145 hours, my attention was turned to my portable radio. One of our fire inspectors told our dispatch center via radio that he was on scene in Chesapeake, Va., at a commercial building fire. He reported that the Chesapeake Fire Department was requesting mutual aid immediately. It was unclear at first how many pumpers they were requesting. Our dispatch then received a call from Chesapeake dispatch requesting a full-alarm assignment.

At 1152 hours, a full-alarm assignment was made, requesting Engines 10, 19 and 23; Ladder 9; Battalion 4; and Safety 1. Since I am dispatched on all mutual-aid alarms and requests when any Virginia Beach Fire Department units are sent out of the city, I left my office at the municipal center. As I was leaving, I could see smoke from the fire, which was at least 10 miles to the southwest.

The dispatcher had said: "there are still people in the building, and a Chesapeake pumper is on fire." Never in my wildest moments did I envision that "the people" in the building would turn out to be firefighters from the Chesapeake Fire Department.

I arrived on scene at an auto parts retail store that was 75% destroyed. I parked in the middle of Indian River Road, put on my protective clothing and equipment, and went to the command post. There was no roof on the building, no mansard, no windows or doors, just a burning shell.

I said to myself, we'll set up the master streams and be out of here in an hour. I gave the deputy chief of Chesapeake my accountability tag and asked for an assignment. He said, "Talk to my safety officer," and then turned away. I did a face-to-face with the Chesapeake incident safety officer and then did a walk-around of the building, as I always do at any incident.

## Confusion in Back

The picture was completely different when I reached the back of the building. The front had been relatively tranquil. At the back, confusion reigned. I slowly began to realize that something was wrong—terribly wrong.

Chief Harry Diezel of the VBFD then arrived on the scene and, in cooperation with Chesapeake command, directed several rapid intervention crews from Virginia Beach to enter the building to locate the missing firefighters. The building was 120 feet long by 50 feet wide and cluttered with auto parts, chemicals, parts of the collapsed roof, storage racks and about a foot of water.

Side "A" was the front of the building facing the parking lot. Side "B" was surrounded by parking lot and an add-on portion of the shopping center. Side "C" was the rear access area that was cluttered with personnel and apparatus. Side "D" was the fire wall adjoining the shopping center. After about 30 minutes of searching, one of our rapid intervention crews found two bodies under a pile of debris. I will never forget the radio transmission that they had found the two bodies, both Chesapeake firefighters.

I do not describe this incident to place blame on the Chesapeake Fire Department or any other fire department involved, but only to say that the fire service has to face the fact that *this* is reality. It hits close to home. I'd talked with friends who had experienced line-of-duty deaths in their departments, but nothing can ever prepare you for an actual incident. It wasn't even my department, but I still felt the pain and sorrow, and I still ask why.

An irony, especially for me, was that the VBFD had, with the Fire Industry Equipment Research Organization and the Virginia Organization for Fire Service Safety and Health, sponsored a firefighter safety and health seminar only a week before. One of the speakers was Chief Richard Arwood, who spent five hours depicting the excruciating situation that the Memphis Fire Department had encountered on April 6, 1994, when they lost two firefighters in a high-rise apartment building fire [Ed: See "Memphis high-rise firefighter deaths: Few new lesson," Sept. 1994.]

Only two weeks after the fatalities in Chesapeake, I would sit in a meeting with Chief Charles Dickinson of Pittsburgh and listen to him describe the terrifying events of Feb. 14, 1995, when the Pittsburgh Bureau of Fire lost three members in a house fire. As an incident safety officer, I asked myself over and over, what would *I* do if I were faced with a situation such as these? The fire service has to learn from its mistakes and provide the safest possible working environment for its members.

## Safety and Health Issues

Firefighting presents risks to our members. I don't think anyone will argue that point. But through an effective risk management program, and an occupational safety and health program, risks can be reduced. The ultimate goal is to eliminate firefighter fatalities and reduce the number and severity of accidents and occupational injuries.

The fire service experienced a safety and health revolution with the development and implementation of NFPA 1500, Fire Department Occupational Safety and Health Program in 1987. This document did much to awaken the fire service to the need for a structured occupational safety and health program. Previously, firefighter fatalities, injuries and illnesses had been considered part of the job and accepted as occupational hazards.

Fortunately, a group of fire service safety and health proponents believed there was a better way to do things. The end result of their perseverance and hard work was a consensus standard that could be implemented by departments to improve the safety, health and welfare of their members. NFPA 1500 was a proactive approach to help eliminate firefighter fatalities, reduce occupational injuries and illnesses, and provide a standard approach to safety and health for firefighters, yet the standard has only scratched the surface in dealing with fire service occupational safety and health.

Fatalities continue to plague the fire ground and recent firefighter fatality investigations have revealed several common factors that generally precipitate such incidents:

- An inadequate incident management system.
- A lack of a personnel accountability system.
- Inadequate incident scene communications and radio procedures.
- Poor pre-incident planning.

This is not an all-inclusive list by any means, but it points out that we keep making the same mistakes again and again. Other issues that need to be addressed are:

- Incident scene risk management.
- Effective standard operating procedures.
- Use of personal alert safety systems.

The leadership of the American fire service has to address these issues through some forum that the fire service as a whole can agree on. Is this through national consensus standards, federal and/or state legislation, a combination of both, or some other forum that will provide a proactive approach to these issues?

### Laws, Codes and Standards

Thus far, various levels of government have taken an interest in firefighter safety. At the federal level, the Occupational Safety and Health Administration has become concerned with fireground operations, particularly in having an appropriate number of members on scene before the starting of interior operations. In the near future, the agency will be issuing the revised respiratory protection standard (29 CFR 1910.134) that's the source for the "two in/two out" language.

Also OSHA is reviewing the use of consensus standards as a source for its regulations. Rather than generate a new mandate of its own, OSHA would use a consensus standard that's currently being used by a particular industry, such as NFPA standards. This approach may prove to be the way of the future: regulations that reflect government/industry cooperation rather than governmental fiat.

State regulators are struggling with the same sorts of safety issues that the feds are. The Commonwealth of Virginia's Department of Labor and Industry has formed an ad hoc committee of fire service members and other interested parties to develop a solution for implementing the "two in/two out" rule. This group has been working over the past nine months to develop procedures that will provide safer fire ground operations for all departments—career, volunteer and combination. Other states are working on developing similar procedures.

Outside of government, consensus standards themselves are constantly evolving. The "two-in/two-out" safety requirements are reflected in the final draft of Chapter 6 of NFPA 1500, under operations at emergency scenes. The Technical Committee for Fire Service Occupational Safety and Health formulated this final draft based on the public comments received. The standard will be voted on at the NFPA annual meeting in May in Los Angeles.

### Key Components

What are the key components to improving the safety and health of our members? There are solutions that the fire service can implement. The managers of the fire service must provide the leadership to ensure that these solutions are implemented and administered effectively within their departments. The solutions that I believe are paramount are:

**Training.** Training is the foundation of any organization, because it tells you how well members will function in a real incident. It's a basic, yet critical, component that's often forgotten after recruit training. Training must be a proactive process that serves members *throughout* their time at a department. When new training or retraining is necessary, the department must meet this need.

**Standard operating procedures.** SOPS are organizational directives establishing a specific policy that must be followed. They address issues of administration, training, driving, protective clothing and equipment, emergency operations, and other matters that affect members. To operate effectively and safely, a department must develop and implement standard operating procedures.

Departmental SOPS are based on current laws, codes or standards used by an industry. They must be reviewed and updated on a regular basis, and a department must also make sure that they're complied with. A written SOP, such as a personnel accountability system, is totally useless unless the members covered by the procedure actually follow it.

**Incident management system.** This policy serves as a basis for safely and effectively managing members during emergency operations. Issues such as personnel accountability, risk management, and rapid intervention crews are all part of this system. Without an incident management system, chaos and confusion can easily prevail at an incident.

**Communications.** Effective communications are essential to managing an incident. Members must be trained to use their radio equipment competently, especially when an emergency occurs, such as a firefighter becoming trapped or lost.

**Protective clothing and equipment.** Even with the quality of protective clothing and equipment available today, members still aren't using full protective clothing, respiratory protection and PASS devices.

**Risk management.** During emergency operations, command officers, company officers and members must use basic risk-benefit analysis. Rather simply put, they have to assess the situation and decide whether to:

- Risk a lot,
- Risk a little, or
- Risk nothing.

**Incident safety officer.** The fire service must place more emphasis on this function. The incident safety officer acts as the on-scene risk manager, monitoring the risks present at an incident and managing them with effective control measures.

**Post-incident analysis.** This process serves as a method for evaluating the operations at an emergency incident. Department criteria and the type of incident will determine the extent of the PIA or critique, but it starts on the company level and continues upward to all members who participated in the incident. The operational procedures, issues that need to be improved, and safety and health issues are all topics that need to be discussed in this structured process. It's a way to learn about and improve department operations.

Though the focus of this article relates to safety at emergency operations, there are other components of safety and health that we have to consider. Health and wellness is one of these, and a comprehensive occupational safety and health program is the way to approach it. The health and safety officers should manage this kind of program, but leadership and direction must come from the chief.

With an effective risk management plan and occupational safety and health program, departments can provide effective services while protecting their work force. There may be some capital outlay involved, but the benefits will be shown in reductions of accidents, occupational injuries and illnesses; insurance premiums; workers' compensations costs; lost work time; and disability retirements. In the not-so-long run, risk management will save money, and more importantly, the lives and health of our members.

**Review Questions**

1. Identify the factors that create grounds for fatalities in firefighting operations.

2. Discuss the key components for improving the health and safety of firefighters.

# Lead Poisoning
*Eugene Nielsen*

Lead poisoning is a very real safety hazard that every agency and officer needs to be aware of. The risk is much greater than most people realize. All shooters may be at risk.

Lead is a toxic heavy metal that shooters are exposed to every day. Indoor shooting ranges pose the greatest risk. According to studies, lead exposure can rise dramatically during firing practice at indoor shooting ranges. Permissible exposure limits can literally be exceeded within minutes.

Range personnel and others who work or shoot regularly at indoor shooting ranges are at greatest risk from lead poisoning. Firearms instructors have died as the result of airborne lead exposure at firing ranges.

Lead causes severe health effects at even relatively low levels in the body. It damages the brain, nervous system, kidneys, heart, reproductive system, and interferes with hemoglobin production. It also affects behavior. At typical levels of exposure, the blood, brain, and nervous system are primarily affected. The effects are often irreversible.

The gradual onset of symptoms of lead poisoning and the lack of specificity of the symptoms, which often affect more than one part of the body at a single time, results in lead poisoning often being misdiagnosed. The classic textbook physical signs of lead poisoning may not even be present. The symptoms of lead poisoning are often vague. Unless the patient raises the issue of lead poisoning or the doctor is extremely suspicious and the appropriate testing is done lead poisoning will go unrecognized.

Exposure to lead during pregnancy can cause birth defects and miscarriages. Lead in the mother's bloodstream easily passes through the placenta to the fetus and may cause gross deformation in development.

The margin of safety between measured blood lead levels and the levels that cause clinical symptoms is small. Children are more at risk than adults, as harmful effects from lead begin at lower blood levels. Although lead blood levels in children have been declining as a result of regulations designed to cut lead exposure, studies of the blood lead levels in children show concentrations of lead that are already above the levels that are known to cause changes in blood enzymes.

Shooters and their families are exposed to lead residues from two sources: three-fourths lead in the cartridge priming compound and lead in the bullet. When a cartridge primer detonates and the powder charge is ignited, a cloud of lead particles is expelled into the air and onto the shooter's hands. Additional lead particles are sheared off the bullet as it travels down the barrel and expelled into the air at the muzzle. Lead is also expelled into the air when the bullet impacts the target.

When lead particles are inhaled into the lungs they are absorbed into the bloodstream. Approximately 50% of the lead that's inhaled reaches the bloodstream. Lead residues on the skin or in the hair can be absorbed through the pores. If any lead is ingested through the mouth, it will be absorbed through the intestines and enter the bloodstream.

The amount of ingested lead that reaches the bloodstream will vary depending on the form of the lead. While approximately 10% of ingested lead reaches the bloodstream, 100% of ingested lead salts reaches the bloodstream.

According to the National Bureau of Standards, lead bullets are the source of 80% of the airborne lead at indoor firing ranges. Although primers are the source of only 20% of the airborne lead, the airborne lead from primers is much more fine and more easily absorbed into the bloodstream when inhaled. The risks from ingestion of lead is also greater since lead salts are formed when a conventional lead syphnate primer is ignited.

Although this article deals with lead, readers should be aware that lead isn't the only health hazard from conventional primers. Although most US suppliers have non-toxic primers, styphnate primers, and some lead-free primers contain barium nitrate as an oxidizer. Antimony is another health hazard in conventional primer mixes.

It doesn't take much lead to cause lead poisoning. Only 0.16-grain of lead in the bloodstream can result in acute lead poisoning. That is just 1/1000th of the amount of lead in a single .38 Special/.357 Magnum 158-grain lead semi-wadcutter bullet!

Chronic poisoning from exposure to low-levels of lead is more common than acute poisoning. Lead exposure is cumulative. Lead can gradually build up in the body over time, reaching toxic concentration after years of exposure.

The body treats lead like calcium. Approximately 94% of the lead that enters the bloodstream is deposited in the bone. The remaining 6% is deposited in the blood and soft body organs. Stored lead can be mobilized from the bone and reenter the bloodstream during times of calcium deficiency or increased calcium requirements, such as during pregnancy or lactation.

The body does have the ability to gradually eliminate lead. The amount of time that is required is measured by what is known as "half-life." Half-life is the amount of time required by the body to excrete one-half of the lead dose. Lead in the blood and soft body tissues has a half-life of about 30 to 40 days. Lead in the bone has a half-life of about 20 years. Most lead excretion is through the kidneys. Lesser amounts are excreted through the bile, sweat, hair, and nails. Factors such as the total dose and length of time of exposure also play a factor in the elimination of lead from the body.

## Prevention

There are two basic ways in which the risk of toxic effects from lead can be minimized 75% by reducing exposure and through proper nutrition. Obviously, the best way to reduce the risk is to take precautions to reduce exposure to lead. However, since some exposure to lead is unavoidable, proper nutrition is also essential to reduce the risks from exposure.

## Reducing Exposure

There are a number of simple precautions officers can take to reduce the risk of exposure to lead. Shoot at well-ventilated ranges. Indoor shooting ranges have a greater problem with lead dust and airborne lead residues than outdoor ranges. Ranges should be monitored for lead and conform to OSHA standards. Unjacketed ammo poses a greater problem than jacketed ammo. Shotgun ammunition poses a greater problem than handgun or rifle ammo.

Use lead-free ammo with non-toxic primers and either a TMJ bullet or a non-toxic bullet, such as CCI/Speer Lawman RHT* (Reduced Hazard Training) "Clean-Fire" ammo, whenever possible for qualification and shooting practice, especially when firing on indoor shooting ranges.

Lead-free ammo was first introduced in the US by CCI over 20 years ago. Today, lead-free ammo is available from a number of manufacturers. The primers contain no lead and the bullets either contains no lead or, if the bullet has a lead core, the bullet is totally enclosed in copper. Many agencies have transitioned to lead-free ammo for training use. Important note: Generally non-toxic primers are less reliable than conventional lead styphnate primers. For this reason, lead-free ammo is not recommended for duty use.

Don't collect fired brass in caps. Lead residues on the brass can contaminate the cap and be absorbed into the skin when the cap is later worn. And don't eat, drink or especially smoke on the range. Lead residues on your hands and face can be ingested. Airborne lead can also contaminate food, drinks and tobacco products and be ingested. Smoking increases the absorption of inhaled lead into the blood stream.

Thoroughly wash your hands and face after shooting with soap and cold water. Warm water shouldn't be used since it will open the pores in the skin and enhance absolution of any lead residues. Wash your hands and face before eating, drinking or applying cosmetics. Your hair should also be shampooed to remove residues.

Change your clothes and shoes before entering your residence. As an alternative, protective apparel, such as coveralls and disposable shoe coverlets can be worn while at the range. Clothing and shoes can transport lead into your home.

Wash contaminated clothing separately from other clothing to avoid cross contamination. Contaminated clothing shouldn't be shaken to remove lead residues as this will result in lead particles becoming airborne.

Carefully clean firearms in a well-ventilated area, preferably outside of your residence. It's a good practice to wear disposable gloves while cleaning firearms. Gun cleaning solvents can increase the absorption of lead through the skin.

Avoid physical contact with others until after showering and changing clothes. Lead residues can be transferred to others by casual contact. If possible, shower and change into clean clothes and shoes before returning to your residence to prevent carrying any lead contamination home.

When cleaning or repairing indoor shooting ranges, or in other situations where airborne lead may pose a hazard, respiratory protection should always be worn along with disposable outer garments.

Select respirators based on the hazards to which one will be exposed. An air-purifying respirator with a high-efficiency particulate (HEPA) filter can be used in environments where the concentration of lead is not in excess of 0.5 mg/m$^3$.

Never dry sweep firing ranges. Standard vacuums shouldn't be used to remove lead dust, either, since they will only circulate the lead into the air. A HEPA vacuum with a three-stage particulate air filter should be used for this purpose. Dispose of lead properly as hazardous waste.

## Proper Nutrition

Deficiencies in dietary minerals can speed the absorption of lead into the bloodstream from the gastrointestinal system. Adequate amounts of calcium and phosphorus are especially important, as too are adequate amounts of copper, iron and magnesium. Milk may not be a good source of dietary minerals when lead is present, since recent research indicates that lactose (milk sugar) may hasten the absorption of lead.

Some research indicates that vitamins C and E may help prevent brain damage caused by high exposures to lead. Both vitamins are essential to keep blood cells healthy. Research in Russia indicates that pectin, a polysaccharide occurring in plant tissues, such as apple skins, may also help protect blood cells from damage due to lead.

## Symptoms of Lead Poisoning

Symptoms of lead poisoning typically develop slowly. They are often vague and may resemble "flu-like" illnesses. Symptoms of lead poisoning may include headache, poor appetite, dizziness, irritability, anxiety, constipation, pallor, excessive tiredness, numbness, metallic taste in the mouth, muscle and joint pain or soreness, sleeplessness, hyperactivity, weakness, reproductive difficulties, nausea, fine tremors, insomnia, "lead line" on the gums, and weakness of extensor muscles ("wrist drop"). If lead poisoning is suspected, prompt medical attention should be obtained.

## Testing for Lead Levels

There are several tests that may be performed to test for lead levels in the body. A blood lead level (BLL) test may be performed to detect recent exposure to lead. The BLL does not provide information on past or long term exposure. A test known as the zinc protoporhyrin (ZPP) test is often performed in conjunction with the BLL to determine longer term exposure. The ZPP measures the amount of zinc in the blood. Lead interferes with the absorption of iron in blood and allows zinc to replace the iron. An elevated ZPP is indicative of concentration of lead in the bone marrow. The chelating agent disodium edetate (EDTA) may be used to test for bone lead levels. Because of potentially harmful side effects the EDTA chelating agent test is only used in more extreme cases of lead poisoning.

**Medical Treatment of Lead Poisoning**

Treatment of lead poisoning consists of avoiding further exposure to lead. Under certain circumstances, drugs called chelating agents are prescribed by a physician to bind with the lead in the blood and help the body excrete in the urine it at a faster rate. The chelating agent penicillamine may be used alone in mild cases. In more severe cases, penicillamine may be used in conjunction with other chelating agents, such as edetate calcium disodium (calcium EDTA) and dimercaprol (BAL).

All of us are exposed to lead from a variety of sources on a daily basis. Since we can't get away from lead in our modern, industrialized environment, it's essential that we take precautions whenever possible to lessen our exposure.

**Review Questions**

1. Describe the health effects of lead poisoning.

2. What are the sources of lead dust found in indoor firing range?

3. Discuss the prevention strategies to reduce lead poisoning for officers using an indoor firing range.

# Lead Poisoning: Still a Concern for Indoor and Outdoor Ranges

*Chuck Klein and Anthony M Gregory*

A generation or so, ago, police officers were lucky if they fired their guns once a year. Any practice between "qualification" meant shooting wadcutter reloads. Later, it was determined that it was best to fire the same ammo for practice and qualification as what you carry for duty.

By the start of the 1990s, officers, in response to litigation fears, began practicing more often—often monthly. The word was out to burn more powder. But with burning powder comes the risk of toxic lead exposure. Also, there are now many instructors who log hours of range time.

Range instructors, due mostly to increased line time and quantities of rounds fired, are exposed to greater amounts of toxic pollutants than ever before. The most dangerous of these toxins is lead. Not the lead bullet/pellets, per se, but the lead compounds sprayed into the air with the firing of the primer.

With the exception of lead-free cartridges, projectiles are made up of lead, copper, zinc and antimony.

The common properties of a primer are: copper, zinc, lead antimony, barium, lead styphnate and tetazene. Unless the bullet is totally encased in a non-lead product [copper], elemental lead is shaved as it passes through the barrel and then dispersed into the air.

When this bullet impacts with a steel backstop it breaks up throwing more elemental lead into the air and onto the ground. This form of lead, in its elemental state, is not the major concern. Elemental lead, in the form of dust from the fragmented bullets [after hitting steel back plates] is mostly a problem for clean-up crews at indoor ranges.

It's the compound leads that are vaporized and formed by the burning powder that are of greatest risk to shooters and range officers. These dangerous gases come from two sources. First, the burning powder sears the base of the lead projectile causing lead gases to be expelled with the powder residue. It is this compounded lead, along with the second source, the vaporized lead and lead styphnate [from the discharge of the primer], which possess the greatest danger to those on the shooting line.

It has always been known that long term and/or short intense exposure to lead particles and dust can cause lead poisoning. Until recently the effect of the sports of shooting and reloading and required certification/practice for police officers to incidence of lead poisoning has been ignored. Reports of toxic levels of lead in officers assigned to range duty, including one recent death, have raised the awareness. It's time for police administrators and instructors to take note.

Lead, when introduced to the human blood stream is very toxic. Even the tiniest amount, 1/2 of 1/10 of one grain [.05], dissolved in your blood can produce adverse reactions—try measuring that on your powder scale. Though most cases of plumbism are treatable, the treatment, like the cumulative toxic condition, takes a long time. If you have had or are experiencing any of the below symptoms you might re-examine your shooting/gun/ammunition handling practices and be tested by a doctor.

We learned the lesson of wearing hearing protection from older shooters who go around saying "Huh" a lot.

Those who lost an eye are testimony to the prudence of shooting glasses. Lets hope today's heavy shooters aren't the lead poisoning lesson for the next generation. If you're around the range a lot, be it indoor or outdoor, or you handle fired cases, take precautions and encourage your range officers to set the example.

**Reprinted from** *Law and Order Magazine,* Jan. 2000, pp. 62–66 with permission of *Law and Order Magazine.*

**Symptoms of Lead Poisoning Include:**

- Loss of memory and difficulty in concentrating (usually the first noticeable symptom);
- Fatigue in various degrees, including a pallor, malaise, loss of appetite, irritability and sudden behavioral changes;
- Insomnia, which may exacerbate fatigue;
- Headaches, which may be accompanied by depression;
- Neurological disorders such as muscle spasms;
- Brain deterioration. This, the most serious condition inasmuch as damage done, is not treatable and usually is permanent. Symptoms include limb paralysis, confusion, disorientation, coordination problems and/or insanity;
- Amyotrophic lateral sclerosis (degenerative disease of the nerve cells that controls the muscles);
- Digestive difficulties and abdominal pains, with or without weight loss;
- Elevated blood pressure;
- Joint pains;
- Anemia (hemolysis—rupturing of red blood cells);
- Menstrual irregularity and decreased fertility;
- Kidney and/or liver damage;
- Sore or bleeding gums and marked by a blue line at the junction of the teeth and gums.

**Note:** The symptoms and the severity of such are different in each person. Children are particularly susceptible due to their smaller size in relation to amount of ingested/absorbed lead. Also, because lead poisoning symptoms are so varied and mimic other maladies it is difficult to self-diagnose.

Though other heavy metals such as gold and iron are present (and needed) in the human body, lead, in any amount, is not. Lead is toxic to all persons, but is easily detected with a BLL (blood lead level) test available at most clinics, hospitals or doctor's offices. Lead contamination on clothing, skin, or other objects can be tested for with test kits such as the HybriVet Systems lead check swabs. These analysis tools are inexpensive and are readily available from most paint supply stores.

Outdoor range shooting is no less a concern than indoor ranges when it comes to inhaling lead dust. However, indoors or out, lead poisoning is just as serious when produced by other factors. A few hours of shooting outdoors during a humid, breezeless day where the expelled gasses hang in the air, or shooting into a head wind, might be far more hazardous than all day at a well ventilated indoor range.

We tested Winchester's new SuperX, Super Unleaded load in 9mm Luger. The 115-grain load contains a totally heavy-metal-free primer and a fully encapsulated lead core bullet. The only exposed lead is the tip of the bullet. The base is fully covered by the copper jacket thus eliminating the source of lead gases that come from vaporization of a lead base bullet during ignition.

The Super Unleaded cartridge is not to be confused with their Super Clean lead-free ammunition. The latter consists of a tin core bullet and the same lead-free primer used in the Super Unleaded. Though the tin core bullet, in 9mm, weighs 105 grains, its sectional density is significantly lower [than lead core bullets] and therefore energy and trajectory are adversely affected. The physical properties and ballistic comparisons of the Winchester SXT and the Super Unleaded, however, are very similar.

The 3M Company provided us with their 6000 series Low-Maintenance Half Facepiece with particle filters, and their #8233 N100 Particulate Respirator. These protect the wearer from both elemental and compound lead and other toxic gases. The #8233 is a disposable mask while the 6000 series face piece utilizes disposable filters snapped on each side.

One problem facing range instructors while wearing any form of breathing filter is the muffled effect of their commands. For ranges that use voice amplification equipment this should not be a problem.

The test weapon was the KEL-TECH P-ll in 9mm. fitted out with a new barrel so as not to contaminate the lead-free tests. We covered the top of the shooting bench with clean white paper. Before firing any ammo we ran the HybriVet lead check swabs over the bench paper, gun barrel, the shooter's hands and face. This preliminary checking done, we then fired 75 rounds of the Super Unleaded.

Following the shooting we again tested the barrel, bench paper and shooter for residual lead. The results yielded no evidence of lead—the Winchester Super-X, Super Unleaded rounds are truly lead free.

For comparison, and to observe if lead does settle on shooting benches and human body parts, we then fired 10 rounds of Winchester 9mm 115 grain "regular" cartridges. Running the lead check swab over the bench paper, and the shooter's hands and face most assuredly indicated the presence of lead— and that after only 10 rounds and with a 5–10 MPH tail wind!

**Sources of Lead Poisoning**

- From Firearms Related Activities Airborne residue from the discharge of primers, Lead styphnate, a common element of primers is lethal due to its ready absorption into the body. Only about 10% of elemental lead is absorbed, but nearly 100% of ingested lead compounds, such as from a fired primer, are absorbed.
- Shaved lead particles from bullets as they pass through the barrel,
- Dust from cleaning the range area,
- Handling fired cases, lead bullets or lead shot,
- Vaporized lead gases from the base of partially jacketed bullets,
- Eating food touched by unwashed hands after shooting or handling fired cases,
- Food and drink that pass through a beard or mustache that hasn't been washed after shooting,
- Absorption via exposed skin, especially on a hot day,
- Cigarettes exposed to lead contaminated air are an easy way to ingest lead directly into the lungs,
- Lead dust formed from fragmenting bullets as they strike a hard backstop.
   **Preventive Measures:**
- Blow your nose after shooting,
- After any shooting or reloading session wash your hands and face before eating or smoking,
- Wash hair before bed. Lead particles in the hair can transfer to the pillow and thus be ingested during sleep,
- Use lead free primers (though not as popular as the common lead styphnate primers, they are available from most makers),
- Have your doctor test you for lead levels as part of your regular checkups,
- Change out of your shooting clothes and footgear so as not to contaminate car, home or office— especially important if you have small children,
- Wear breathing masks (rated for lead dust) if you are going to spend much time on the range— especially instructors. It might seem silly to wear breathing masks, but remember how "silly" it was to wear ear protection 2030 years ago?

**Range Rules and Procedures**

Post signs forbidding consumption or storing of food, tobacco, beverages and cosmetics on the firing range. Anyone exposed to lead by handling fired cases or shooting should wash their hands and face before eating, drinking or smoking.

Plastic bags should be available for shooters to place their contaminated clothes for transport to their home laundry facilities.

Shooters using the kneeling or prone position should cover the ground with heavy paper.

Range maintenance workers should be required to change clothes, shower and shampoo daily. Separate lockers should be provided to keep clean street clothes separate from contaminated work clothes.

Encourage the use of lead-free ammunition.

After each use the range floor should be vacuumed with a unit designed for collecting lead. Dry sweeping should never be practiced.

On indoor ranges, the ventilation system should be in operation during all shooting, clean up and maintenance operations.

Range officers, maintenance workers, clean-up crews and anyone who engages in shooting activities on a substantial basis should wear breathing masks or respirators.

These same high exposure officers, workers, and shooters should have a BLL [blood lead level] test every six months.

Lead poisoning is serious business. Department administrators must be aware of the danger and take aggressive measures to insure their agency members are not exposed to the possibility. Prevention is the only way to go.

## Bibliography:

Anthony M. Gregory, Risks of Lead Poisoning in Firearms Instructors and Students, *The Law Enforcement Trainer*, Sept/Oct 1998.

*NOISCH Health Hazard Evaluation Report*, U.S. DEPT OF HEALTH & HUMAN SERVICES, HETA 91-0346-2572, FBI ACADEMY Michael Barsan, Aubrey Miller, April 1996.

Robert Leonard Goldberg, et al., Lead Exposure at Uncovered Outdoor Firing Ranges, *Journal of Occupational Medicine*, Vol. 33, No. 6 June 1991.

Material Safety Date Sheet Remington Arms POB 700 870 Remington Road Madison, NC 27025-0700 1-800/243-9700.

## Sources of Supply:

3M Occupational Health and Safety Products Div. 220-3E-04, 3M Center St. Paul, MN 55144-1000 1-800/364-3577 Disposable respirators and lead dust/mist masks: Model 8710 & Model 9920

HybriVet Systems, Inc. POB 1210 Framingham MA 01701 1-800/262-LEAD Lead Check Swabs for instant lead test.

Winchester Div, OLIN CORP 427 N. SHAMROCK STREET EAST ALTON, IL 62024-1197 1-618/258-2000 http://www.winchester.com Lead free ammunition.

KEL-TEC ARMS POB 3427 Cocoa, Florida 32924-3427 1-407/631-0068; Fax 1-407/631-1169.

## Review Questions

1. Discuss the different sources of lead poisoning for a police officer doing shooting practice.

2. Explain the preventive measures to be applied by officers to reduce lead poisoning.

# HEALTH: Recognizing and Preventing Heat-Related Illnesses
*Michael Savasta*

Heat-related illnesses are more common during the summer months but can also occur in moderate climates. Heat production is affected by multiple environmental factors including temperature, humidity, sun exposure, wind, and clothing. During physical activity, the body keeps cool by evaporating moisture through perspiration.

When you sweat, and the water evaporates from your skin, the heat that evaporates the sweat comes mainly from your skin. As long as blood is flowing properly to your skin, extra heat from the core of your body is "pumped" to the skin and removed by sweat evaporation.

When heat gain exceeds the level the body can remove, or when the body cannot compensate for fluids and salt lost through perspiration, the temperature of the body's inner core begins to rise and heat-related illness may develop.

Ranging in severity, heat disorders share one common feature: the individual has over-exposed himself or over-exercised for his age and physical condition in the heat environment. Anyone who exercises or works outdoors is susceptible to heat-related illnesses and should become familiar with the following illnesses and their symptoms.

## Heat Cramps

Heat cramps are the most common but least serious of the heat-related illnesses. Although no conclusive evidence is available, heat cramps seem to be connected to heat, dehydration, and poor conditioning, rather than to lack of salt or other mineral imbalances. Heat cramps are characterized by spasms of the muscles of the arms, legs or abdomen and are sometimes forceful and painful.

Treatment consists of rest, moving to a cool environment and drinking plenty of fluids. Use cool, moist towels to speed the cooling process, and gently massage the affected muscles to loosen them up. You may also want to do some light stretching exercises.

## Heat Exhaustion

Heat exhaustion is caused by excessive heat and dehydration, leading to volume depletion. Symptoms include profuse sweating, paleness, headaches, nausea and vomiting and muscle weakness.

Treatment consists of rest, moving the person to a cool environment and replacement of fluids. You may also want to remove any excess clothing, and place cool, moist towels on the head, neck, armpits and groin. While recovery should be rapid and the person should fed better in two or three hours, more severely exhausted patients may need IV fluids, especially if vomiting keeps them from drinking enough.

## Heat Stroke

Heat stroke is the most severe form of heat illness, as it may be fatal. It occurs primarily in the elderly and very young but may also occur in healthy, physically fit individuals. A core temperature of at least 104.9 degrees Fahrenheit, cessation of sweating, rapid pulse and usually hot and dry skin characterize heat stroke. These symptoms are usually preceded by mental changes ranging from disorientation to unconsciousness.

If you suspect someone is suffering from heatstroke, call 9-1-1 immediately. Move the person indoors or into a shady place at once.

Be careful about giving the person liquids by mouth, as the person may slip out of consciousness or experience convulsions unexpectedly. Heat stroke is a true emergency that requires immediate intervention by qualified medical personnel.

**Reprinted from** *Law and Order Magazine*, Aug. 2005, pp. 106–109 with permission of *Law and Order Magazine.*

## Prevention

You can prevent heat-related illnesses by staying well hydrated and be sensible about exertion in hot, humid weather. The hotter and more humid it is, the harder it will be for you to get rid of excess heat. The increased moisture in the air slows the evaporation of sweat. Check the temperature and humidity conditions before exercising. Even if the dry temperature is only 65 to 75 degrees Fahrenheit, a high humidity will increase the heat stress.

Other guidelines include wearing light colored clothing that is loose to allow air circulation, exercising in the cool of the morning, and drinking fluids periodically even though you are not thirsty. Additionally, wear a hat if working in the intense sun and limit your food intake to small meals. Avoid foods that are high in protein which increase metabolic heat. You should also take time to get used to a new climate before becoming very active or staying in the sun.

When dehydration is the major threat, water replacement is the primary consideration. In prolonged events or exercising in the heat with heavy sweat loss, sport drinks such as Gatorade or PowerAde may be essential to prevent heat injury. Pay special attention to the sugar content of these types of drinks. In general, sport drinks having 10 to 12% sugar content should be limited. They may significantly delay gastric emptying and possibly cause gastrointestinal distress.

In addition, gastric emptying increases in proportion to the volume of fluid ingested. Intake greater than 500 to 600 milliliters at one time may actually retard emptying. In other words, if you drink too much fluid at one time, the stomach will be inhibited and rehydration will be slowed.

According to the American Academy of Pediatrics Committee on Sports Medicine, all heat-related illnesses are preventable. Heat cramps, heat exhaustion and heat stroke are either the result of extreme fluid loss over a period of a few hours or fluid loss that is never completely replaced over a period of several days.

It is often said that the thirst mechanism is not a reliable indicator of when we should start replacing fluids. Proper hydration should begin prior to exercising or venturing outside in hot and humid weather. Prehydration provides a fluid cushion and delays the onset of dehydration.

## Review Questions

1.  Describe the following terms:

    *   Heat cramp
    *   Heat exhaustion
    *   Heat stroke

2.  Discuss the precautionary measures to prevent dehydration, when working outdoors in a hot, humid environment?

# PART NINE
## Safety Issues

## SAFETY

### The Future of Officer Safety in an Age of Terrorism
*Michael E Buerger and Bernard H Levin*

Traditionally, most people consider officer safety in terms of an individual officer, in extreme circumstances, facing a "bad guy" intent upon doing harm to that officer. The armed encounter—and the possibility of death—puts into high relief the entire range of tactical defenses that have constant application: awareness of the environment, including reading "cues" from subjects; threat assessment; and approach and contact techniques, such as handcuffing, weapons retention, and firearms handling and use. The elements that officers must focus on are concentrated in time and, usually, space, with the majority of violent encounters occurring within a 10- to 20-foot radius.[1]

We do not intend to denigrate or underestimate the importance of incident-specific tactical defenses, which remain critical parts of police training. Rather, as futurists, we proffer that the potential for terrorist activity on American soil demands new conceptual understandings and practical applications of officer safety. The elements of safety expand across time and space, broadening the threshold beyond the potential for incident-based contacts. Our offerings here add to the existing canon of safety concerns, building upon it in some instances and supplementing it in others.[2]

If a terrorist incident occurs as a large-scale public event-an attack with conventional, chemical, biological, or nuclear weapons against symbolic or densely populated targets—officer safety concerns change. Individual safety will be subsumed as an element of large-scale concern for survival. Officers will have to take on additional risks in managing the public's safety, as well as dealing with the perpetrators.

Looking at the issue broadly, three main categories, or theaters, of terrorism-related safety concerns exist. The first, intelligence gathering, is a prevention activity. The second involves direct contact with known or suspected terrorists in which the individual officer's safety becomes as acute as in the standard armed encounter. The third, the wake of a successful terror attack and its aftermath, joins the officer's safety with that of the larger public. In addition, a fourth category spans the other three: administrative and supervisory responsibility for management of the long-term and large-scale concerns.

### Intelligence and Prevention

Training to prevent terrorist attacks is essentially a matter of intelligence gathering. Officers best protect themselves by helping to ensure that no terror attack succeeds. To this end, individual officers must perceive their duties to be more than merely handling calls.

Information gathering and, perhaps more important, information seeking represent ongoing efforts that have secondary benefits.

Armed encounters are relatively rare events in most police careers; acts of terror will be even more so. An important theme (and an ongoing lament) of traditional officer training is the need to maintain constant vigilance, even under conditions that seem to belie that edict. Maintaining peak mobilization for long periods of time proves difficult, as Aesop's timeless fable of the boy who cried wolf and the contemporary "orange alert fatigue" demonstrate.[3] A conceptual change must occur to mount a sustained, focused intelligence-gathering effort to intercept a devastating event.

Law enforcement agencies can incorporate many of the precepts of community policing into their intelligence-gathering efforts, such as developing cultural awareness, initiating contact with and identifying sympathetic guides and mentors among new immigrant and alternative cultural groups, and maintaining the respect and sympathy of the people being policed. New information concerning potential trouble is much more likely to come from the communities than from patrol-based observation. The ability to act upon intelligence developed outside the locality most likely will require some form of community assistance.

Many of the fundamental activities of traditional policing also will attend the endeavor. Agencies must continue to keep an eye on known perpetrators and identify new players, develop informants and information from the fringes of the underworld, and maintain a baseline understanding of how the neighborhoods live and move to detect when something is "just wrong."

At the intellectual level, officers must maintain an awareness that the targets of their suspicion almost certainly belong to a larger organized enterprise. While officers involved in multijurisdictional task forces and RICO-based investigations understand the demands of enterprise crime investigation, most local officers are trained and indoctrinated with an incident-based frame of reference. Officers will require a longer time frame and broader set of resources to identify a suspect's or a cell's contacts, support bases, and potential targets.

This perceptual shift also places action-oriented officers in a new and unsatisfying role. Instead of intervening directly and "solving" the problem through arrest of an individual, officers will need to remain near-invisible elements in a larger and more deliberate network. Premature individual heroics simply may alert the terrorist network to surveillance and deflect or postpone any planned attack. Critical portions of the network may escape not only arrest but even detection.

These concerns apply only to those few officers who encounter an ongoing or imminent terrorist action. Most of the officers charged with intelligence seeking will contribute little or nothing to any antiterrorist action; those who report activity into the gathering endeavor never will receive positive feedback in the form of an arrest or thwarted attack because they did not cross paths with a terrorist network or associate. This lack of feedback on even local events constitutes a long-standing complaint of local officers; the needle-in-a-haystack nature of terrorism intelligence undoubtedly will exacerbate that problem.

To counter skepticism and disgruntlement, the efforts to develop intelligence on terror must be transformed into a larger understanding of the intelligence function. The same activities will have a local payoff in terms of criminal activity in the officers' jurisdictions, if managed correctly. Clear- and far-sighted officers should make the connection between their activities and traditional (if underserved) functions, such as preventing crime, nipping developing problems in the bud, and integrating new residents into the larger community. A strategic understanding of community vulnerability will identify critical infrastructure (e.g., power plants, bridges, transportation facilities, and manufacturing concerns) that would make tempting targets for terror attacks.

## Interception

Antiterrorist preparations must anticipate the possibility that a patrol officer, a detail officer from another assignment, or even an off-duty officer of any rank will encounter one or more terrorists preparing or launching an attack. While most of the interceptions of terrorists have been intelligence based and conducted by federal authorities, officer safety concerns are framed in terms of "it's only a matter of time" before an officer or deputy encounters terrorists on the way to or in the act of mounting an attack. In such an event, the individual officer becomes a secondary but immediate target-someone the terrorists must eliminate to achieve their primary objective. Unplanned interception contacts involve protecting the individual officer's safety in an incident-specific context, similar to the armed encounter but with a wider range of threat.

The possibility of unplanned interception increases if officers take their intelligence duties seriously, particularly a focus on infrastructure sites. Nevertheless, even everyday enforcement actions may instigate the contact. After all, one of the great "What if?" moments in American policing involves the course that history would have taken had authorities stopped Timothy McVeigh in the rental truck on the way to Oklahoma City, rather than afterwards as he fled the area in a car.

Much of the contingency preparation for unplanned interception rests on the nature of the attack contemplated by the terrorists. Conventional assaults, such as the North Hollywood bank shooting on February 17, 1998 (a "shock and awe" takeover robbery in support of militia groups in eastern Europe), may involve a variation of the traditional armed encounter. Discovery of terrorists planting explosives at a critical juncture creates other risks, as do the various scenarios for launching chemical or biological attacks. Officers must anticipate armed terrorists in any encounter, but chemical and biological ones pose special hazards.

Both biological and chemical incidents, as well as the more distant concern of a nuclear "dirty bomb" weapon, require considerable preplanning with public health officials and other emergency responders. Most preplanning events assume a successful or partial attack, however, with little emphasis on serendipitous discovery. Developing a curriculum to prepare officers for such an eventuality remains a pressing need.

Officer safety at the point of discovering a suspected biological, chemical, or nuclear device reflects a new dimension. Effective training should be diverse, able to accommodate the variety of biological and chemical threats ranging from the terrorist to the transportation accident. The likelihood of the latter is considerably greater in the multiple police jurisdictions of the country and provides a more suitable cognitive platform on which to build antiterrorist training.

At the present time, clandestine drug labs and industrial or transportation accidents constitute the primary viable model for chemical attacks but with considerably different surrounding circumstances. These incidents are localized; are accidental, rather than designed to inflict mass casualties; and have smaller areas of danger than a successful terrorist attack. Nevertheless, they form a logical and practical framework for adapting antiterrorist safety training.

A variation on the interception model involves law enforcement officers attacked by terrorist groups or agents. Right-wing separatist groups have targeted public officials with threats, nuisance lawsuits, and, in some cases, violence. While the current public model of "terrorist" is an al Qaeda affiliate, multiple models of potential threats could be transplanted to American soil and used either by foreign or domestic groups.

The potential for incorporation of terrorist methods into criminal actions coexists with terrorist aspirations. Although the ideology that fuels suicide bombings under the guise of "martyr actions" has not been associated with American radicalism, some U.S. cults have embraced suicide (from the Jonestown slaughter to the Heaven's Gate apotheosis); the barrier between the two may be very thin. The threat of sleeper cells may turn out to be more potential concern than actual threat, but law enforcement training should anticipate the arrival or emergence of newer, more lethal assaults.

The Iraqi situation has shown the devastating results of the improvised explosive device (IED) and the vehicle-borne improvised explosive device (VBIED). While domestic officers have some experience with bomb training and bomb squads exist, law enforcement agencies should anticipate new wrinkles beyond the Oklahoma City scenario. For example, three Irish nationals with IRA connections were arrested in Colombia in 2001, thought to be teaching bomb-making techniques to the Revolutionary Armed Forces of Colombia.[4] In the wake of the robbery of the Northern Bank in Belfast, police suspect that some element of the IRA is turning to organized crime.[5]

Resources for coping with any such new threats already exist. Prior to its dissolution, the Royal Ulster Constabulary of Northern Ireland learned to contend with the constant threat of assassination of its officers. The Israeli police have dealt with the potential for renewed suicide bombings on an almost daily basis. Americans training Iraqi police, like those engaged in similar peacekeeping missions in other parts of the globe, have encountered and adapted to variations of similar threats. New and modified training regimens can capitalize on the antiterrorist lessons already learned throughout the world.

## Aftermath

The odds that terrorists will succeed in launching an attack are slightly greater than those of serendipitous interception. In that event, officers' safety becomes a subordinate part of the general welfare of the citizenry in the attack area. Even more pressing, perhaps, is the fact that officers will have to function under circumstances that also pose a threat to their loved ones, from whom they will be separated by duty.

Americans have few exemplars of mass panic, the worst-case scenario. Most of the prior examples involve serious but geographically bound events. Wide-scale civil disorders and antiwar protests in the late 1960s had specific geographic dimensions and involved only a portion of the populace. Large-scale mass evacuations from hurricane-threatened areas are implemented with several hours' warning and along preplanned, well-publicized routes.

Even the unexpected attacks on the Murrah building in Oklahoma City and the World Trade Center, catastrophic as they were in terms of casualties, remained localized in time and physical dimensions. The longer-term environmental impacts of the collapse of the Twin Towers may have greater ramifications, but they were overwhelmed by the horror of the main incident. Additional lessons may be derived from the Aum Shinriyko cult's attack on the Tokyo subway or the Chernobyl nuclear accident, even though they occurred in foreign countries and have become increasingly distant in time.

None of these predecessor events can provide a reliable road map for an event that instigates mass panic. Americans must travel back to a much different age, Orson Welles' broadcast dramatization of *War of the Worlds*, to find a real-life event involving open panic. The most vivid portrayal of cataclysmic events is found in motion pictures, and that image is of sheer panic. One of the concerns will be how to avoid modeling fictitious behavior. Preplanning (not seen publicly since the civil defense plans for nuclear attack during the Cold War) will be necessary for both the guides (police, emergency medical services, and other public safety entities) and the guided (the general public).

Ideally, the public's reaction will be more disciplined, along the lines of the evacuation of projected hurricane landfall sites. Even in such a case, provisions should be made in advance and not left to ad hoc solutions. Evacuation will be a natural reaction to any mass-casualty possibility; therefore, preplanning for evacuation; alternative routes in the event of artery-choking accidents or inclement weather conditions; and logistics of communication, shelter, and remobilization of the affected communities will require multiple layers of contingency planning adaptable to multiple scenarios, not just terrorist attacks.

## Management

Traditional focus on individual officer safety to survive a single encounter proves insufficient in the face of mass attack. The lesson of the World Trade Center attacks is that the entire agency must be prepared. Communications and the ability to work with other agencies responding to the same emergency represent organization-level considerations, as do the procurement of proper equipment, provision of adequate training, and commitment to coordinated preparations.

Police managers also will have to prepare for and cope with officers' very human need to see to the protection of their families and loved ones in case of a general disaster. Creation of a plan-within-a-plan for evacuation of families to a central protected shelter, for instance, may help relieve anxieties and allow officers to focus on larger duty concerns.

In addition, a series of long-term questions about safety must be asked, incorporating not only the demonstrated threats of today but the potential threats on the horizon, such as the impact of nanotechnology, the possible disasters resulting from corruption of the Internet and other cyberattacks, and the remote but possible geological cataclysms similar to the December 2004 earthquake and tsunami. These questions include how the perception of officer safety may change over time. Would law enforcement agencies be satisfied today with 1970s-level training? If not, what training would the profession expect to develop, change, and deliver over the next decade? For patrol officers, what has changed and what will change?

Deeper questions are embedded in the safety issue. Over the next decade, what changes will occur in the jurisdiction of the police? Will the police role become altered? What is the profession developing, products or lifelong learners? Is the patrol officer of tomorrow a combatant; a peace officer; an information warrior; a community builder; or a flexible, agile public servant who needs the attributes of all of those roles? The distinct survival disadvantages of going one-on-one against a terrorist armed with chemical or biological agents should turn the focus back onto prevention, the gathering of intelligence that will prove useful across a broad spectrum of issues affecting the police.

Looking at management itself, what is the proper role of hierarchy? Is it primarily information systems serving the line officer? Or, must it remain an industrial-age artifact of controlling behavior? Is it possible to adapt and do both? What applicant must an agency hire today who can lead it 15 years hence? What will those leaders look like?

## Conclusion

The future of officer safety in an age of terrorism raises many questions. Some may prove extremely hard to answer. Ultimately, though, the unifying question is, Will we in law enforcement continue to venerate our dysfunctional past, or will we see change as our friend? If crisis does indeed present an opportunity for positive change, the crisis of global terrorism offers us a chance to use an issue of deep emotional significance to all officers, regardless of other interests, to begin to move larger questions forward.

## Endnotes

1   For additional information, see Anthony J. Pinizzotto, Edward F. Davis, and Charles E. Miller III, "Escape from the Killing Zone," *FBI Law Enforcement Bulletin,* March 2002, 1–7.

2   Both authors have extensive experience in the law enforcement profession and have actively participated in the Futures Working Group, including Dr. Levin's recent contribution as the futurist in residence at the FBI Academy.

3   Bryan Vila and Dennis J. Kenney, National Institute of Justice, "Tired Cops: The Prevalence and Potential Consequences of Police Fatigue," NU Journal 248 (2000): 17–21; retrieved on May 3, 2005, from http://www.ncjrs.org/pdffdesl/jr000248d.pdf.

4   Juan Forero, "IRA Men Accused of Aiding Rebels to Go on Trial in Colombia," *The New York Times;* retrieved on October 5, 2002, from http://www.nytimes.com/2002/10/04/international/americas/04BOGO.html.

5   Lizette Alvarez, "Police Fear IRA Is Turning Expertise to Organized Crime," *The New York Times;* retrieved on January 19, 2005, from http://www.nytimes.com/ 2005/01/19/international/europe/19ireland.html.

## Review Questions

1.  Discuss the essential strategies to include in officer training to prepare them for safety in an age of terrorism.

# 6 Elements That Form a Context for Staff Safety
*Jesse W Doyle*

One of the important elements of maintaining an effective correctional organization is to address key staff concerns. Throughout my 25-year career in juvenile corrections, one of the issues that has consistently concerned staff, particularly those who work the front line, is personal safety.

When a facility becomes unstable and the number of staff injuries begin to rise, many staff look to someone other than themselves to make their environment feel safer. Whether perceived threats to safety are real, such as several documented group disturbances, or unreal, including false stories of a group disturbance or a riot that occurred five years ago in an otherwise trouble-free environment, staff look to management for answers. More often than not, management reacts to staff concerns by addressing them piecemeal. For example, if staff on a particular unit have been involved in an increased number of resident restraints and some staff have expressed concern for their safety, an immediate response may be to transfer those employees to another location or temporarily increase staffing on the unit until the problems subside.

Managers often are reactive, rather than proactive, when it comes to staff safety. Although addressing an immediate problem is a quick fix, management periodically must step back to look at staff safety from a systemic point of view. Managers must consider the fact that staff safety occurs within the context of the organization's total environment.

Likewise, the context for staff safety in a juvenile correctional facility is the environment in which the facility operates. The various structures that are created within the facility support all its elements, including staff safety. In this article, six elements of environmental structure that form a context for staff safety are discussed: physical plant, behavior management, staff relationship with youths, policies and procedures, supervision and staff training.

## Physical Plant

**Building.** The building defines structure by limiting the movement of inmates within its walls. A well-designed building will enhance staff safety in many ways. One example is Ahat the building's structure can be used to separate occupants into small groups, which will minimize contagion behavior that may occur when an isolated incident affects the larger groups. In a dormitory-type situation, even a small disturbance can lead to everyone in the dormitory getting involved. Living quarters with individual rooms can be used to isolate inmates. On the other hand, a poorly designed building may diminish staff safety. If the building is designed with blind spots, inmates may conspire away from staff supervision behind blind corners or walls that are not designed with good sight lines. Staff also can be isolated and overpowered in places where blind spots exist. Many older institutions were inadvertently designed with blind spots.

**Security system.** In this article, the physical security system is described as part of the physical plant because it generally is attached to the building's structure. These devices extend the listening and viewing ranges of security personnel. Visual and audio equipment can enhance staff safety by adding an additional pair of eyes and ears to a work area. The presence of video cameras allows staff to monitor inmate activities in real time. As a result, their response time can be reduced during emergencies.

**Reprinted from *Corrections Today Magazine,* Oct. 2001, pp. 101–105 with permission of the American Correctional Association, Lanham, MD.**

**Perimeter barriers.** Whether a wall or a fence, a perimeter barrier keeps residents in a defined space and keeps out intruders. Perimeter barriers define the spatial limits of those enclosed by the defined physical boundaries. The barriers greatly reduce attempted escapes, at the same time, reducing the chance that staff will get hurt running after and stopping attempted escapees.

**Rooms, doors and locks.** Rooms, doors and locks serve as limited defined structural barriers. As with perimeter barriers, doors and locks help keep inmates in and intruders out. In terms of safety, doors and locks protect staff from out-of-control inmates. When used wisely, they help to modify offenders' behavior and help them conform to social standards espoused in their environment.

## Behavior Management

A behavior management system helps structure the inmates' environment and achieve desired outcomes. A behavior management system gives its participants rewards for socially accepted behavior. A good system provides clear guidelines for socially acceptable behavior and rewards to reinforce expected behavior. When residents buy into the behavior management system, they learn to delay gratification to achieve external rewards. The inmates' ability to repeatedly delay immediate gratification lays the groundwork for self-discipline, which will lead to an ordered way of life once discipline is internalized.

Behavior management systems help improve staff safety by having inmates take part in their own behavior control. In a well-implemented system, the authority of all staff to authorize desired rewards for positive behavior equalizes their worth across the board. This means that regardless of the staff member, there is equal opportunity to authorize rewards and sanctions as stated in the behavior management system.

Long ago, when people entered the juvenile corrections field, they were interviewed and given start dates. When they first reported to work, they were given keys and directions to a residential unit, which did not have a behavior management system. All too often in such an environment, a person's success depended on his or her size and physical prowess. What counted was the ability to stand up to youths and if necessary, overpower them if they got out of control. For the people who did not have brute strength or street skills, their authority and value were limited.

During that time, a well-implemented behavior management system would have been beneficial. Staff gained value by virtue of the organization. Staff safety is increased when residents view them as having value. Further, the tangible and intangible rewards given to residents support a stable environmental structure.

## Staff and Resident Relationships

The structure of staff relationships with the juvenile offenders in their care is the most critical component for staff safety in a juvenile corrections environment. Unlike the adult system, in which the structure of the environment is supported by an abundance of aids, such as cell extraction devices, and weapons, such as stun guns, the juvenile system is excluded, often by law or public mandate, from using many such items. They also do not use lethal weapons, such as firearms, and although the use of chemicals, such as pepper spray, is on the rise throughout the country, only a small group of organizations allows the use of such agents.

For the most part, juvenile corrections staff must depend on their relationships with offenders to create a safe environment for themselves and others. Healthy relationships between staff and juveniles form the basis of a safe and secure environment. No matter how much correctional knowledge staff have, they must be able to generate the warmth and strength needed to make contact with juveniles. Most juveniles will gravitate toward their peer group and bond with staff if they feel valued by them.

There are many ways staff can encourage juvenile offenders to value them without violating policies and procedures or personal integrity. The type of relationship staff form with the juveniles depends on the role they play—the expected behavior they agreed to display when they were hired. The operational idea is appropriateness of behavior.

How do staff behave in the context of a juvenile corrections setting? As soon as the juveniles meet staff, they begin to define their relationship with staff in their environment. The juveniles determine what is expected of them and if they will be able to "get one over" on staff.

As offenders increase their interactions with staff, their uncertainty diminishes as they receive feedback from staff as well as their peers. Exchange of information between staff and juveniles clarifies and structures the relationship accordingly. Staff often develop relationships based on role behavior. For example, a juvenile may ask a staff member to make a phone call and although the staff member knows the youth does not deserve the privilege, he or she will allow it based on fear or an inability to handle conflict. As a result, the staff member has acted "out of role" or outside the expected behavior associated with his or her position. As actors learn roles in theatrical productions, staff can teach juveniles how to function as members of a juvenile correctional institution.

Correctional staff must treat juveniles with respect and compassion. At the same time, they must set appropriate limits and enforce the organization's rules and procedures. When staff enforce expected roles for juveniles and treat them with respect, they make it possible for youths to conform to rules and behave even before they are capable of understanding and controlling their behavior. For example, a youth may not understand the value of an education but may attend a class because he or she has a friendly relationship with a supervising staff member. The importance of relationships in juvenile correctional settings cannot be understated.

Unfortunately, there are staff who are verbally and physically abusive to juveniles throughout their stays in institutions. Those people tend to wonder why the juveniles return the abuse whenever the opportunity arises. For example, a staff member in a juvenile correctional facility complained during a staff meeting that he feared for his safety in the community. He said he had encountered several juveniles who he had supervised before they were released. He explained that the juveniles had accosted him outside a store, shouted expletives at him and reminded him of how he treated them while they were in custody. Although several other staff members stated they had had positive experiences with juveniles they ran into outside the facility, this staff member refused to acknowledge that his treatment of the juveniles inside the facility had a direct bearing on their attitude toward him in the community.

Staff's role is to set boundaries for juveniles and to hold them accountable for their behavior while maintaining a safe environment, which must be done in a humane and caring manner. Staff must discipline the juveniles, but they also can help the youths acquire new skills that will help them be successful in the facility and eventually in the community.

Another staff role is to help juveniles develop confidence. Staff who model appropriate behavior for youths to emulate help youths embrace the organization's way of life and follow its values.

The development of interpersonal competencies helps youths negotiate their needs. As juveniles increasingly meet their needs as a result of their interpersonal competence, they are less likely to risk their gains by going against facility norms. Youths need a sense of worth and belonging, as well as values clarification—a sense of right and wrong. Experiences with staff and other youths influence and shape their behavior along with attitudes about themselves and others. The experience teaches youths how to be responsible and relate to others in their environment - both adults and peers. When staff relate to juveniles positively by setting limits and demonstrating fairness, consistency and caring, juveniles develop healthy interpersonal skills, which lead to competence. Competence leads to confidence and confidence helps youths try newly learned skills. Skills acquisition begets more competence and confidence and leads to increased skill acquisition. When staff develop relationships with juveniles that reinforce this cyclical process, they help to create and maintain a safe environment for themselves and everyone around them.

## Policies and Procedures

Every organization must develop policies and procedures to maintain a standard for consistent implementation of rules and regulations. A policies and procedures manual provides staff with a systematic method for implementing the mission, goals and objectives of the organization. Policies reflect organization philosophy, provide a framework and structure for the activities of the facility and guide decision-making. Procedures determine the tasks that will be completed, define who will carry out the tasks and when they will be implemented, and provide the step-by-step process of how to complete the policy. It also ensures conformity in the organization. Further, a policies and procedures manual is the authority on how things are done, eliminating guesswork. Policies and procedures provide structure to the organization by minimizing potential conflicts among staff. For example, each staff member brings a different set of values, beliefs and behaviors to the job. Without the guidance provided by policies and procedures, staff are left to make their own varied decisions.

They begin to create their own rules and behaviors. This situation creates the perfect environment for juveniles to manipulate staff and eventually leads to unsafe conditions. Clear and consistent communication among staff and between staff and juveniles is essential. Clearly written, thoughtful, thorough and consistently implemented policies and procedures enhance the opportunity for safe conditions.

## Supervision

An effective supervisor must reflect a guiding vision, strong values and organizational beliefs. His or her job is to remind staff of the rules that are needed to shape their behavior for their benefit as well as the organization's. The supervisor must consistently and clearly communicate what the system requires to maintain its structure, form and stability. This task is deceptively simple: It is easy to articulate but difficult to implement. For example, in many organizations, each time a crisis occurs, the tendency is to create a new policy or change parts of the system. In most cases, when an in-depth review of a crisis is completed, it is not the lack of written policies that created the crisis, it is the failure of supervisors to effectively and consistently direct staff to implement system processes.

## Staff Training

Before an organization can move forward, it must have an adequate number of well-trained staff and supervisors, particularly at critical junctures, such as the nexus between front line staff and supervisors.

Effective recruitment is the best way to develop a well-trained staff. If self-centered, ill-tempered, abusive people are hired, no amount of training will make them effective. After staff are carefully screened and hired, training is essential. First, a proper assessment of the knowledge, skills and abilities needed for corrections must be completed. Once training needs have been determined, use of adjunct trainers from the organization's various disciplines have proved effective.

Classroom training enables staff to gain knowledge and, to a smaller degree, skills and abilities, but it does not fully prepare them for the day-to-day events they will face in the actual workplace. The dilemma is how do staff transfer classroom learning to practical application?

Two methods used to transfer learning are on-the-job training and direct supervision. On-the-job training allows staff to complete tasks under the supervision of more experienced staff and receive direct feedback. Also, it allows them to observe the more experienced staff. For the organization to work well, it must generate replication. On-the-job training and continuous supervision help support this process.

## Conclusion

When large organizational structures are developed as a context for staff safety, staff are able to look at emerging themes and patterns as well as isolated causes. Viewed this way, they begin to see how multiple forces work together to shape the organization. Effective implementation of the structures of the organization is an integral part of its safety. When effective structures are designed and put in place, the organization replicates itself on all levels. Implementing systems to develop structures helps staff come together in their various disciplines to effectively and efficiently perform their jobs. It also creates a context for staff safety.

## Reference

Wheatley, Margaret J. 1992. *Leadership and the new science.* San Francisco: Clear Communication/The Graphic Solution.

## Review Questions

1. Discuss the 6 elements that form the foundation to enhance correctional officer safety.

# Officer Survival
*James Hurley*

The number of attacks on law enforcement officers has increased dramatically. Not only are officers being attacked more frequently, the attacks are also more vicious and deadly.

Officers need to hone their survival skills-particularly in the area of identifying the indicators of aggression—so that they can be prepared for an attack before it happens. Identifying indicators of aggression early on will provide valuable seconds to plan for the attack as well as planning to win the confrontation.

Following are some of the most common indicators of aggression. Being able to identify them quickly is imperative to being prepared for an assault:

**Bladed Stance.** A person standing with his hands in the bladed position is indicative of an impending strike.

**Folded Arm Stance.** This is symbolic of several forms of resistance and aggression. Folded arms create a physical barrier between the officer and the subject. The folded arms, symbolic of personal space that the suspect is defending, are a barrier to communication and a defiant show of the subject's lack of respect for the officer and his authority.

**Hands On Hips.** This is a strong indicator of aggression where the subject is representing his authority during the situation.

**Invasion of Personal Space.** Space is indicative of confrontation. Invasion of personal territory is often a test to see how far the subject can push the officer. Immediate response by the officer is critical. Quickly and firmly push the subject away, reinforcing the action with a strong verbal command of "GET BACK." This creates distance and sends the message that the officer will not allow his space to be compromised.

**Finger Pointing.** This is a sign of impending aggressive action. The officer needs to deal with this behavior immediately and decisively in order to establish his authority and avoid a physical confrontation.

**Wandering Attention.** A subject looking around instead of paying attention to the officer is a common indicator remembered by officers who were assaulted. It may be the subject's final assessment of his chance to succeed in the attack.

**Ignoring Verbal Commands.** This is a sign of defiance and indicates a willingness to physically challenge the person issuing the command. This is commonly seen in subjects who ignore the command to stop and walk away from an officer. If the officer pursues the subject, the subject is in control of the situation, not the officer. The subject knows what his next move will be-placing the officer at a considerable disadvantage as he attempts to apprehend the subject.

**Other Indicators.** Several other common indicators are the subject who continues to pace; subject standing with fists clenched; and subject talking through clenched teeth.

**New Indicators of Aggression.** With the growth of organized gangs there are certain gang-related indicators of aggression that need to be recognized. Some are associated specifically with the gang culture but will certainly find their way into the mainstream of society.

**Spitting.** A subject who spits on the ground in the presence of a police officer is indicating his defiance of the officer's authority.

**Reprinted from** *Law and Order Magazine,* **June 2000, pp. 112–114 with permission from** *Law and Order Magazine.*

**Grabbing the Groin Area.** A subject who grabs his groin area and then lifts his arm in an upward motion is giving the officer the "F--- Off" salute. It is the ultimate sign of defiance in many gang cultures.

**Emotional Mood Swings.** Officers should pay special attention to suspects who display dramatic mood swings such as going from laughing to crying in a relatively short period of time.

There are other important factors to consider also. Studies indicate that 70 percent of police deaths in the line of duty involve alcohol. Officers should pay extra attention to intoxicated suspects, who are statistically more likely to become involved in violent physical confrontations with officers.

Every police officer needs to be prepared to win physical or armed encounters at all times. Mental alertness can mean the difference between winning and losing an encounter. The following four-step strategy can assist officers in winning physical and armed encounters.

*Recognizing the Threat.* Officers need to constantly survey every situation they encounter for threat indicators. The majority of attacks on police officers are preceded by body language such as those mentioned that indicate aggressive behavior is imminent.

*Accept the Threat.* By recognizing signs of aggression, officers will be able to accept that there is an imminent threat to their safety. With this knowledge they can readily move to tactical preparation.

*An Action Plan.* An officer who recognizes a threat and accepts that it is going to happen can formulate a plan to survive and win the encounter. A plan of action should include creating distance and being conscious of possible cover, as well as being prepared to use diversionary tactics. The best defense is to have a planned strategy to overcome an attacker before he takes aggressive action against you.

*Execute Plan.* As an assault or armed encounter begins, execute your plan in order to survive and win. Move to previously identified cover. Use distance and movement to make yourself less of a target. Create diversions to effect your escape to safety. Most subjects do not expect officers to be prepared for attacks or to have a pre-planned response. A planned response Will likely defeat the aggressive or armed suspect.

Officers must continually train and educate themselves in the techniques that provide a tactical edge, particularly when conducting investigative and traffic stops. These are situations where officers are commonly attacked and there are specific tactical advantages that officers should adhere to maintain the edge.

Never give field sobriety tests alone. Alcohol impairs the suspect's judgment, which increases the likelihood of an assault. A lone officer monitoring a field sobriety test is not focused on identifying signs of danger and may become an easy target. A second officer present can monitor the suspect's behavior while the first officer conducts the sobriety tests.

Conduct traffic stops from the passenger side. This approach puts the officer at a tactical advantage as creates distance between the officer and the driver. The officer is less of a target and provides more time to perceive and react to danger.

Avoid the "hamburger zone." Never cross between the front of the patrol vehicle and the rear of a suspect's vehicle. This eliminates the possibility of being pinned in between the two vehicles.

The importance of being prepared cannot be stressed enough. As assaults on police officers continue to rise, it is important for every officer to be able to identify the signs of aggression and be prepared for an attack before it happens. The early identification of these indicators can provide the opportunity to defeat an attack.

While most officers are trained in tactics to survive attacks and armed encounters, trainers must focus on training officers not only to survive but also to win these encounters.

**Review Questions**

1. Identify and explain 10 indicators of aggression officers should look out for in the line of duty.

2. Describe the 4-step strategies that can assist officers in winning physical and armed encounters.

# Surviving an Off-Duty Encounter
*Michael T. Rayburn*

It is the duty of police administrators and law enforcement trainers to guide and train officers in the tactics they need to survive on the street. Much training time is spent on how to react and survive while working in this profession. Any officer will tell you that the most important thing is that he goes home at the end of his shift. However, being a police officer is a 24-hour job—and not just an eight-hour tour of duty.

Being a police officer is a way of life. To neighbors you're the "cop who lives next door." To the people who recognize you out in the grocery store or at the mall shopping, it's "How are you today, Officer?" To the average citizen you're the police—it makes no difference to them whether you're wearing your uniform or not.

Yet little training time is spent on off-duty survival techniques. Administrators and trainers alike seem to minimize the fact that police officers are recognized as such 24 hours a day—regardless of whether your jurisdiction states that you do not have police officer status 24 hours a day and are not required to act off-duty. To the EDP neighbor who lives down the street or the criminal element who recognizes you in the mall, you are the police. Many of us have had neighbors knock on our doors looking for police assistance or legal advice.

That's why officers must be trained in the tactics necessary to survive an off-duty encounter. To do this we must draw on the basic tactics used each day while on duty. The case histories of officers killed in the line of duty while off-duty show that these officers failed to employ some basic officer safety fundamentals—basic fundamentals that they all practiced while on duty.

First and foremost, always be aware of your surroundings. This doesn't mean that you become paranoid and constantly look over your shoulder. But stay aware of where you are and who is around you.

An officer from an upstate New York department was vacationing with his family in Florida. While waiting in line with his children to get onto an amusement park ride he heard his name called out from the back of the line. The officer turned around to see a hometown drug dealer along with a group of friends waving at the officer.

Along with being aware of your surroundings, mentally prepare yourself and your family for an off-duty encounter. Have a plan of action and discuss it with your family so they know exactly what is expected of them. We teach family members what to do in case of a fire in the home, yet we neglect to teach them what to do in the event we have to become involved off-duty.

Being mentally prepared and having a plan may mean simply going to a safe location from which to call the police and being a good witness. No jurisdiction requires that an officer intervene in a situation where it would be suicidal for the officer to do so.

Consider the case of the off-duty State Police Officer who was shopping at a local grocery store with his wife when a masked robber entered the store armed with a sawed-off shotgun. With the assistance of his wife the officer was able to usher the store patrons to a safe location. The unarmed Trooper then ran back to the front of the store and tackled the armed robber, causing both of them to fall through a plate glass window. The gunman rose to his feet and fatally shot the officer in the chest.

Before you put that plan into action, think about what you are about to do and know your limitations.

Are you mentally prepared to handle the situation? Can you physically handle the situation and physically control the suspect if need be? What are your equipment limitations? Most off-duty officers don't carry portable radios and ballistic vests with them-a number of officers don't even carry a weapon off-duty. Or, if they do, the weapon is not readily available.

Two off-duty Sheriff's deputies were waiting in a beauty salon for a friend to finish work when two armed men entered demanding money and valuables. The officers had their badges and identification

**Reprinted from** *Law and Order Magazine,* **Aug. 2000, pp. 99–102 with permission from** *Law and Order Magazine.*

with them but had left their weapons in their vehicle. When the robbers discovered the officers' identities they fatally shot the male officer in the back of the head with a revolver.

Always carry a weapon with you and carry it in a location that is easily accessible. It's better to have a gun and not need it, than to need a gun and not have one.

Many officers who work the streets carry their duty weapon and a backup weapon and keep extra ammo in their duty bag. Yet they leave the stationhouse without any weapons on them at the end of their shift.

Some jurisdictions don't allow their officers to carry off-duty. If you are authorized, always carry a weapon with you and go to the range to practice drawing and shooting that weapon while wearing street clothes. Be familiar with the weapon and the difficulties of drawing that weapon from the location you've chosen to conceal it.

Also consider carrying a ballistic vest in the trunk of your car. If you've been on the job for a while, you probably have an old vest lying around. Dust it off and have some large "POLICE" patches sewn onto it or get a new cover made for it.

Body armor manufacturers claim the ballistic capability of vests deteriorates over time. I took a vest out to the range that had been worn by an officer every day that he was on duty for 15 years. The vest was shot multiple times with different caliber handgun ammunition with no penetration. I have never heard of even an old vest failing to stop a round for which it was rated.

If the situation warrants it and you have time, put that old vest on. You may not have 100 percent confidence in the vest, but it's better than nothing. It can also identify you as a police officer to other officers on the scene or those who arrive after the incident is over.

If other officers are already on the scene and you are off-duty and in plain clothes, discretion may tell you to wait on identifying yourself and drawing your weapon. The other officer may still mistake you for a second gunman, but you also have given yourself away and lost the element of surprise if there is a second bad guy.

Use the principles of contact and cover. If the other officer has the situation somewhat controlled, stay back and act as a cover officer, watch his back. If the situation starts to go downhill you will have to identify yourself and get involved. But until that happens, for your safety and his, stay back and act as a cover officer.

Recently an off-duty police officer lost his life to "friendly fire." While he was getting a snack at a late night eatery a fight broke out among a group of females. The fight spilled out into the parking lot as 911 was called. When one of the combatants yelled to her boyfriend, "Get the gun," the career criminal grabbed a small caliber handgun. He was brandishing it as two uniformed officers arrived. Apparently wanting to assist the uniformed officers, the off-duty officer exited the restaurant with his gun drawn. The uniformed officers commanded the career criminal to "Drop the weapon."

Mistakenly identifying the off-duty officer as a second gunman, the officers repeated their command to him. The criminal complied but the off-duty officer held onto his weapon and pointed it at the criminal. The uniformed officers felt they were "close to his line of fire" and perceived the off-duty officer as a threat. The off-duty officer, who either didn't hear the command or thought it was directed at the criminal, held onto his weapon and the two uniformed officers opened fire. The off-duty officer died later in a hospital.

Identifying yourself should be a big concern if you decide to get involved in a situation while off-duty. Too many officers have been wounded or killed by other officers who did not recognize them as law enforcement personnel. If possible get your badge out there side by side with your weapon. Obviously you won't always have the time to get your badge out with your weapon, but as soon as possible get your badge out to identify yourself.

In high stress situations officers get tunnel vision, reducing their vision by up to 70 percent. They focus on the threat-and the threat is the weapon. Getting the badge out there side by side with your weapon will help to reduce the risks of an accidental shooting.

Use loud verbal commands when you are involved off-duty. If you have to confront someone, shout in a loud clear voice, "Police—don't move!"

If another officer confronts you, don't ever turn towards the officer with your weapon. Respond by saying, "Don't shoot, I'm a police officer!" They may still require you to put your weapon down. They may even handcuff you until your identity can be confirmed. For everyone's safety, do what the officers tell you to do. Apologies will come later. Any uniformed officer on the scene is in charge until the scene is deemed safe for all those concerned.

Officers seem to forget the survival basics taught them or think they don't apply when they are off the clock. How else to explain the lack of tactical thinking?

They are the simplest of mistakes, but they are costing officers their lives. According to the FBI, between 1986 to 1995 one out of seven officers killed in the line of duty in the United States was off-duty. Administrators and trainers alike need to rethink attitudes toward off-duty officers and incorporate off-duty survival tactics into training.

This is not just a chosen profession, it is a chosen way of life. You're a police officer every minute of each day.

## Review Questions

1. Discuss the off duty survival tactics that should be included in police training program.

# Inmate Transportation: Safety Is the Priority

*Carlos Jackson and Sharon Johnson Rion*

Sheriffs, jail administrators, police chiefs, public safety directors and wardens share a common challenge—the safe, secure and humane transfer of hundreds of thousands of inmates per year. Although inmate transportation has been a part of corrections and law enforcement since the inception of America's criminal justice system, the demand to move so many, so often and so far, has increased in the last 10 to 15 years, thus, further challenging existing resources to meet the need, often instead of, or in competition with, other equally essential operations.

Prior to 1990, few state departments of correction had centralized transportation units. Similarly, county sheriffs, local law enforcement and detention personnel did not incorporate specialized transportation units or transportation overtime as major budget items. However, units and overtime now are in the budget, and the U.S. Marshals Service has established its own air service to accommodate the increased demand.

While there is not an easy solution for balancing agency goals and objectives with diminishing resources, there are some fundamentals to be considered in establishing an inmate transportation operation, program or unit. Whether one is moving a detainee from the local jail across town for a court appearance, transferring an inmate from one prison to another, or extraditing a fugitive cross-country, the basic principles of good security and inmate management apply.

## Policies and Procedures

It is hard to imagine any agency establishing and maintaining fundamental security and offender management without first developing a game plan. Policy and procedures must be developed with and coordinated among all principals and agencies involved. Think of the challenges federal, state and local officials face when transporting high-profile in-mates. Also consider the routine movement of large numbers of inmates across jurisdictional lines by the Federal Bureau of Prisons, U.S. Marshals Service and private inmate transportation companies. Such work is not accomplished by happenstance.

However, simple a move may appear, each requires planning. An established game plan, known to and complied by all concerned, will ensure an assessment of a potential escape or disruptive behavior, reduce possible miscommunication between staff and should circumvent inefficient time in court, missed medical appointments and overtime.

There are innumerable factors to be considered when moving inmates outside correctional facilities. While the scope and complexity of some factors of transport are relative to the number of agencies involved, jurisdictions to be traversed and miles traveled, the fundamentals are the same. Therefore, it is not possible to ensure that adequate equipment, staff, inter/intra-agency communication and information exchange, subject-specific training and applicable regulations have been addressed without developing policies and procedures.

## Communication

Communication between agencies and staff is challenging. Needless to say, that difficulty is magnified as agencies involved in the transportation of one or more inmates increase. Consequently, when multiple agencies—courts, doctors' offices, hospitals, other correctional facilities and law enforcement agencies—are involved, it is essential to share and confirm information to eliminate inefficiency and risky events.

Lines of communication must be established and shared with all applicable agencies and individuals. Staff members from each organization exchanging information about all or specified aspects of the

Reprinted from *Corrections Today Magazine,* July 2001, pp. 110–113 with permission from American Correctional Association, Lanham, MD.

transport need to know the game plan and work accordingly. If staff on one shift initiate the move, but staff on the next shift process the inmate back into the facility, all necessary information must be shared between personnel on both shifts. Likewise, when reception center staff members use a centralized transportation unit to initiate moving an inmate to another facility, they should provide transportation officers with appropriate information and inform staff at the receiving facility. Ensuring that everyone is in the communication loop will promote cooperation and prevent miscommunication, which often is the root cause of lax security.

Communication should be proactive and, at the same time, maintain appropriate information and record confidentiality. For example, while it is essential for transportation staff to know the exact location and time of a doctor's appointment, it is not appropriate for staff to read confidential medical records. Corrections personnel and extradition staff need to be advised of and comply with applicable rules and regulations regarding confidentiality of all aspects of adult and juvenile detainee and inmate information. Interestingly, discussions of inmate transportation communication often exclude the verbal exchange between staff and offenders. Personnel transporting inmates should be trained in interpersonal communication skills in order to assist staff in establishing expectations, resolving conflicts and maintaining professional distance.

## Risk Assessment and Reduction

The best opportunity for escape is when inmates are transported outside correctional facilities. Thus, the rule is simple: Know inmates' risk factors and plan accordingly. The goal is equally simple: retain custody and contain disruptive behavior.

When preparing to transport an inmate, it always is necessary to assess the individual's potential for escape, unruliness, assault or other safety threats. Through assessment practices, include an examination of any and all of the following information that is available and applicable: criminal history, length of sentence, severity of current charges, outstanding charges, assault and escape history, behavior during confinement, mental health status and medical condition. In the absence of necessary information to adequately assess an inmate, assume the highest level of risk and deploy security accordingly.

Although security is a primary risk, there are other risk factors to be considered, such as medical condition, medication requirements and vulnerability. In order to increase staff and public protection, established procedures should require universal precautions, medical review and clearance for travel. Appropriate medical personnel should provide written instructions for transportation staff regarding each and every inmate. Medical stipulations need to be clear, legible and easily understood by nonmedical personnel.

When it is necessary to transport male and female offenders at the same time, gender separation is essential. Likewise, if juveniles and adults are transported in the same vehicle, separation must be maintained. To further reduce risk and ensure protection of transportation personnel from allegations of sexual impropriety, it is recommended that female staff transport female offenders.

## Staff and Equipment

Staff assigned to transportation duties require specialized training, including use of restraints and force, searches, universal precautions, offender rights, transportation of special management inmates, first aid/CPR, interpersonal communications, applicable weapons certification, self-defense, record-keeping, map reading, emergency response and applicable regulations.

Transportation personnel job expectations also should specify responsibilities for: receiving and maintaining proper paperwork, timely arrivals and departures, proper maintenance and use of equipment, compliance with medical instructions, confidential handling of inmate records, emergency preparedness, and maintaining positive communication with the public, court officials and staff from other agencies.

One component of required equipment for inmate transportation is communications equipment. Using more than one type of communication equipment must be considered. Some equipment can be permanently installed in the vehicle, however, personnel also need to be able to communicate outside the vehicle.

The array of security equipment available to transport inmates ranges from handcuffs, leg irons, chains and black boxes to stun belts, hand guns, pepper spray and other weapons. Regardless of the equipment, staff must be trained how to properly use and subsequently document use of this equipment.

Transportation staff assigned to drive vehicles that require more than a standard driver's license must maintain current certification and licensing consistent with applicable state and federal Department of Transportation and Federal Aviation Administration (FAA) regulations. Likewise, all vehicles must be registered, licensed and maintained consistent with good safety practices. Agency administrators and transportation staff need to be familiar and comply with mandated vehicle maintenance and usage record-keeping.

The decision to transport inmates by commercial air carriers should take into account custody level and requisite security, airline rules and FAA requirements. The decision to move inmates by private transport should consider the company's history of compliance with applicable regulations. All inmates transported by commercial carriers should be restrained. Technology is available to provide secure methods of restraint that will minimize unnecessary attention when inmates are being transported in and among the general public.

## Emergency Preparedness

While proper planning will address most contingencies, it is impossible to predict and prepare for every possible occurrence. Nevertheless, it is essential to have a backup plan coordinated with other agencies. Clearly, emergency preparedness is a must for staff training and retraining. It is particularly useful for staff to conduct training exercises during which they respond to mock emergencies.

The importance of prepared staff is amplified by their isolation from normal support systems. When an emergency is the result of an inmate assault or other disruptive behavior, this isolation results in increased staff vulnerability. When the emergency is caused by a source outside the control of staff and inmates on board the vehicle, a ready response from prepared staff may minimize the vulnerability of both.

It may be helpful, while planning emergency responses to predictable scenarios, to determine the extent and type of communications equipment needed during routine inmate transport. This is the time to ensure that there are no "dead spots" for radio or cellular equipment or, if there are, how to compensate for them. It is better to find out these deficiencies during the planning stage than when an emergency occurs.

## Federal and State Regulations

Moving a single inmate or several inmates from one location to another may be the mission at hand, however, maintaining public safety is the ultimate goal. Popular television and Hollywood stereotypes notwithstanding, most local, state and federal correctional agencies have long since addressed the growing need to transport inmates from town to town or cross-county. The result has been that thousands of juvenile and adult inmates are moved daily without incident, with little, if any, notice by the public. However, like so many other aspects of correctional work, it only takes one escape of a violent offender during a transportation run to increase public scrutiny. When this occurs, it is in everyone's best interest that staff step back and re-examine policies and procedures.

This subject matter is important enough that it is has been regulated by statute in some states for several years. More recently, federal legislation—the Interstate Transportation of Dangerous Criminals Act of 2000—was passed in late December and mandates the establishment of minimum standards for the transportation of violent inmates.

The following provisions are included:

- Background checks and pre-employment drug testing for potential employees;
- Minimum standards for the length and type of training that employees must undergo before they can transport inmates;
- Restrictions on the number of hours that employees can be on duty during a given time period;
- Minimum standards for employee uniforms and identification;
- Requirement that violent offenders wear brightly colored clothing clearly identifying them as inmates;
- Minimum standards for restraints to be used;
- Advance notification to local law enforcement officials of scheduled stops in their jurisdictions;
- Notification requirements in the event of escapes; and Minimum standards for the safety of violent offenders.

Many look at these requirements as par for the course or inherently found in correctional hiring practices and well-developed policy and procedures. Nonetheless, all can benefit from a comprehensive review of internal practices. A self-regulated industry with solid procedures encompassing the scope of the above-referenced legislation will go a long way toward continuing to solidify correctional professionalism. There are ample and appropriate procedures, long established by both the public and private agencies handling inmate transportation, to serve as models for these federally mandated requirements.

**Review questions**

1. Discuss the safety precautions you need to apply during transportation of inmates.

# Firefighter Hydration During Rehab
*Derek Williams*

Fighting fire is hard work. This has been a universal truth since the inception of the fire service. No amount of tactics, resources, or technological progress will change this fact. One thing that has changed over the past 100-plus years of the modern day fire service is that firefighter rehab is absolutely necessary. We have come a long way in the concept of firefighter rehab, but there is always room for improvement. Specialty apparatus with comfortable seating, air-conditioning, misting systems, and other amenities specifically designed for rehab are certainly a plus. However, you don't need to spend millions to have an effective rehab sector.

Following National Fire Protection Association (NFPA) 1584, *Recommended Practice on the Rehabilitation of Members Operating at Incident Scene Operations and Training Exercises*, does not require that you have a huge budget at your disposal.[1] An effective rehab area can be set up using very simple concepts and tools. This article addresses one component of rehab: firefighter hydration.

## The Definition And Function of Hydration

What is dehydration, and what does it do to the body? Our bodies are made up of about two-thirds water. When someone gets dehydrated, it means the amount of water in the body has dropped below the level needed for normal body function. Under normal circumstances, we lose about two to 2.5 liters of water a day through body waste, sweat, and breathing. Nutrition experts recommend a daily fluid intake of about 1.5 to 2.5 liters for healthy adults under normal living circumstances to prevent a liquid deficit. Small decreases don't cause problems and go completely unnoticed in most cases. Losing large amounts of water (in excess of 2 percent of body weight) can be a problem.

Strenuous work, particularly in protective clothing and in hot environments, can result in a loss of one to two liters of water an hour. At this rate, a firefighter may rapidly lose a significant amount of body water weight (the amount of water the body contains under normal conditions based on the size and weight of an individual). A loss of 1 to 2 percent of body water weight will compromise work performance, a loss of 2 to 3 percent will compromise mental alertness, and a loss of 3 to 5 percent can compromise the body's ability to sustain life.[2] Thirst is one indicator of dehydration, but it is not an early warning sign. By the time you feel thirsty, you may already be dehydrated.[3] Other symptoms of dehydration include the following:

- ☐ dizziness and lightheadedness;
- ☐ headache;
- ☐ a dry or sticky mouth;
- ☐ nausea/vomiting;
- ☐ excessive fatigue, general discomfort, irritability, and unusually decreased work performance; and
- ☐ production of less urine and darker urine.[4]

Urine color is the best low-tech monitoring tool for detecting possible dehydration. *Note*: If you are taking a vitamin supplement, this method will not be an accurate indicator; vitamins affect urine color. Clear urine is an indicator that you are very well hydrated. If the urine is light yellow or straw colored, you are sufficiently hydrated and not in any immediate danger. However, if your urine is a dark yellow color, you are already in the early stages of dehydration. Beginning a firefight at this stage may be the precursor to advanced dehydration or worse.[5] Dehydration often leads to heat cramps, heat exhaustion, and possibly even heat stroke.

**Reprinted from *Fire Engineering Magazine*, Dec. 2006, pp. 81–84 with permission from *Fire Engineering Magazine*.**

Along with water, the body loses sodium and potassium through sweat. These electrolytes are critical to maintaining the body's performance level. Without sodium and potassium, the body cannot function properly, and symptoms will appear.[6]

## Heat Cramps

Heat cramps are the mildest form of heat/dehydration-related illness and are characterized by painful muscle spasms usually in the abdomen, hamstrings, or calves. These cramps can come on very suddenly and are excruciating. Heat cramps are caused by failure to replace the body's lost sodium, although poor physical conditioning can also play a key role. Heat cramps can be relieved by drinking liquids (what liquids will be discussed in depth later) or through IV therapy. Light massage and application of ice packs to the affective area may also help to relieve muscular pain during these cramps.

## Heat Exhaustion

Heat exhaustion is a more serious form of heat/dehydration illness. It is the result of even more severe levels of water and sodium losses through sweat. Symptoms generally include weakness and fatigue and clammy and moist skin that may appear flushed or pale. The body will continue to produce sweat at this stage, further depleting itself of electrolytes and water.

## Heat Stroke

The most serious heat/dehydration-related illness is heat stroke. This is very serious and possibly life threatening. It is brought on by a combination of the aforementioned dehydration factors as well as the body's failure to regulate its core temperature. Sweating now stops. It is followed by mental confusion, delirium, loss of consciousness, convulsions or seizures; if left untreated, it could lead to coma or death. The core temperature of an individual experiencing heat stroke can be greater than 106°F; the patient will present with hot, dry, and mottled skin.

Dehydration and all the aforementioned related medical problems can further be complicated by age, physical fitness level, stimulant use (such as caffeine), and preexisting medical problems. Even if none of these risk factors exist, we firefighters are already predisposed to dehydration by the very nature of what we do. Turnouts raise the body's core temperature as well as eliminate the body's primary method of cooling itself. The body produces sweat, which evaporates and cools the skin, helping to regulate body temperature. When encapsulated in turnouts, this evaporation cannot take place. The body's temperature continues to rise as we vigorously exercise (firefighting).

We sweat more, losing more electrolytes and water, while still not being allowed to cool off. It is a vicious cycle that can rapidly overheat and dehydrate even the most physically fit firefighters.

## Preventing Dehydration

Dehydration must, for all these reasons, be combated before the firefight begins. Limiting the use of stimulants such as caffeine, maintaining physical fitness, and keeping yourself adequately hydrated throughout your shift are ways to stop dehydration before it starts.

Avoid caffeine throughout your shift. It has been proven to cause major changes in the kidneys known as a diuretic effect. Caffeine increases the blood flow in the kidneys while inhibiting the reabsorption of sodium and water. Caffeine also has been known to weaken the detrusor muscles in the bladder, which provokes the need to urinate.[7] In a nutshell, caffeine makes you dispose of the electrolytes your body so desperately needs. The liquid you consume in the form of caffeinated drinks, such as coffee or soda, is not enough to overcome dehydration, and the diuretic effects make what little liquid your body takes in less effective.

There is some controversy surrounding caffeine and dehydration. A Web search on this topic reveals several proponents of caffeine use and sports activity. However, the majority of the debate surrounding caffeine focuses on athletes and their use of caffeine as a sports stimulant. In these cases, the athletes were prehydrated and under the supervision of sports trainers in a regimented training program. For this reason, it is recommended that firefighters use caffeine in moderation.

A high level of physical fitness helps combat dehydration before it starts. Fitness improves heat regulation, creates a greater blood volume, and allows you to adjust more easily to vigorous exercise in a hot environment. Fit firefighters typically carry less body weight and are acclimated to intense physical activity. Furthermore, in general, firefighters engaging in fitness-related activities throughout their workday typically maintain an adequate level of hydration by consuming water or sports drinks during and after workouts.

Maintaining an adequate level of hydration throughout your workday is of the utmost importance. Unlike most athletes, when and for how long we are expected to perform is an unknown factor for firefighters. At a moment's notice, we may be called to engage in very strenuous activity in a hot environment. Once the alarm sounds, it is too late to try to prehydrate for a fire. Maintaining hydration throughout a shift is the only way to ward off dehydration later.

Prehydrating begins the day before a shift. If engaging in physical activity during your day off, it is vitally important to stay hydrated. Drinking alcohol or large amounts of caffeine before a shift will potentially affect your performance when called to duty. For on-call volunteer firefighters, staying hydrated while "off duty" is an absolute must. Approach your days off from the mindset of "the night before the big game." Athletes certainly would not allow themselves to become compromised by dehydration, drinking alcohol, or consuming an excessive amount of caffeinated drinks the night before they want to perform at their best. To be at the top of your "game," you must have the same mindset before a shift.

As discussed before, urine color is an easy way to measure your hydration level. Throughout your day, this simple method may be used to stay prepared. Here at the Mesa (AZ) Fire Department, dehydration, especially during the summer months, is a major concern, as you can imagine. For this reason, we have placed charts (SNTTM Handout #14, Web site listed in endnotes) (5) in the bathrooms of the stations that help firefighters gauge their hydration levels. This simple tool illustrates what hydration level you currently have based on a color chart. We have had great success with this simple regulatory method.

### Selecting Sports Drinks

What you drink to prevent dehydration can be very important. A good rule of thumb is, if physical activity has lasted for less than 40 minutes, drink water; if the activity has lasted for more than 40 minutes, drink a sports drink to replace energy and electrolytes. Picking sports-drink type products to stock in the station and in the rehab sector can be very confusing. They are not all created equal, and cost is always a factor. So how do you pick a good sports drink to place in rehab? With some simple baseline knowledge, choosing a sports-type drink can be easy. First, let's discuss what a sports drink is and what it does.

A sports drink is a combination of water, carbohydrates, and electrolytes. The water replaces the water the body loses through sweat. The carbohydrates replace energy stores in the body to increase performance and stamina. Electrolytes replace those that the body has lost and needs for continued performance. The glucose and sodium also enhance fluid absorption in the small intestines, thus rapidly replacing what the body has lost. The water, carbohydrates, and electrolytes work together to keep the body's thirst mechanism active. Thirst prods firefighters to drink more, thus they become better hydrated. Water alone tends to eliminate the body's thirst mechanism.[8]

Picking a sports drink that will rehab firefighters properly is not that difficult. All the information you need to make a wise choice is on the bottle label. Start with the calories the drink provides. A good sports drink should provide between 50 and 80 calories per serving, which will properly replenish the energy stores of firefighters recovering in rehab. Additional calories will cause the absorption rate to slow and the body's metabolism to become inefficient.

Next, look at the electrolytes contained in the drink. The sports drink should contain between 100 and 170 mg of sodium to adequately replenish the body's electrolytes. A lesser quantity may cause firefighters to become electrolyte depleted (hyponatremic), which may lead to heat cramps or worse.

Finally, look at the carbohydrate content. Research has shown that a 6 percent concentration of carbohydrates allows for rapid fluid absorption and improves performance. To calculate the carbohydrate percentage of a beverage, divide the amount of carbohydrates in one serving (usually listed in grams) by the amount of fluid in milliliters (8 oz. = 240 milliliters) per serving, and then multiply by 100. The label may list this value for you next to the total grams of carbohydrates per serving.[9]

The type of carbohydrate is very important. Choose a drink that has glucose or sucrose as the carbohydrate source, because they are quickly absorbed by the body and easily utilized as energy. Drinks with high-fructose corn syrup or galactose can upset the stomach and can be a far less effective energy source.[10] In general, the less expensive sports drinks (typically store-brand types) contain corn syrup as the carbohydrate. This falls into the "you get what you pay for" category. Although the drinks may be cheaper, the minimal cost savings may not be worth it if crews in rehab have stomach discomfort (and in some cases nausea from gastrointestinal distress) and possibly may not be able to return to the firefight.

Some manufacturers are now adding protein to sports drinks. The theory behind this is that protein aids in recovery time following strenuous muscular work. However, the sports nutrition community is divided on this subject. Protein will certainly not hinder firefighters' recovery time; however, the amount of carbohydrates, electrolytes, and calories a drink contains should be of primary concern.[11] Until there are further studies done defining the attributes of protein in sports-type drinks, protein should not be a major determining factor when choosing drinks for firefighter hydration.[12]

Avoid fruit juices. Although healthful, they are not ideal fluid replacement beverages because of their high carbohydrate and low sodium content. Fruit juice is absorbed at a slow rate and can cause stomach discomfort and gastrointestinal distress. Even when diluted with water to help absorption rates, they still do not contain enough sodium to be effective rehab choices.

Do not choose drinks with carbonation, which can cause a burning sensation in the throat (discouraging drinking), cause gastric distention and discomfort, and slow the absorption of liquid into the small intestines.

As noted, avoid drinks with caffeine. Many "energy drinks" are sold in health food stores and are marketed as energy boosters for pre- or post-workouts. However, energy-type drinks do not contain the carbohydrates and electrolytes needed for rehab and should not be used. Some sports drinks may contain caffeine, which is not plainly stated on the front of the bottle. That's why it is important to take the time to research products before buying them to stock a rehab unit or area.[13]

Taste, of course, is an important factor. The flavoring in sports drinks encourages consumption. Factor taste in when looking at products to purchase for rehab. Provide a wide variety of flavors to encourage members to consume the drinks often. Taste, however, should not be the most important factor. Consider the caloric intake, type of carbohydrates, and sodium levels first; taste should be a secondary concern.

There is a common misconception that sports drinks should be diluted with water before consumption. This is not so. Water can and should be stocked with sports-type drinks in rehab (keeping the 40-minute exertion rule in mind). However, sports drinks are formulated to provide the greatest benefit when consumed without dilution. The theories behind dilution of sports drinks most likely stemmed from individuals trying to limit calories when "dieting" and not fully understanding how and why sports drinks are designed the way they are. Dilution of sports drinks will not provide the proper amount of carbohydrates and electrolytes for firefighter rehab when exertion has been more than 40 minutes.

Once you have selected the sports drinks your department will purchase, decide where and when they will be available to firefighters. Placing these drinks on a rehab unit along with water and snacks is a good start, but it does not completely address firefighter hydration and rehab.

Since, as stated, combating dehydration starts before the fire, drinks should be available in the stations so firefighters can maintain an adequate level of hydration throughout their shift. Mesa Fire has made bottled water and sports drinks available to our members in this way for many years. The policy has been well received and is considered a privilege that has not been abused. Along with placing these drinks in the stations, remind members of the importance of maintaining their hydration level throughout their shift. Placing the color charts in the bathroom at the beginning of the summer months as well as sending out yearly dehydration educational material has been an effective way for the Mesa Fire Department to remind our membership of how important these concepts are.

Make sports drinks and water available on each apparatus to facilitate company/crew level rehab (also referred to as self-rehab by the NFPA). By placing sports drinks and water on each unit, crews may hydrate throughout their day. Rehab units often are called only to scenes where a large number of resources are required. However, the activities that crews engage in throughout the day as single units can be just as taxing on their hydration levels as a large incident. Their hydration level is steadily attacked throughout a shift as crews engage in activities such as drills, business inspections, single-unit response calls, and equipment maintenance. Having the ability to rehydrate at the crew level is critical. On each Mesa Fire Department apparatus, we have placed a small store-bought ice chest. Each morning during the apparatus check, the engineer (driver/operator) places sports drinks and bottled water in the cooler along with fresh ice. This concept has been an easy fix for our hydration needs and has proven to work effectively at the company level.

NFPA 1584 lists the following as basic rehab practices:

- ☐ medical evaluation (heart rate, blood pressure, and temperature) and treatment,
- ☐ food and fluid replacement,
- ☐ relief from climatic conditions (out of smoke, shade, air-conditioning, for example),
- ☐ rest and recovery, and
- ☐ member accountability.

Using these simple concepts as guides, every department can achieve effective rehab. Although we here at Mesa Fire are fortunate enough to have several specialty vehicles designed specifically for rehab, often it is the simple things such as those described above that truly make a difference. With some basic research into sports drinks and their contents, you can be well on your way to providing adequate firefighter rehab for your members. There is a wealth of information on the Internet on this subject as well as in NFPA 1584. I encourage you to continue to investigate sports drinks and rehab concepts.

To learn more about dehydration, firefighter heat stress, and rehab concepts, go to www.city ofmesa.org/fire/default.asp; select "personnel and wellness" division, and click on the "heat stress" link for a very funny and informative DVD production available for viewing or downloading.

*I would like to thank Captain Holly Button and Captain James Johnson of the Mesa Fire Department Wellness Office for providing some of the research for this article.*

## Endnotes

1   NFPA 1584, *Rehabilitation of Members Operating at Incident Scene Operations and Training Exercises*, NFPA Technical Committee on Fire Service Occupational Medical and Health, Feb. 6, 2003.

2   Glen A. Selkirk and Tom M. McLellan, "Physical Work Limits for Toronto Firefighters in Warm Environments: Defining the Problem and Creating Solution," WSIB Research Grant #01 005: Final Report. Defense R&D Canada—Toronto, Sept. 2003, 4–5.

3   Elizabeth Joy, M.D., FACSM, "Heat Illness," Sports Medicine Tip Sheet," University of Utah, Salt Lake City, 1–2.

4   Inter-Association Task Force on Exertional Heat Illnesses, "Consensus Statement: Overall Strategies for the Prevention of Exertional Heat Illness," http://www.nata.org/statements/consensus/heatillness.pdf, accessed on 08/15/2006.

5   SNTTM Handout #14 "Am I Dehydrated? Urine Color Chart" http://www.owlnet.rice.edu/~heal103/docs/Am%20I% 20Hydrated%20-%20Urine%20Color%20Chart.pdf, accessed 08/13/06 (may also be accessed by typing "SNTTM Handout #14" into "Google" search engine).

6   AWC Executive Wellness Center "Hydration and Heat Disorders," http://www.au.af.mil/au/awc/health/centersite/hydration.htm Accessed on 08/10/06.

7   Jack Hartley, "Caffeine and Sports Performance," Vanderbilt University Research Paper, http://www.vanderbilt.edu/AnS/psychology/health_psychology/caffeine_sports.htm, accessed 08/15/2006.

8   City of Mesa (AZ) Fire Department, Firefighter Wellness Office, "Heat Stress Awareness" DVD, 2006, directed/produced by Captain Holly Button.

9   Gatorade Sports Science Institute, "How To Read a Sports Drink Label" flyer, 2000.

10  Leslie Bonci, "A Quick Boost," a guide to energy drinks and bars. T&C Sept. 2002 at Athleticbid.com.

11  "The verdict is in: Most of us can skip drinking protein-enhanced sports beverages during exercise," Julie Deardorff, *Chicago Tribune*, www.chicagotribune.com/features_julieshealthclub/2006/08/gatorade_vs_acc.html, accessed 9/13/06.

12  "Studies Divided on Value of Adding Protein to Sports Drinks," Robert Preidt, www.medicinenet.com/script/main/art.asp?articlekey=63522, accessed on 9/13/06.

13  "Fluids 2000, How Sports Drinks Work," Gatorade Sports Science Institute, 07/27/2000.

## Review Questions

1. Describe the symptoms of dehydration.

2. Discuss the methods for preventing dehydration.

# Bibliography

Aaron, T. (March, 1991). AIDS education in law enforcement. *Law and Order*, pp. 35–36.

Ahrens, C. (Oct. 1996). "Checking up" on staff health education. *Corrections Today*, pp. 102–107.

Anderson, K. and Brown, J. (March 27, 1998). Emotional overload. *Police Review*, pp. 22–23.

Arliss, R. M. (July, 1991). Healthy hearts for New York City Cops. *The Police Chief*, pp. 16–22.

Armstrong, D. (Jan/Feb.1999). Stress of the job takes a terrible toll. *American Police Beat*, Vol VI, No. 1, pp. 1, 10, 34 & 35.

Armstrong, J. J. (Oct. 2001). Staff safety and wellness—an evolving commitment. *Corrections Today,* Vol. 63, Issue 6, pp. 8–10.

Bahrke, M. (April, 1996). Eating on the run. *Muscles and Fitness*, Vol. 57, No. 4, p. 77.

Baker, T. E. and Baker, J. P. (Oct. 1996). Preventing police suicide. *FBI Law Enforcement Bulletin*, pp. 24–27.

Barba, J. (Jun. 2005). Crossfit physical training. *Law and Order,* Vol. 53, Issue 6, pp. 60–66.

Beckley, A. (Dec. 1996). Health and safety: The future role of federation reps. *Police: The Voice of the Service*, pp. 20–22.

Biermann, P. J. (Feb, 2006). Improving correctional officer safety: Reducing inmate weapons. *Corrections Today,* Vol. 68, Issue 1, p. 68.

Bigbee, D. (May, 1993). Pathogenic microorganisms: Law enforcement's silent enemies. *FBI Law Enforcement Bulletin*, pp. 1–5.

Bilton, V. (Sept. 2008). Protect the protectors … Wear body armor. *Law and Order,* Vol. 56, Issue 9, pp. 40–44.

Black, S. (Oct. 2001). Correctional employee stress & strain. Corrections Today, Vol. 63, Issue 6, pp. 82–87.

Buerger, M. E. and Levin, B. H. (Sep. 2005). The future of officer safety in an age of terrorism. *FBI Law Enforcement Bulletin,* Vol. 74, Issue 9, p. 2.

Burke T. W. (Oct. 1995). Dispatcher stress. *FBI Law Enforcement Bulletin*, pp. 1–6.

Catlin, D. et al. (August 1993). Assessing the threat of anabolic steroids. *The Physician and Sports Medicine*, Vol. 21, No. 8, pp. 37–44.

Caudill, C.B. and Peak, K.J. (Oct. 2009). Retiring from the "Thin Blue Line": A need for formal preretirement training. *FBI Law Enforcement Bulletin*, Vol. 78, Issue 10, pp. 1–7.

Champion, D. J. (1998). *Criminal Justice in the United States*. Chicago, Nelson-Hall Inc.

Chapola, C. (Dec. 2002). Good nutrition benefits all officers. *Law and Order*, Vol. 50, Issue 12, pp. 90–94.

Clark, D. F. el. al. (March 1998). Heat stress in the training environment. *Fire Engineering*, March 1998 Vol. 151, Issue 3, p. 163–167.

Connors, E. F. (January, 1990). Hazardous chemicals from clandestine labs pose threat to law enforcement. *The Police Chief*, pp. 37–41.

Collingon, J. (Feb. 1995). Assessing officers' lifestyle: The importance of health risk appraisals. *The Police Chief*, pp. 48-52.

Collingwood, T. R. (Feb. 1995). Physical fitness standard: Measuring job relatedness. *The Police Chief*, pp. 31–47.

Cornell, S. (Feb. 2003). New for 2003: Body armor. *Law & Order Magazine*, Vol. 51, Issue 2, pp. 44–49.

Cross, C. L. and Ashley, L. (Oct. 2004). Police trauma and addiction: Coping with the dangers of the job. *FBI Law Enforcement Bulletin*, pp. 24–33.

Cummings, J. P. (Oct. 1996). Police stress and the suicide link. *The Police Chief*, pp. 85–96.

Davis, E. F. and Pinizzotto, A. J. (April, 1996). Above and beyond the call of duty: Preventing off-duty officer deaths. *FBI Law Enforcement Bulletin*, pp. 1–5.

Dart, R. C. III and Ferranto, D. A. (July, 1991). Anabolic steroid abuse among law enforcement officers. *The Police Chief*, p. 18.

Department of Labor, Occupational Safety and Health Administration, Occupational Exposure to Blood borne Pathogens. 29 CFR, Part 1910.1030, Docket no. H-370 (Washington, DC: US Department of Labor, Occupational Safety and Health Administration, 1992).

Dezelan, L. A. (Feb. 1997). Firefighter fitness is now on the front burner. *Fire Chief*, pp. 56–57.

Dittmar, M. J. (Dec. 2006). Firefighters and heart diseases: Beyond the Statistics. *Fire Engineering*, pp. 49–62.

Dorman, R. V. (1998). Drink or die. *Law and Order*. August 1998, pp. 45–48.

Doyle, W. J. (Oct. 2001). 6 elements that form a context for staff safety. *Corrections Today*, Vol. 63, Issue 6, pp. 101–104.

Editor. (August 1998). Your health: Hepatitis B. *GateLodge*, pp. 42–43.

Egbert, B. et al. (April 30, 1998). Bravest dies on the job. *Daily News*, p. 7.

Epps, C. A. (March 1992). OSHA issues regs on AIDS and hepatitis. The Police Chief,. pp. 14–15.

Fix, Charles. (Oct. 2001). Critical incident stress management program: Responding to the needs of correctional staff in Pennsylvania. *Corrections Today*, Vol. 63, Issue 6, pp. 94–96.

Fletcher, T. (April/May 1997). Stay alert & comfortable on the job. *Canadian Security*, pp. 19–20.

Fox, R. (Feb. 2007). Stress management … And the stress-proof vest. *Law and Order*, Vol. 55, Issue 2, pp. 352–356.

Friel, J. K. and Stones, M. (August 1992). Firefighters and heart disease. *American Journal of Public Health*, Vol. 82, No. 8, pp. 1175–1176.

Gates, D. F. and Lady, K. E. (March 1991). Enhancing AIDS awareness in Los Angeles. *The Police Chief*, pp. 44–47.

Garner, G. W. (Mar. 2006). Things I wish somebody had told me. *FBI Law Enforcement Bulletin*, Vol. 75, Issue 3, pp. 22–24.

Gayle, R. (Oct. 2001). The emotions hidden behind a badge. *Corrections Today*, Vol. 63, Issue 6, pp. 98–102.

Garland, B. (Dec. 2002). Prison treatment staff burnout: Consequences, causes and prevention. *Corrections Today*, Vol. 64, Issue 7, pp. 116–122.

Gondles, J. A. (Oct. 2001). Editorial: Public safety in action. *Corrections Today*, Vol. 63, issue 6, p. 6.

Gordon, J. (Jan./Feb./March 1998). Handling stress. *Police Times: The Voice of Professional American Law Enforcement*, Vol. XXXVIII, Issue 1, pp. 1–3.

Haberman, C. (Dec. 13, 1996). The dangers when police turns to drink. *New York Times*, p. B1.

Hart, S. V. (Apr. 2003). Making Prisons safer through technology. *Corrections Today*, Vol. 65, Issue 2, pp. 26–28.

Heglund, J. (Sep. 2009). Helping first responders withstand traumatic experiences. *FBI Law Enforcement Bulletin*, Vol. 78, Issue 9, pp. 1–4.

Hill, K. Q. and Clawson, M. (1988). The health hazards of street level bureaucracy: Mortality among the police. *Journal of Police Science and Administration*, Vol. 16, No. 4, pp. 243–248.

Hilton, L. (Jun. 2009). Bloodborne pathogens training is a lifesaver for correctional staff. *Corrections Today*, Vol. 71, Issue 3, pp. 22–23.

Hodges, R. (June 1997). Safety on the line. *Fire Chief*, pp. 42–49.

Hoffman, B. (April, 1996). How today's law enforcement officers rank. *Muscles and Fitness*, pp. 76–79.

Hoffman, J. (April 2000). Body armor improvements. *Law and Order*, pp. 90–94.

Holgate, A. M. and Clegg I. J. (1991). The path to probation officers burnout: New Dogs, old tricks. *Journal of Criminal Justice*, Vol. 19, pp. 325–337.

Honig, A. L. and White, E. K. (October 2000). By their own hand: Suicide among law enforcement personnel. *The Police Chief*, pp. 156–160.

Hostetter, A. (2007). The donut dilemma: The impact of obesity on today's police. *Journal of California Law Enforcement*, Vol. 41, Issue 3, pp. 13–22.

Hurley, J. (Jun. 2000). Officer survival. *Law and Order*, Vol. 48, Issue 6, pp. 112–114.

Hyams, M. (1998). Fitness for duty evaluation: A sample policy. *The Journal of California Law Enforcement*, Vol. 32, No. 1, pp. 10–13.

Jackson, C. and Johnson Rion, S. (Jul. 2001). Inmate transportation: Safety is the priority. *Corrections Today*, Vol. 63, Issue 4, pp. 110–114.

Johnson, R. R. (Jan. 2009). Officer fitness. *Law and Order*, Vol. 57, Issue 1, p. 18.

Johnson, R. R. (Oct. 2005). Middle Management stress. *Law and Order*, Vol. 53, Issue 10, p. 16.

Jones, G. R. (July, 1992). Health and fitness programs. *FBI Law Enforcement Bulletin*, pp. 6–11.

Jones, R. D. (Oct. 2003). Hepatitis not just corrections' problem. *Corrections Today*, Vol. 65, Issue 6, pp. 78–80.

Kelly, P. and Martin R. (March 2006). Police suicide is real. *Law and Order*, Vol. 54, Issue 3, pp. 93–96.

Kennedy, D. B. et al. (1990). AIDS concern among crime scene investigators. *Journal of Police Science and Administration*, Vol. 17, No. 1, pp. 12–19.

Klein, C. and Gregory A. M. (Jan. 2000). Lead poisoning. *Law and Order*, Vol. 48, Issue 1, pp. 62–66.

Koehler, R. J. (Jan/Feb. 1994). HIV infection, TB, and the health crisis in corrections. *Public Administration Review*, Vol. 54, No. 1, pp. 31–35.

Kureczka, A. W. (Feb./March 1996). Critical incident stress in law enforcement. *FBI Law Enforcement Bulletin*, pp. 10–16.

Levitin, H. W. and Socher, M. M. (Oct./Nov. 1997). Attacking the nervous system. *Fire International*, pp. 13–14.

Levitan, H. W. and Socher, M. M. (June 1, 1997). Nerve Agents—They can take your breath away! Find out how to respond correctly. *IAFC On Scene*, Vol. 11, Issue 10, pp. 6–7.

Lindsey, D. (Aug. 2007). Police fatigue: An incident waiting to happen. *FBI Law Enforcement Bulletin*, Vol. 76, Issue 8, pp. 1–8.

Lindsey, D. and Kelly, S. (Jul. 2004). Issues in small town policing: Understanding stress. *FBI Law Enforcement Bulletin*, Vol. 73, Issue 7, pp. 1–7.

Loeb, D. L. (Nov. 1997). Have we gone too far? *Fire Chief*, pp. 60–65.

Loflin, M. E. (February, 1997). Safety means learning from our mistakes. *Fire Chief*, pp. 60–63.

Mayhead, G. (Dec. 1997). When you look good, you are good. *Police Life*, pp. 28–30.

McCormack, W. U. (July 1994). Grooming and weight standards for law enforcement: The legal issues. *FBI Law Enforcement Bulletin*, pp. 27–32.

McDiarmid, M. A. and Agnew J. (Oct/Dec.1995). Reproductive hazards and firefighters. *Occupational Medicine*, Vol. 10, No. 4, pp. 829–839.

Meese, E. III (Oct. 1987). AIDS poses special concerns for law enforcement. *The Police Chief*, p.11.

Melius, J. M. (Oct/Dec. 1995). Cardiovascular disease among firefighters. *Occupational Medicine*, Philadelphia, Hanley & Belfus Inc. Vol. 10, No. 4, pp. 821–827.

Milam, T. (Sep. 2010). Officer safety: Making the vision a reality. *The Police Chief*, Vol. 77, Issue 1, pp. 1–8.

Miller, A. (July, 1987). A fireman's heart. *Public Management*, pp. 24–26.

Miller, L. (March 2006). Practical strategies for preventing officer suicide. *Law and Order*, pp. 90–93.

Moore, E. (Jul. 2004). A common sense approach to staff safety. *Corrections Today*, Vol. 66, Issue 4, p. 72.

Morris, A. F. (Feb. 2006). Pointed workout. *Fire Chief*, pp. 4–8.

Mueller, J. (Oct. 1996). Locking up tuberculosis. *Corrections Today*, pp. 100–101.

Mulroy, D, E. (Sep. 2000). Stress: How it contributes to poor performance. *Law and Order*, Vol. 48, Issue 9, pp. 67–69.

Murray, E. R. (Apr. 2009). Improving communication between public health and corrections. *Corrections Today*, Vol. 71, Issue 2, pp. 26–28.

National Institute of Justice Staff (Author Anonymous). (Feb. 2007). Helping probation and parole officers cope with stress. *Corrections Today*, Vol. 69, Issue 9, pp. 70–71.

Ness, J. J. and Light, J. (August 1992). Mandatory physical fitness standards: Issues and concerns. *The Police Chief*, pp. 74–79.

Nielsen, E. (Jan. 2005). Lead poisoning. *Law and Order*, Vol. 53, Issue I, pp. 46–49.

NIJ Staff. (Feb. 2008). Making corrections safer with technology. *Corrections Today*, Vol. 70, Issue 1, pp. 62– 63.

Norvell, N. et al. (June 1989). Perceived stress levels and physical symptoms in supervisory law enforcement personnel. *Journal of Police Science and Administration*, Vol. 16, pp. 75–79.

Nowicki, E. (Mar. 2002). Handcuffing. *Law and Order*, Vol. 50, Issue 3, pp. 14–16.

Oldham, S. (Jun. 2001). Physical fitness training for police officers. *Law and Order*, Vol. 49, Issue 6, pp. 75–78.

Peak, K. et al. (January, 1992). Physical abilities testing for police officers: A flexible, job-related approach. *The Police Chief*, pp. 51–56.

Pilant, L. (Nov. 1995). Infection control. *The Police Chief*, pp. 53–56.

Pilant, L. (Aug. 1995). Physical fitness. *The Police Chief*, pp. 85–90.

Pilant, L. (July 1993). Preventing infectious disease. *The Police Chief*, pp. 34–42.

Potter, K. (Sept. 1997). Gym'll fix it. *Police:The Voice of the Service*, pp. 12–13.

Potter, R. H. and Moseley, K. (Jul. 2006). HIV and corrections: Every statistic tells a story. *Corrections Today*, Vol. 68, Issue 4, pp. 76–77.

Pounder, B. (March 1998). Alcohol dependency and ill health retirement. *Firefighter*, Vol 26, No. 2, pp. 3–4.

Ramos, O. (May 2010). Police suicide: Are you at risk? *FBI Law Enforcement Bulletin*, Vol. 79, Issue 5, pp. 21–23.

Rayburn, M. T. (Aug. 2000). Surviving an off-duty encounter. *Law and Order*, Vol. 48, Issue 8, pp. 99–102.

Sanow, E. (Mar. 2008). Fitness: An ethical obligation. *Law and Order*, Vol. 56, Issue 3, p. 6.

Sanow, E. (Feb. 2001). Body armor? Require it! No excuse. *Law and Order*, Vol. 49, Issue 2, p. 4.

Sardinas, A. et al. (Sept. 1986). Ischemic heart disease mortality of firemen and policemen. *American Journal of Public Health*, Vol. 76, No. 9, pp. 1140–1141.

Sauter, C. (Oct. 2001). Health and wellness programs available to Maryland correctional employees. *Corrections Today*, Vol. 63, Issue 6, pp. 110–112.

Savasta, M. (Aug. 2005). Health: Recognizing and preventing heat related illness. *Law and Order*, Vol. 53, Issue 8, pp. 106–108.

Schanlaub, R. (Jun. 2004). Safe searches. *Law and Order*, Vol. 52, Issue 6, p. 126.

Sharp, A. (Feb. 2003). Wellness: A new trend in fitness standards. *Law and Order*, Vol. 51, Issue 2, pp. 58–62.

Shearer, R. W. (August 1993). Police officer stress: New approaches for handling tension. *The Police Chief*, pp. 96–99.

Sheridan, K. et al. (Sept/Oct. 1989). Effects of AIDS education on police officers' perceptions of risk. *Public Health Reports*, Vol. 104, No. 5, pp. 521–522.

Spaulding, D. (Feb. 2002). Body armor 2002. *Law and Order*, Vol. 50, Issue 2, pp. 78–82.

Spawn, M. A. (Apr. 2010). Officer safety during police-on-police encounters. *The Police Chief*, Vol. 77, Issue 4, pp. 24–30.

Standfest, S. R. (May 1996). The police supervisor and stress. *FBI Law Enforcement Bulletin*, Vol. 65, pp. 7–10.

Stewart, J. D. (May 1993). Blood borne Diseases: Developing a training curriculum. *FBI Law Enforcement Bulletin*, pp.11–15.

Stewart, T. L. and Brown, D. W. (Jul. 2002). How about a national staff safety web site? *Corrections Today*, Vol. 64, Issue 4, pp. 16–18.

Stewart, T. L. and Brown, D. W. (Oct. 2001). Focusing on correction staff safety. *Corrections Today*, Vol. 63, Issue 6, pp. 90–94.

Storch, J. E. and Panzarella, R. (1996). Police stress: State-trait anxiety in relation to occupational and personal stressors. *Journal of Criminal Justice*, Vol. 24, No. 2, pp. 99–107.

Sudetic, C. (May 29, 1995). When alcohol and silence mix. *New York Times*, p. A25.

Tate, H. (Mar. 2001). Stress during SWAT training. *Law and Order*, Vol. 49, Issue 3, pp. 77–82.

Valway, S. E. et al. (August 1989). Lead absorption in indoor firing range users. *American Journal of Public Health*, Vol. 79, No. 8, pp. 1029–1032.

Violanti, J. M., Vena, J. E. and Marshall, J. R. (1986). Disease risk and mortality among police officers: New evidence and contributing factors. *Journal of Police Science and Administration*, Vol. 14, pp. 17–23.

Violanti, J. M. (Feb. 1995). The mystery within: Understanding police suicide. *FBI Law Enforcement Bulletin*, pp. 19–23.

Violanti, J. M. and Aron, F. (1995). Police stress: Variations in perception among police personnel. *Journal of Criminal Justice*, Vol. 23, No. 3, pp. 287–294.

Violanti, J. M. (Jan. 1999). Alcohol abuse in policing. *FBI Law Enforcement Bulletin*, Vol. 68, Issue 1, pp. 16–19.

Violanti, J. M. (Oct. 1992). Police radar: A cancer risk? *FBI Law Enforcement Bulletin*, pp. 15–16.

Volpe, J.F. (Oct. 2000). A guide to effective stress management. *Law and Order*, Vol. 48, Issue 10, pp. 183–187.

Vonk, K. (Apr. 2009). Functional fitness, part 2. *Law and Order*, Vol. 57, Issue 4, pp. 15–17.

Vonk, K. (Mar. 2009). Functional fitness, part 1. *Law and Order*, Vol. 57, Issue 3, pp. 17–19.

Vonk, K. (Feb. 2009). The nitty-gritty of proper nutrition. *Law and Order*, Vol. 57, Issue 2, pp. 14–17.

Vonk, K. (Jan. 2009). Law enforcement and nutrition. *Law and Order*, Vol. 57, Issue 1. pp. 10–12.

Vonk, K. (Oct. 2008). Police performance under stress. *Law and Order*, Vol. 56, Issue 10, pp. 86–92.

Weiss, J. and Dresser, M. (Apr. 2000) Learning to survive. *Law and Order*, Vol. 48, Issue 4, pp. 113–117.

Wheeler, J. B. and Lando, C. M. (Oct. 2002). Safety awareness for public-contact employees. *FBI Law Enforcement Bulletin*, Vol. 71, Issue 10, pp. 1–13.

Williams, D. (Dec. 2006). Danger in the station: Drug-resistant infections. *Fire Engineering Magazine*, Vol. 159, Issue 12, pp. 1–12.

Williams, D. (Dec. 2006). Firefighter hydration during rehab. *Fire Engineering*, Vol. 159, Issue 12, pp. 81–84.

Wright, L. N. and Northrup, M. K. (Oct. 2001). Examining the health risks for corrections professionals. *Corrections Today*, Vol. 63, Issue 6, pp. 106–109.

Wright, L. N. (April, 1998). Staff health and wellness: Protecting the health of correctional employees is a long-term endeavor. *Corrections Today*, pp. 134–135.

Young, A. T. and Brumley, N. (Sep. 2009). On-scene mental health services establishing a crisis team. *FBI Law Enforcement Bulletin*, Vol. 78, Issue 6, pp. 6–11.

# Index